SCHOLASTIC

ENCYCLOPEDIA

OF THE

PRESIDENTS

AND THEIR TIMES

SCHOLASTIC

ENCYCLOPEDIA OF THE PRESIDENTS

AND THEIR TIMES

DAVID RUBEL

An Agincourt Press Book

SCHOLASTIC REFERENCE

For Julia

Design: Tilman Reitzle/Oxygen Design
Maps: Geoff Notkin, Tilman Reitzle
Photo Research: Diane Hamilton, Nora E. Malek
Production: Mike Hortens, Mark Lewis

We would like to thank Allan Shrem and Lee Schogel of the World Collectible Center for kindly allowing us access to their collection of presidential campaign memorabilia.

PHOTO CREDITS

All images are from the Library of Congress, the National Archives, and the Steele Collection, except for:
Liaison Agency, Inc.: cover (top right); Corbis Images/The Bettmann Archive: cover (bottom left, bottom right), 213 (bottom); Beverly R. Robinson Collection/U.S. Naval Academy Museum: 17 (bottom); World Collectible Center: 52, 116, 120, 128, 130 (bottom), 132, 136 (bottom), 140, 144, 156, 168, 172 (center, bottom), 183 (bottom), 185 (bottom), 196 (bottom), 200, 204; Levi Strauss: 66 (bottom); Alaska State Library: 79 (top); Utah Division of State History: 81 (bottom); American Heritage Center, University of Wyoming: 86 (bottom); Arizona Historical Society/Tucson: 94 (bottom); Kansas State Historical Society: 103 (bottom); Hogan Jazz Archive: 111; Sophia Smith Collection/Smith College: 131 (bottom); New York Stock Exchange Archives: 141 (bottom); Franklin Delano Roosevelt Library: 145 (top), 146 (top), 153 (top); Veterans of Foreign Wars of the United States: 153 (bottom), 179 (top), 187 (bottom); National Archives of Canada: 155; Harry S. Truman Library: 159 (bottom); Schomburg Center for Research in Black Culture: 167 (bottom), 171 (top); Soviet Life: 169 (bottom); E.C. Publications, Inc.: 171 (bottom); John Fitzgerald Kennedy Library: 172 (top), 174; U.S. Air Force: 173 (bottom); Lyndon Baines Johnson Library: 178 (top), 179 (bottom); National Aeronautics and Space Administration: 181 (bottom), 197 (bottom), 207 (bottom); New York Public Library: 182 (bottom); Jimmy Carter Library: 189 (bottom), 190; Dori Jacobson/Sophia Smith Collection/Smith College: 191 (top); Con Edison: 191 (bottom); Ronald Reagan Library: 193, 198 (bottom); Apple Computer, Inc.: 195 (bottom); National Safe Kids Campaign: 199; Earth Times: 201 (bottom); Office of George Bush: 202 (bottom); African National Congress: 203 (top); Magic Johnson Foundation: 203 (bottom); White House: 205 (top), 206, 209 (top); Tilman Reitzle: 205 (bottom); 207 (top); Senate Historical Office: 209 (bottom); White House Historical Association: 218 (bottom); Rutherford Hayes Presidential Center: 221 (bottom). The Mount Rushmore cover of MAD is used with permission. © 1956, 1984 by E.C. Publications, Inc.

Library of Congress Cataloging-in-Publication Data

Rubel, David.
The Scholastic encyclopedia of the presidents and their times/David Rubel.
p. cm.
Includes index.
1. Presidents—United States—Encyclopedias, Juvenile. 2. United States—
History—Encyclopedias, Juvenile. [1. Presidents—United States—
Encyclopedias. 2. United States—History—Encyclopedias.] I. Scholastic
Inc. II. Title.
E176.1.R88
973'.099—dc20   93-11810
                                                                 CIP

ISBN 0-590-25986-5

Table of Contents

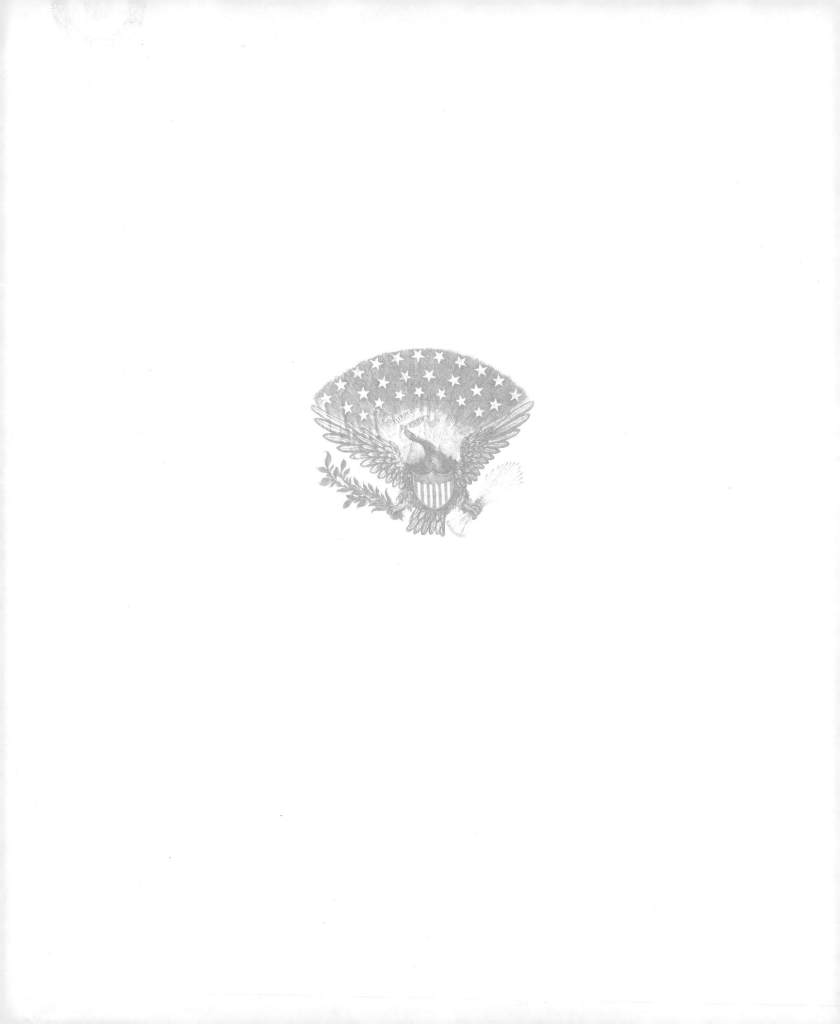

IN 1789, GEORGE WASHINGTON became the first president of the United States. More than forty others have followed him. The ninth president, William Henry Harrison, served less than a month. Franklin Roosevelt, the thirty-second president, served for twelve years. During Roosevelt's term, which spanned the Great Depression and World War II, the country changed a great deal. But the same can be said for almost any president. Each president's term in office is usually shaped by important events both inside and outside the United States.

This book tells the story of the United States through its presidents. It is organized by year, with one page for each year there has been a president. The year is marked at the top outside corner of each page. The book begins in 1789 and ends for now in 2001, at the start of President George W. Bush's first term. The pages for each president generally correspond to the years of his administration. But not every event happened during the year of the page on which it is described. Using one page per year is just a useful way to give a sense of time as it passes.

This book also tells the story of ordinary Americans. In the outside column of each page, you can read about the political events occurring in Washington, D.C., and around the world. But on the inside, you can read features that describe events happening in the rest of the country. Words and pictures describe the arts, medicine, and the sciences as well as trends in daily life.

How to Look Up...

★A PRESIDENT – Look up the president's name in the Table of Contents and turn to the page listed.

★WHO WAS PRESIDENT DURING A PARTICULAR YEAR – Find the page corresponding to that year. At the bottom of the page, you will find the president's name and his years in office.

★PRESIDENTIAL ELECTION RESULTS – A chart listing the results of every presidential election begins on page 214.

★IMPORTANT EVENTS AND PEOPLE OTHER THAN PRESIDENTS – Look up the subject in the index at the back of the book. The index will list the numbers of the pages on which that person or event is discussed.

★PRESIDENTIAL CAMPAIGNS – To find out about a particular campaign, turn to the page corresponding to the year of the campaign in which you are interested.

★PERSONAL STATISTICS ABOUT EACH PRESIDENT – The birthdate, birthplace, death date, political party, vice president, first lady, children, and nickname of each president are listed on the first page of that president's term.

WORDS IN RED mean that a subject is discussed in greater detail elsewhere in the book. To find out where, look up the subject in the index. The most detailed entry will also be marked with red.

THE MANIFEST DESTINY MAPS (appearing on pages 1, 9, 29, 41, 73, 105, and 177) show the territorial growth of the United States, beginning with the thirteen original colonies and ending with statehood for Alaska and Hawaii in 1959. The first time each state appears on a Manifest Destiny Map, it is shown in red and labeled with the year of its admission. States already in the Union are shown in blue. Territories that have not yet been admitted as states are shown in white.

GEORGE WASHINGTON

1ST PRESIDENT

★

FROM 1789 TO 1797

BORN: February 22, 1732

BIRTHPLACE: Pope's Creek, Va.

DIED: December 14, 1799

PARTY: Federalist

VICE PRESIDENT: John Adams

FIRST LADY: Martha Dandridge Custis

STEPCHILDREN: John Parke Custis, Martha Parke Custis

NICKNAME: Father of His Country

The first president to appear on a postage stamp.

BILL OF RIGHTS ALLOWS PASSAGE OF CONSTITUTION

THE FRAMERS OF THE Constitution were concerned that the new government they were planning might become too powerful. Americans had fought hard for their freedom, and no one wanted it taken away so soon.

The government was divided into three branches that could check and balance each other. But the Constitution did very little to protect individual rights. Critics of the Constitution vowed to fight its ratification unless individual liberties were spelled out clearly.

The first ten amendments, adopted in 1791, formed the Bill of Rights. They guaranteed to all citizens the freedoms of speech, religion, and assembly. They also protected citizens from having to testify against themselves and from having their homes searched without cause.

Most Americans trusted George Washington, but they were worried about giving any one person too much power. History has been full of modest people corrupted by power. The Bill of Rights was intended to protect the rights of every individual no matter who became president.

In the years after the American Revolution, the retired general George Washington became so popular that some people wanted to make him king. Washington, however, had no intention of becoming an American monarch. He didn't even want to be president.

Instead, he was quite content to enjoy the peaceful life of his Mount Vernon, Virginia, plantation. But the new nation that he had helped to create needed him.

When the American colonies declared their independence from Great Britain in 1776, their first task was to win the Revolutionary War. But they also had to create a new form of government. Great Britain was ruled by a king, but most Americans wanted to be governed democratically by leaders the people elected.

The first plan for such a government was set forth in the Articles of

The Thirteen Original Colonies

Confederation. It included some features that linked the states together, but it lacked a strong central government with a president to run it. Individual states could still pass their own laws, issue their own money, and levy their own taxes.

The powerlessness of the federal government under the Articles of Confederation became obvious to everyone in 1786 during a revolt in Massachusetts. Farmers there rebelled because they were being jailed for their debts. The federal government could neither put down the uprising nor force the other states to help.

THE CONSTITUTIONAL CONVENTION

Because the Articles of Confederation weren't working, a national meeting was called to develop a new plan. Delegates from the states gathered in Philadelphia on May 25, 1787. George Washington presided over this group, which became known as the Constitutional Convention.

The Constitution that thirty-nine delegates signed in September set up a new federal government with three distinct branches. The legislative branch included two chambers, the House of Representatives and the Senate. The judicial branch would be headed by the Supreme Court. Finally, the executive branch would be led by the president.

CHOOSING THE FIRST PRESIDENT

Presidents have never been elected by the direct vote of the people. Instead, each state chooses a number of electors equal to its representation in Congress. These electors then vote for the president. Until 1832, electors were chosen by state legislatures. After that, electors were chosen directly by voters, except in South Carolina.

When the electoral college met for the first time in January 1789, George

The Early Years

IN 1753, GEORGE WASHINGTON WAS WORKING AS A surveyor in Virginia and serving as a major in the colonial militia. In October, Virginia's colonial governor sent the twenty-one-year-old Washington on a mission to demand that French troops leave land in the Ohio Valley claimed by Britain. The French refused, leading to the French and Indian War.

Because of his military experience during this war and his service to the Continental Congress, Washington was chosen in 1775 to command the new Continental Army. Washington experienced many more defeats than victories, but he never lost badly enough to lose the war completely. Instead, his real task was to keep the army together.

★MYTHS ABOUT GEORGE WASHINGTON

There are many stories that people tell about George Washington. One is that he lost all his teeth and had to wear wooden ones. In fact, he did wear false teeth. But they weren't made out of wood. Instead, he had sets made from gold, lead, and ivory. One set was even made from hippopotamus teeth.

Another myth about Washington was that, as a boy, he chopped down his father's cherry tree. When asked whether he did it, Washington supposedly said, "I cannot tell a lie. I did it." This is certainly not a true story. Rather, it was invented by Parson Mason Weems for his book *The Life and Memorable Actions of George Washington*, first published in 1800. Weems's intention was to create legends for the new country.

★ THE COTTON GIN

Before Eli Whitney invented the cotton gin in 1793, farmers and slaves who cleaned cotton picked the seeds out by hand. Whitney's invention saved a tremendous amount of work because it picked the seeds out mechanically. One person operating a cotton gin could clean as much cotton as fifty people working the old way.

With this new technology, southern farmers were able to expand their plantings by thousands of acres. Cotton soon became so important to the region that it was called King Cotton.

★ CHIEF RED JACKET

One of the most pressing problems facing Washington was trouble along the frontier. Whites who were anxious to farm the rich land in the nation's interior were settling native lands illegally. Soon enough, the Creek, Chickasaw, Cherokee, and Seminole tribes decided to fight back.

In 1792, Washington met with the Seneca chief Red Jacket, to whom he gave a silver medal as a token of respect. Red Jacket believed that the Indians would inevitably have to make peace with the powerful whites. However, later in his life, the chief fought vigorously to protect the Senecas' customs, religion, and language.

★ THE FIRST LADY

When George Washington became president, his wife, Martha, was wary of living a public life. As time went on, however, she grew fond of her role as the first lady. She hosted state dinners every week, and on Friday afternoons, she and Abigail Adams, the vice president's wife, held casual receptions for anyone who might want to attend. The informality of these receptions was supposed to show that the new government was not above the people. But visitors to the president's house still wore fine clothes and called Martha "Lady Washington."

Washington was the clear choice of the electors. But the retired general was still reluctant to serve, a fact that probably helped him win.

Americans continued to worry about one man having too much power. If there had to be a president, people thought, it should be someone who didn't want the job. When the vote for president was taken, Washington was the unanimous choice.

HAMILTON AND JEFFERSON One of the president's first tasks was to appoint people to head each of the four executive departments: Foreign Affairs (later called State), War, Treasury, and Justice. For the first secretary of the treasury, Washington chose Alexander Hamilton, who had played an important role at the Constitutional Convention. Later, along with James Madison and John Jay, Hamilton had written the *Federalist Papers*, which had urged ratification of the Constitution.

Hamilton's political rival, Thomas Jefferson, became the first secretary of state. Unlike Hamilton, Jefferson feared a strong federal government. As ambassador to France, he had seen how the ruling classes there lived in luxury, while poor people dressed in rags and begged on the streets. He blamed the problems of France on its powerful central government.

Jefferson worried that a strong government in the United States might oppress people, too. From the opposite point of view, Hamilton worried that a weak federal government would accomplish nothing. Usually Washington sided with Hamilton.

At first, Washington asked each of his four department heads to meet with him separately. But this took up a lot of time and was not very effective. Eventually, the president came up

GEORGE WASHINGTON 1789-1797

3

with a better way. In late 1791, he instructed the secretaries to meet with him as a single group. This group became known as the cabinet.

PAYING THE STATES' DEBTS One of the most important issues faced by the cabinet during Washington's first term was the public debt owed by the states. During the Revolutionary War, most states had borrowed money from foreign and American investors to pay their soldiers. This money had to be paid back. Early in 1790, Hamilton came up with a plan. He proposed that the federal government pay off the states' debts.

Hamilton had two reasons. The first was that he wanted to establish the federal government's credit. The best way to encourage people to lend money is to show the ability to pay off a debt. Paying off the states' debts would encourage citizens and foreign governments to lend money to the federal government in the future.

The second reason was to bring the states closer together in the new union. If the debts became the responsibility of the federal government, the states would be motivated to work together to pay them off.

IMPLIED POWERS The problem with paying off the states' debts was that the Constitution had not given the federal government the power to do it. On the other hand, the Constitution had not specifically withheld that power, either. Hamilton argued that by not forbidding it, the Constitution implied the existence of such a power. Hamilton's theory has been called the doctrine of implied powers.

Jefferson thought that Hamilton's argument was dangerous. He believed the more power the government took,

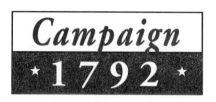

WHEN THE ELECTORAL COLLEGE MET IN 1789 AND again in 1792, each elector voted for two people. The person getting the most votes became president, as long as that total represented a majority. In both elections, the winner was George Washington. In 1789 and again in 1792, not a single elector cast a vote against him. Washington was the only president ever to be elected unanimously.

The person with the second highest electoral vote became vice president. In both the 1789 and 1792 elections, John Adams received the second highest total, so he became Washington's vice president.

Under the Constitution, the vice president had not much responsibility or power. His role was to break tied votes in the Senate and take over if the president resigned or died. Adams called the job the "most insignificant office that ever the invention of man contrived or his imagination conceived."

Buttons were made to honor George Washington's first inauguration on April 30, 1789. One design consisted of his initials and the words "Long Live the President." Another featured an eagle. The buttons played no role in the campaign, but they are believed to be forerunners of the campaign buttons used today.

Martha and George Washington with John and Martha Custis (left).

WAR IN EUROPE

Can the United States Stay Neutral?

THE WAR between France and Great Britain that began in 1793 had an immediate effect on the United States. Both Britain and France still held territory in North America, and the naval battles they fought off the West Indies continually disrupted U.S. shipping.

During the Revolutionary War, the Continental Congress had signed a treaty with King Louis XVI of France. In exchange for military aid, the Americans promised to defend the French West Indies against British attack.

In 1793, the French government asked for American help. But the U.S. refused, believing the treaty no longer applied because Louis XVI had been overthrown and executed.

Meanwhile, Britain, which had never fully accepted American independence, also began provoking the U.S. In 1794, the Royal Navy began boarding American ships that were suspected of carrying British deserters. During these raids, the British kidnapped not only former British sailors, but also innocent Americans. The practice was called impressment.

the less freedom the people would have. In response to Hamilton, Jefferson argued that unless the Constitution explicitly granted the power to do something, it couldn't be done. Hamilton and Jefferson's debate has continued throughout the history of the United States.

THE FIRST NATIONAL BANK Part of Hamilton's plan included the establishment of a national bank to hold federal deposits and issue paper money. Many people, especially farmers, conducted business by trading goods. When they did use money, it was in the form of gold and silver coins. Because America had only small stores of these precious metals, most people used coins that had been minted in other countries. Everything from English pounds to Russian kopecks passed from hand to hand.

The national bank met with a great deal of opposition, especially from Jefferson, who feared any concentration of governmental power. In exchange for Jefferson's acceptance of the national bank, which Congress approved in 1791, Hamilton agreed to move the nation's capital so that it would be closer to Jefferson's native Virginia.

New York City was the nation's first capital. With a population of thirty-three thousand, it was the largest city in the country. Its streets were jammed daily with city residents and country farmers who had come to sell their goods. The wagons that clattered along the cobblestone streets made a terrible racket.

Besides these drawbacks of New York, some members of the government thought it would be wiser to move the nation's capital to a district outside the control of any one state. For the new capital, George Washington chose a site on the Potomac River between Maryland and Virginia. Each of these states donated a share of the land for the new District of Columbia within which the capital city of Washington would be built. In the meantime, Philadelphia became the temporary capital.

THE PROCLAMATION OF NEUTRALITY

America's foreign policy was first tested during Washington's second term. Soon after the French Revolution began, France declared war on Great Britain. The French had greatly aided the American cause during the American Revolution, and now they asked for help in return. Jefferson was inclined to say yes. But many officials, including Alexander Hamilton, argued against supporting France. Almost every American agreed on one point, however. No one wanted to get involved in the actual fighting.

In April 1793, knowing it would be best to stay out of a European war, Washington issued the Proclamation of Neutrality. In it, he advised the states to remain friendly with both sides. But he also warned them against smuggling weapons and other contraband, which might pull the United States into the war.

Jefferson generally supported Washington's conduct of relations with France and Britain. But he grew increasingly tired of fighting with Hamilton. In late 1793, he resigned as secretary of state.

★THE SLAVE TRADE

The slave trade between Africa and North America began in the 1600s. By the 1790s, there were about seven hundred thousand slaves in the United States. Although the northern states all outlawed slavery between 1777 and 1804, the South became even more dependent on slave labor

after the invention of the cotton gin led to more cotton planting.

Some slaves were taught skills, such as how to read and write. A few even managed to earn enough money to buy their freedom. But most slaves were beaten into obedience. Some slaveholders convinced themselves that Africans were less than human, which made it seem acceptable to treat African slaves brutally.

★THE FRENCH REVOLUTION

By 1789, the French government was almost bankrupt. Peasants in the countryside and poor people in the cities were on the verge of rioting for food. Only the aristocracy of titled landowners remained rich.

In May 1789, the government convened an emergency meeting of the Estates-General, a special parliament made up of delegates from the clergy, the aristocracy, and the

common people. Both the clergy and the aristocracy wanted to protect their privileges. But the representatives of the common people wanted to eliminate these advantages.

Alarmed by the people's demands, King Louis XVI sent twenty thousand soldiers to Versailles, where the Estates-General was meeting. News of this troop movement enraged Parisians, who responded by attacking the Bastille prison and capturing the weapons stored there. The storming of the Bastille on July 14, 1789, is considered the beginning of the French Revolution.

★**PAINTING IN AMERICA** The most promising art students in America were usually sent to Europe for their training. The two most famous American painters of this time, Benjamin West and John Singleton Copley, both settled in London, where they followed the fashion of painting scenes from history.

In America, the most popular paintings were portraits. Most American artists painted little else until the 1840s when photography reduced the demand for them. The leading portrait painters of the time were Gilbert Stuart and Charles Willson Peale. Both men painted George Washington, who was known to be a patient subject. The most famous of these works is an unfinished portrait of Washington begun by Stuart in 1794. An etching based on this portrait appears on the dollar bill.

★**ROYAL GIFT** Despite his achievements as a general and president, George Washington saw himself primarily as a farmer. Throughout his life, he remained interested in the breeding of animals. His specialty was breeding mules.

A mule is the offspring of a male donkey and a female horse. Washington was always trying to improve the strength of his mules.

Learning of Washington's passion, the king of Spain sent him an excellent donkey as a gift. Washington named the donkey Royal Gift and used him to breed many fine mules. He occasionally mated Royal Gift with female donkeys and sent the offspring all over the country to raise the quality of breeding stock nationwide.

★**FAMILY FARMS** Farming was the most important industry in the United States until the twentieth century. George Washington called it "the most healthy, the most useful, and the most noble employment of man." In Washington's time, most farms were small and self-sufficient, producing only a tiny surplus of crops that could be traded for manufactured goods. Women played a particularly important role on these small farms.

Girls worked with their mothers on family farms to make everything from beeswax for candles to yarn for clothing. What little extra they made they traded at the local country store for items they couldn't make themselves, such as printed cloth and sugar.

THE WHISKEY REBELLION Although Washington was very successful in keeping the United States out of the war, he was much quicker to use military force at home. An important example was the Whiskey Rebellion.

In 1791, Congress ordered a tax on whiskey. This tax outraged farmers who made whiskey from their extra corn. (Otherwise, it would spoil.) Some people in the countryside even used whiskey for money.

When federal officers tried to collect the whiskey tax in western Pennsylvania, farmers there rebelled. When the governor refused to punish the farmers and collect the tax himself, the problem became a national one.

Because the Whiskey Rebellion represented a direct and immediate challenge to the authority of the national government, Washington decided to form a volunteer army to enforce the law.

In fact, the incident never posed a serious military threat. Most of the rebels turned and ran when they saw Washington's army coming. But the incident was an important test of the new government. In putting down the Whiskey Rebellion, Washington proved that the federal government had the power to enforce its laws.

Meanwhile, Washington's policy of neutrality was being tested by the British, who began to stop and search American ships that were allegedly carrying supplies to the French. Britain also began encouraging Indians to attack American settlers along the nation's northwest frontier.

In order to avoid war, the U.S. minister to Great Britain, John Jay, negotiated a new treaty with the British government. In exchange for Britain's promise to withdraw troops from the Northwest Territory, the

United States agreed to permit the inspection of its ships on the high seas. Many people criticized Jay's Treaty for bargaining away the nation's neutrality rights. But it did postpone a war that America was not prepared to fight. Washington signed the treaty and managed to get it ratified by the Senate.

THE NORTHWEST TERRITORY

Disputes between settlers and native peoples on the nation's frontier were a constant problem for Washington. At first, he tried to solve the problem militarily. He sent General Arthur St. Clair into the Northwest Territory in 1791 to build a fort there.

Washington warned St. Clair to watch for surprise attacks, but St. Clair didn't listen. His two-thousand-man army was ambushed by Indian warriors on November 4, 1791, on the site of present-day Fort Wayne, Indiana. The Americans suffered more than nine hundred casualties.

When Washington found out, he was furious. But he didn't try to cover up the blunder. Instead, he immediately informed Congress and sent General "Mad" Anthony Wayne to replace St. Clair.

Wayne was more careful. Before fighting the Indians, he spent time training his men in the methods of Indian warfare. On August 20, 1794, he engaged the tribal armies at the Battle of Fallen Timbers, where he won a decisive victory. Then, during the summer of 1795, Wayne spent six weeks negotiating a peace treaty with delegates of the Great Lakes, Mississippi River, and Ohio River tribes.

George Washington announced his retirement in his Farewell Address, which was published on September 19, 1796. In it, he warned the nation against becoming permanently allied with foreign powers.

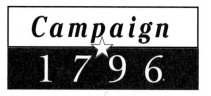

Campaign 1796

AS MOST PEOPLE expected, Vice President John Adams announced that he would run for president in 1796. Like Washington, Adams was a member of the Federalist party, which supported a strong central government and life terms for senators.

Adams's opponent, former secretary of state Thomas Jefferson, had very different political ideas. He led a new party, the Democratic-Republicans, that favored more power for the states and limited terms for public office.

Out of personal respect for George Washington, the Democratic-Republicans had been relatively quiet during his two terms. Now that Washington was retiring, they were ready to fight.

During the American Revolution, Adams and Jefferson had been friends and colleagues. But the rough campaign of 1796, the first to be contested, turned them into enemies. The Democratic-Republicans claimed that Adams wanted to become an American king, while the Federalists condemned Jefferson as a demagogue—that is, someone who manipulates popular fears for his or her own political ends.

It was probably Washington's endorsement that won the election for Adams. Jefferson came in second, however, and became Adams's vice president. This was the only time in history that the president and vice president were members of different political parties. In 1804, the Twelfth Amendment to the Constitution changed the way the president and vice president were elected so that it wouldn't happen again.

JOHN ADAMS

2ND PRESIDENT

★

FROM 1797 TO 1801

BORN: October 30, 1735

BIRTHPLACE: Braintree, Mass.

DIED: July 4, 1826

PARTY: Federalist

VICE PRESIDENT: Thomas Jefferson

FIRST LADY: Abigail Smith

CHILDREN: Abigail, John Quincy, Susanna, Charles, Thomas

NICKNAME: Duke of Braintree

The first president to live in the White House.

ALIEN AND SEDITION ACTS PASSED BY CONGRESS

In 1798, as the United States moved closer to war with France, John Adams signed into law the Alien and Sedition Acts to protect America's security.

There were four bills: The Naturalization Act made it harder for immigrants to become U.S. citizens. The Alien and Alien Enemies acts gave the president the power, especially during wartime, to deport or imprison foreigners he considered dangerous. Finally, the Sedition Act outlawed attacks against the government.

Jefferson saw these new laws mainly as a way for Adams to control his political rivals. The Democratic-Republicans received a lot of support from recent immigrants, and they believed Adams sought to take away these votes. The Sedition Act also limited their freedom to criticize the policies of the government.

With his opposition to the new laws, Jefferson became the first person to apply the Constitution to an actual dispute. He argued that the Sedition Act was unconstitutional because it violated the freedom of speech guaranteed by the First Amendment.

The most critical problem facing John Adams when he took office involved French raids on American shipping. U.S. neutrality in the war between Britain and France had led to a boom in trade. Both warring nations badly needed supplies from the United States, but neither wanted the other to receive any U.S. goods.

In 1794, the United States signed Jay's Treaty with Great Britain. This agreement, ratified in 1795, gave away some of the nation's neutrality. In retaliation, the French government began encouraging pirates to attack ships headed for Great Britain. As the number of seized merchant ships neared three hundred, the American public demanded war. There was even a wild rumor that the French might be planning an invasion.

Remembering the warning against foreign entanglements in Washington's Farewell Address,

Growth of the U.S. 1791-1797 VT 1791

President Adams held back. Instead of fighting, he sent three diplomats to negotiate with French foreign minister Charles Talleyrand. Refusing to receive the U.S. mission himself, Talleyrand sent three aides to meet the Americans. These Frenchmen were later referred to as "X," "Y," and "Z" by Adams, who did not wish to reveal their names.

Before the Frenchmen would even listen to the Americans, they demanded a bribe of $250,000. This demand outraged Adams, who had long been famous for strictly following the law.

WAR FEVER AT HOME When news of the XYZ Affair reached the United States, the nation caught war fever. A popular slogan was "Millions for defense, but not one cent for tribute." Tribute meant the payment of bribes in order to stop the attacks.

Still, Adams would not declare war. The United States was not yet prepared to fight at sea, and it would take time to build a capable navy. In the meantime, Adams convinced Congress to stop U.S. trade with France. He also made arrangements for the powerful British navy to protect transatlantic shipping.

It was in the wartime atmosphere of 1798 that Adams obtained passage of the Alien and Sedition Acts. These laws made it hard for the Democratic-Republicans to organize opposition to the government. Jefferson's earlier, unpopular support for the French Revolution also hindered the Democratic-Republicans in their efforts to reverse Adams's policies.

Jefferson publicly accused Adams of enacting the laws in order to frustrate his political foes. He was at least partially correct. Over the next year, at least ten Democratic-Republican newspaper editors were jailed under the Sedition Act.

10

JOHN ADAMS GREW UP ON A FARM IN BRAINTREE (NOW Quincy), Massachusetts, where he liked to spend his time hunting in the woods and playing a variety of games. Adams particularly liked flying kites, shooting marbles, and making toy boats.

After graduating from Harvard, he became a lawyer in Boston. His most famous case was argued in 1770, when he successfully defended the nine British soldiers accused in the Boston Massacre. In that pre-revolutionary incident, a resentful mob of Bostonians menaced a squad of frightened redcoats. The soldiers shot and killed five colonists despite orders not to fire.

From 1774 until 1777, Adams served as a delegate to the Continental Congress in Philadelphia. There, he nominated George Washington to be commander-in-chief of the Continental Army. He also helped Thomas Jefferson write the Declaration of Independence.

★**THE FIRST LADY** For long periods of time during the American Revolution and afterward, John Adams lived away from his Massachusetts home in Philadelphia, New York, France, and England. While he was away, his wife Abigail had to manage the family farm and raise their five children. Many of the nation's founders, including Thomas Jefferson, suffered financially because of the time they spent away from home. But Abigail Adams's shrewd handling of her husband's financial affairs kept the family prosperous.

Although she was the wife of one president and the mother of another, Abigail herself felt disappointed at the lack of opportunities she had as a woman. She regretted especially that the women of her time were denied the same education that men received. In letters she wrote to her husband, Abigail charged him to "remember the ladies" who had served the country so well during the revolution.

★**BLACK CHURCHES** Around 1800, churches began to play an important role in the lives of many African Americans in the North. Unable to attend most schools and unwelcome in politics, many black people turned to the church as a center for education and community organizing.

In the South, however, slaves were often not allowed to attend church services. Their white owners were afraid of letting them gather in large groups. Whites also worried about slaves becoming literate, and therefore discontented, through learning to read the Bible.

★**JOHNNY APPLESEED** Sometime about 1800, twenty-six-year-old John Chapman began to collect apple seeds from cider presses in western Pennsylvania. He used these seeds to grow small plants, which he planned to sell to pioneer families on the western frontier.

At that time, homesteaders were still settling the Ohio River valley. During his travels, Chapman sold or gave away thousands of apple seedlings to these people.

Although John Chapman was a real person, his exploits inspired the myth of Johnny Appleseed. Stories were told of a cheerful, generous vagabond with an upside-down pan for a hat, bare feet, and a coffee sack for a shirt. In addition to planting apple trees, Johnny Appleseed was famous for his gentleness with animals, his love for nature, and his peaceful relations with the Indians.

★**RETIREMENT** Although the end to his presidency was quite rocky, Adams enjoyed a peaceful retirement at his family home in Massachusetts. He spent most of his time reading the literature of the world in his library. Once his eyesight began to fail, his eighteen grandchildren and great-grandchildren took turns reading aloud to him. As time went on, he even renewed his friendship with Jefferson.

At the age of eighty-nine, Adams proudly watched his son John Quincy win election as the sixth president. Two years later, he was invited

to participate in Boston's celebration of the fiftieth anniversary of the Declaration of Independence. Adams never made it, dying quietly in the early evening of July 4, 1826. His last words were "Jefferson still survives."

Although Adams had no way of knowing it, Jefferson had died a few hours earlier at his Monticello estate in Virginia.

To protest the Alien and Sedition Acts, Jefferson and James Madison wrote the Kentucky and Virginia Resolves, which argued that the new laws were void because they were unconstitutional. Jefferson and Madison even went so far as to insist that states had the right to reject federal laws. This argument would become much more important in the years leading up to the Civil War.

THE QUASI-WAR From the spring of 1798 through 1800, despite the official state of peace between the two nations, U.S. frigates battled the French navy. Adams hesitated to declare war because he hoped the fighting would soon stop. He thought the French were too busy in Europe to continue bothering with North America.

In September 1800, a second mission to Talleyrand negotiated an end to what had become known as the Quasi-War because it wasn't a declared war. France agreed to recognize the neutrality of U.S. shipping. In exchange, Adams agreed to increase trade with France.

This treaty helped shipbuilders and merchants in port cities along the Atlantic coast. But the new trade policy did little for citizens in the interior, most of whom were either farmers or artisans.

These people lived a self-contained life. Their work kept them cut off from the outside world. Farming left them and their families little time for education.

In contrast, the men from the east coast who ran the government were wealthy, well-educated, and out of touch with the lives and concerns of the rural farmer. One reason that Jefferson opposed life terms for senators was that he feared the creation of a class of politicians completely removed from the needs of the people.

Soon after concluding the treaty with France in the fall of 1800, John Adams and his family moved to the nation's new capital. Although ten years had passed since architects and engineers had first begun work on Washington, D.C., the city was still barely populated, rough, and muddy. The president's house wasn't finished yet, and the wing in which the Adamses lived was quite drafty. The first family stayed only a year, but during that time the damp, poorly heated house and wild, lonely city had a harmful effect on Abigail Adams's health.

Although Adams was widely popular during the Quasi-War, he lost much of that popularity during the last year of his term. People thought his government was too isolated and that it ignored their wishes. They also agreed with Jefferson that the Alien and Sedition Acts limited their personal freedom. The Federalists, too, led by Alexander Hamilton, turned against Adams because he refused to declare war on France.

THE MIDNIGHT APPOINTMENTS

Adams was not surprised when he lost the 1800 election to Jefferson. Still, the president was a stubborn, embittered man. He was determined that the policies of his Federalist administration should continue. To ensure this, he appointed a large number of judges, all Federalists, in the final days of his administration. Because they came so late in his term, they were known as the Midnight Appointments.

Adams's idea was to fill the courts with Federalists who could frustrate the plans of Jefferson and the Democratic-Republicans. Jefferson's refusal to honor these last-minute appointments led to the landmark Supreme Court case of *Marbury v. Madison*.

The campaign of 1800 was a replay of the 1796 election between Adams and Jefferson. Although neither candidate made public appearances or statements, the contest was a bitter one.

In the tradition of early American etiquette, both men pretended they didn't want to be president. But this false modesty didn't stop their supporters from openly insulting the opposing candidate at every opportunity. The Federalists in power even used the Sedition Act to prosecute the Democratic-Republican press.

When the electoral college met, Jefferson and Aaron Burr each received seventy-three votes, defeating the Federalist ticket of John Adams and Charles Pinckney. It had been understood during the campaign that Burr was running as the vice-presidential candidate. But after the election, Burr refused to step down. Instead, because of the tied vote, the election

was thrown into the House of Representatives, which would decide the winner. After thirty-five separate votes, the House remained deadlocked.

Jefferson's old rival, Alexander Hamilton, faced a dilemma. He still had influence with the Federalist members of Congress. Using this influence, he could break the deadlock. But which candidate should he support? Hamilton disliked Jefferson personally, but he didn't trust Burr at all.

In the end, Hamilton decided that his country was more important than his personal feelings. On February 17, 1801, on the thirty-sixth ballot, he persuaded several congressmen not to vote at all. This swung the election to Jefferson, who became the third president of the United States.

THOMAS JEFFERSON

3RD PRESIDENT

★

FROM 1801 TO 1809

BORN: April 13, 1743

BIRTHPLACE: Shadwell, Va.

DIED: July 4, 1826

PARTY: Democratic-Republican

VICE PRESIDENTS: Aaron Burr, George Clinton

FIRST LADY: Martha Wayles Skelton

CHILDREN: Martha, Jane, Mary, Lucy

NICKNAME: Red Fox

Jefferson's grandson was the first baby born in the White House.

JEFFERSON BUYS FRENCH LAND

Louisiana Purchase Doubles Size of Country

The United States got the biggest bargain in history when Robert Livingston and James Monroe negotiated the massive Louisiana Purchase during the spring of 1803.

The Louisiana Territory, which covered 828,000 square miles and stretched from the Mississippi River to the Rocky Mountains, was first explored by the Spanish in the 1600s. The French later colonized the area, founding New Orleans at the mouth of the Mississippi in 1718.

Throughout the 1700s, control of the area passed back and forth between the French and the Spanish. Between 1800 and 1802, Napoleon's victories in Europe forced the Spanish to give the territory back to France. Spain had allowed U.S. ships to travel freely on the Mississippi, but Jefferson feared that the French might revoke this important privilege.

It was the job of Jefferson's envoys to secure this right of free passage and, if possible, to buy New Orleans. When the two American diplomats arrived, however, French foreign minister Charles Talleyrand surprised them by offering the entire Louisiana Territory. Was the United States interested?

Livingston and Monroe were flabbergasted. Although it exceeded their instructions, the two men soon agreed to a price of fifteen million dollars for the land, which worked out to approximately four cents an acre.

John Adams was not in Washington to see Jefferson's inauguration on March 4, 1801. Bitter at his loss, Adams snuck out of town at dawn rather than stay on to watch Jefferson take the oath of office. The transfer of power may not have been a gracious one, but it was the first time in the country's history that political power passed successfully from one party to another.

After the viciousness of the campaign, Jefferson tried to calm the nation by stressing unity and toleration in his inaugural address. To prove that he meant what he said, the president quickly asked Congress to repeal the Alien and Sedition Acts, and people jailed under these laws were soon released.

The election of 1800 was sometimes called the Revolution of 1800 because that year the

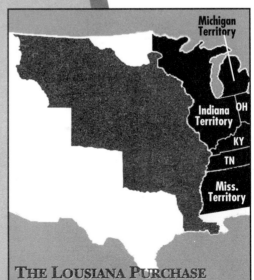

THE LOUSIANA PURCHASE

Michigan Territory · Indiana Territory · OH · KY · TN · Miss. Territory

Democratic-Republicans took control of both the executive and legislative branches of government.

The Democratic-Republicans were able to win the presidency as well as comfortable majorities in both houses of Congress because the campaign had clearly shown the differences between the two parties. The Federalists believed in strong laws to protect business and property. During the campaign, they had warned that a Democratic-Republican government would lead to mob rule, as the French Revolution had.

But the country was tired of Federalist politics. Unlike most Federalists, Thomas Jefferson was more a philosopher than a politician. He was more concerned about democracy and the freedom of the individual than he was interested in the details of government.

In line with his Democratic-Republican principles, Jefferson concentrated on making the government smaller and less involved in the lives of the people. He reduced the size of the military, recalled more than half of the American diplomatic missions in Europe, and ordered a careful review of all government spending. These measures reduced the national debt by one-half.

THE BARBARY PIRATES

Jefferson's first crisis as president came in foreign affairs. The Barbary pirates were vicious buccaneers who operated out of the North African states of Morocco, Algiers, Tunis, and Tripoli. They attacked merchant ships and kidnapped sailors, imprisoning and often torturing them.

For years, the United States had been paying tribute to the leaders of the Barbary states. In exchange for these payments, the Barbary pirates agreed not to attack U.S. ships. By

BEGINNING IN 1762, JEFFERSON STUDIED LAW UNDER George Wythe, who also taught future Supreme Court chief justice John Marshall. Jefferson's apprenticeship ended in April 1767, when he was admitted to the bar in Virginia.

The Early Years

Jefferson served in the Virginia House of Burgesses from 1769 until 1774, and in the Continental Congress after that. Only thirty-three years old, Jefferson was the youngest delegate to the congress in Philadelphia, but he was nevertheless given the task of writing the Declaration of Independence.

The Continental Congress spent almost three days debating Jefferson's work, dissecting every word and phrase. Several changes were made. For instance, a passage attacking slavery was deleted. The document was finally approved on July 4, 1776.

★MONTICELLO

Thomas Jefferson was known as a Renaissance man because he had an extraordinary range of interests. One was architecture. When the government held a competition to design the president's new home, Jefferson submitted a design anonymously. He didn't win.

Jefferson did design his own house, named Monticello, outside Charlottesville, Virginia. The first section of the house, built between 1770 and 1775, was modeled on the Italian villas designed by Andrea Palladio in the sixteenth century. Palladio's villas were in turn based on classical Roman buildings.

★THE *CLERMONT*

On August 18, 1807, people on the banks of the Hudson River in New York saw a very strange sight. A ship, smoking as though on fire, was steadily heading up the river against the current. Even more peculiar were its sails, which were rolled up and therefore useless.

Only later did people find out that the ship, the *Clermont*, was a steamship. Its engineer, Robert Fulton, had been working on the ship's design for more than five years. Although the *Clermont* wasn't the very first steamship, it was the first commercially successful one. Fulton's boat began carrying passengers and freight in September 1807. Within two months, it turned a profit for its owners.

14

★BENJAMIN BANNEKER

Benjamin Banneker was one of the country's first important black scholars. From an early age, Banneker had a talent for mathematics and science. He was almost entirely self-taught. He learned astronomy by charting the movements of the planets in the night sky. He learned mathematics from borrowed textbooks.

President Washington appointed Banneker to the District of Columbia Commission in 1790 so that Banneker could help survey the site of the new capital. Meanwhile, between 1791 and 1802, he published a popular annual almanac. Banneker sent a copy of his first almanac to Jefferson, who was then secretary of state. He included a note asking Jefferson to use his influence to make life better for the country's blacks.

★TRIANGULAR TRADE

Although there was not nearly enough support to outlaw slavery altogether, Jefferson did manage to convince Congress to ban the slave trade. A new law that became effective on January 1, 1808, banned the importation of slaves into the United States. However, tens of thousands of slaves continued to be smuggled into the country illegally.

The slave traders had followed the same triangular route for more than a century. They carried rum from distilleries in New England to West Africa. There, the rum was traded for slaves. The slaves were usually members of rival tribes who had been captured during a war or kidnapped from their villages.

The slaves were kept shackled in the holds of ships for months. Eventually, they were taken to the West Indies, where they were traded for molasses. The molasses was then carried back to New England, where it was made into rum, completing the triangle. The slaves were sold off in the West Indies to North and South Americans.

1801, nearly two million dollars had been paid in tribute.

The situation changed when the ruler of Tripoli decided that the United States wasn't paying enough money. In May 1801, he declared war on the United States, brashly cutting down the flagpole in front of the U.S. consulate in the city of Tripoli.

In response, Jefferson sent the navy to Tripoli. At first, it performed poorly. The pirates captured one ship, the *Philadelphia*, in 1803 and turned its guns against the remaining U.S. ships. It took a daring raid by Stephen Decatur, a young lieutenant, to destroy the *Philadelphia* so that its guns could not be used against the Americans.

In 1805, the U.S. fleet captured Derna, one of Tripoli's main seaports. The loss of Derna forced the ruler of Tripoli to sign a peace treaty that ended the payment of tribute forever. Pirates from the other Barbary states, however, continued to disrupt shipping for another ten years.

THE LOUISIANA PURCHASE

Another foreign involvement also occupied the president's time. Napoleon's military victories in Europe had recently forced Spain to turn over many of its North American colonies to France, including control of the Mississippi River. Jefferson feared that France might now try to deny Americans the right to travel up and down the Mississippi, which would hurt trade dramatically on the western frontier.

The people settling the Mississippi River country at this time were mostly poor farming families. The only land these people could afford was on the untamed western frontier.

Families would usually travel on foot, carrying their belongings on their backs. If they were lucky, they might have a milking cow that could help them with the hauling. Once they found a place to settle, they would build a crude log cabin. The roof, usually made of mud or thatch, often leaked. The final job would be to chop down trees and turn the surrounding forest into fields that could be planted.

Believing that farmers were the key to a stable and productive country, Jefferson wanted to ensure that farmers on the western frontier could ship their goods along the Mississippi River. When a mission he sent to France was offered the entire Louisiana Territory, he was both shocked and excited. The problem was, nothing in the Constitution gave the president the power to buy land.

Throughout his years in government, Jefferson had argued against the Federalists' doctrine of implied powers. In theory, Jefferson believed that larger government meant less freedom for the people. Therefore, the best governments were small, simple, and frugal.

To authorize the purchase of the Louisiana Territory, Jefferson would have to compromise his thinking. But the offer was too good to pass up. Besides adding huge tracts of land to the young nation, the Louisiana Purchase guaranteed free passage along the Mississippi River. The irony for Jefferson was that the purchase also ensured the need for a strong central government to run the huge new country.

MARBURY V. MADISON Back in the capital, Jefferson's ongoing battles with the Federalists led to an important Supreme Court decision. After the election of 1800 (but before the Democratic-Republicans came to power), the Federalist Congress hastily passed the Judiciary Act of 1801, creating a number of new federal judgeships.

THE ELECTION OF 1800 HAD POINTED OUT A serious flaw in the way the president and vice president were chosen. When Jefferson and Burr both received the same number of electoral votes, the stalemate nearly caused a constitutional crisis. Had it not been for Alexander Hamilton's involvement, the House of Representatives might have remained deadlocked indefinitely.

To remedy this oversight in the Constitution, the Twelfth Amendment was passed and ratified in time for the 1804 election. It changed the rules of the electoral college so that the electors now voted separately for president and vice president.

Jefferson was once again the presidential candidate of the Democratic-Republicans. But Burr, the disloyal vice president, was dropped from the ticket and replaced with Governor George Clinton of New York.

The Federalists weren't much of a factor in this election. Their candidate, Charles Pinckney of South Carolina, had run on the same ticket with John Adams in 1800. He was an experienced and qualified statesman, but Jefferson was a popular president and won easily.

Adams filled these positions at the last minute with Federalists whom he believed would frustrate Jefferson's policies. Because these Midnight Appointments were made so late, there wasn't even time to deliver the official commission to one of the new judges, William Marbury. After Jefferson took office, his secretary of state, James Madison, refused to deliver Marbury's commission. Marbury sued.

The case went all the way to the Supreme Court. In his 1803 decision, Chief Justice John Marshall declared that a section of the Judiciary Act of 1789 was unconstitutional. This action established the important principle of judicial review. Marshall's ruling demonstrated that the Supreme Court could void an act of Congress if the law in question violated the Constitution.

THE BURR CONSPIRACY   In his second inaugural address, Jefferson summed up the successes of his administration and looked to the future. He announced plans to build new roads to the western lands as well as canals in the East to connect that region's major waterways. Canals promoted trade by making it easier to transport goods.

What Jefferson didn't know was that his second term would be marred by a dangerous conspiracy. A crisis abroad also contributed to the turmoil that forced him to postpone these plans.

LEOPARD ATTACKS CHESAPEAKE

Four Sailors Impressed as 21 Die

OFF VIRGINIA, June 22, 1807—The British warship *Leopard* fired today on the U.S. frigate *Chesapeake*. The British commander had demanded that the U.S. captain allow his ship to be boarded. When the *Chesapeake*'s captain refused, the *Leopard* opened fire, killing or wounding twenty-one sailors.

After disabling the *Chesapeake*, the captain of the *Leopard* sent over a boarding party, which took four sailors from the *Chesapeake*'s crew. One of these men was indeed a deserter from the Royal Navy, but the other three were U.S. citizens.

President Jefferson expressed his outrage at the continuation of the British policy of impressment, under which the Royal Navy has stopped U.S. ships on the high seas and carried away sailors by force.

As a result of the *Leopard*'s actions, state legislatures all over the country are now demanding war with Great Britain.

17

Aaron Burr was a jealous and bitter man. After losing the fight for the presidency in 1800, Burr was desperate to get even with Jefferson.

While Jefferson ran for reelection in 1804, Burr ran for governor of New York. In order to obtain the support of the Essex Junto, a powerful group of New England Federalists, Burr had to promise that, if he became governor, New York would secede from the union and join Massachusetts in a new Federalist country.

THE BURR-HAMILTON DUEL Alexander Hamilton was shocked to learn of the plan. He didn't wish to see Jefferson reelected. But he couldn't stand the thought of his own state, New York, leaving the Union. When Hamilton began working against him, Burr became enraged and challenged Hamilton to a duel. On July 11, 1804, Burr shot and killed Hamilton.

Burr first fled south after being charged with Hamilton's murder. But when the charges were dropped, he returned to Washington and presided over the Senate until the end of his vice-presidential term in 1805.

Although he lost the election in New York, Burr still pursued his treasonous activities. He met with the British minister to the United States, asking him for half a million dollars and the help of the British navy in taking over the Louisiana Territory. When the British ignored him, Burr went to Louisiana anyway, where he tried to incite a rebellion by himself.

Jefferson was told of Burr's plans by General James Wilkinson, the military governor of the Louisiana Territory. Burr had recently approached Wilkinson with the idea of establishing a new empire.

In 1807, Burr was arrested for treason. Chief Justice John Marshall

★**RELIGIOUS FREEDOM** Of all Jefferson's accomplishments, he was perhaps most proud of the law guaranteeing religious freedom that he helped enact in his home state of Virginia. This law, finalized in 1786, stated that each Virginian was free to attend the church of his or her choice, or no church at all.

Some people attacked Jefferson as an atheist, although he did, in fact, believe in a single creator. Jefferson also admired the teachings of Jesus. But what he really cherished was religious tolerance. "It does me no injury," he once wrote, "for my neighbor to say there are twenty gods, or no god. It neither picks my pocket nor breaks my leg."

★**SACAJAWEA** One of the most important members of the Lewis and Clark expedition was a sixteen-year-old Shoshone girl named Sacajawea. Along with her French-Canadian husband, she joined the expedition in 1804, while Lewis and Clark were wintering in the Dakotas.

As Lewis and Clark continued west during the spring, they encountered a number of different Indian tribes. Sacajawea's ability to communicate with these native people proved to be invaluable in convincing suspicious tribes that Lewis and Clark's intentions were peaceful.

★**NOAH WEBSTER** In 1800, Noah Webster began work on a comprehensive dictionary of the English language. A famous dictionary of English had already been published by the British scholar Samuel Johnson in 1755. But Webster understood that the English language was spoken and written differently in the United States than in England.

In 1806, and again in 1807, Webster published small dictionaries as he kept working on the larger project. Webster didn't publish his complete dictionary until 1828, making his effort truly the work of a lifetime. The 1828 dictionary contained more than seventy thousand words, or twelve thousand more than even Johnson's contained.

★ THE SHAKERS

Cooperative religious communities in the United States date back to colonial times. One of the first was founded by Ann Lee, who came to America in 1774 to escape persecution in England. Her followers were a radical sect of the Quakers known as the Shaking Quakers, or simply the Shakers. They valued hard work, simplicity, thrift, and devotion to God. They also believed in and practiced equality of the sexes.

By the 1830s, there were more than six thousand Shakers living in about twenty communities, mostly in upstate New York and Massachusetts. Because Shakers did not believe in having children, their communities could only survive by recruiting new members.

★ AUDUBON'S BIRDS

The exploits of early nineteenth-century explorers, Lewis and Clark among them, helped to popularize the study of nature in the United States. One man excited by ornithology, or the study of birds, was a failed storekeeper named John James Audubon. After giving up his store on the Kentucky frontier, Audubon became the most famous nature painter in the world. Birds were Audubon's speciality. His four-volume *Birds of America*, published between 1827 and 1838, included 435 full-color illustrations. Audubon's drawings made him a sensation in London, where he would often amuse himself by walking around town dressed as an American frontiersman. For show, he would put on a fringed leather jacket and slick his hair back with bear grease.

presided at his trial. Burr was acquitted because, according to Marshall's strict interpretation of the Constitution, Burr's plotting didn't break any laws.

Although he was found innocent, Burr was completely discredited. After the trial, he left for Europe, where he tried to interest the French in conquering Canada. He finally returned to New York in 1812 under a false name and practiced law there until his death in 1836.

THE LEWIS AND CLARK EXPEDITION

Even before he approved the Louisiana Purchase, President Jefferson, an amateur naturalist, had organized an expedition to explore the Louisiana Territory. To lead this survey, Jefferson chose his secretary, Meriwether Lewis.

With Jefferson's permission, Lewis wrote to William Clark, a seasoned soldier, asking Clark to join him. A month later, Lewis received a reply. Clark believed that the expedition would encounter great difficulties, but he was eager to go along.

On May 14, 1804, Lewis and Clark left St. Louis accompanied by thirty soldiers and ten civilians, including experts in botany, zoology, sign language, and navigation. After six months, they took on a fur trapper and his Shoshone wife, Sacajawea, to help them communicate with the native peoples they would encounter.

The explorers sailed up the Missouri River into what is now North Dakota. They lived on rations of salt pork and biscuits as well as wild game and fish. On November 7, 1805, the expedition reached the Pacific Ocean.

Because the Indian tribes there were in contact with trading ships, Lewis and Clark hoped to catch a ride back east to Washington. They waited for months in the hope that a ship might arrive. Eventually, they decided to make the return journey by land, arriving back in St. Louis on September 23, 1806.

Both Lewis and Clark made maps and kept journals of their trip across the continent. The journals in particular provided a huge amount of new scientific information about the American interior.

Lewis and Clark's diaries included notes about the terrain and people they encountered. The two explorers also brought back some specimens of the hundreds of plants and animals they found along the way. They even presented Jefferson with two grizzly bears, which he kept in cages on the White House lawn.

THE EMBARGO ACT

It was near the end of his second term that Jefferson faced his most dangerous foreign crisis. The trouble began in June 1807, when the British warship *Leopard* fired on the American frigate *Chesapeake*. Despite the public's demand for war, Jefferson wanted to remain reasonable. He told his minister to Great Britain to demand an apology.

When the British refused, Jefferson convinced Congress to authorize an embargo, not just against Britain but against all of Europe. He believed that withholding U.S. goods would force both France and Britain to respect U.S. neutrality. In December 1807, he signed the Embargo Act.

But the embargo was a disaster, hurting Americans much more than the British or the French. Without European buyers, many U.S. crops rotted in storage. Meanwhile, thousands of people in the shipping business, including sailors and shipbuilders, lost their jobs. A year later, Congress passed a bill repealing the embargo, which Jefferson signed on March 1, 1809, three days before leaving office.

JAMES MADISON RAN AS THE DEMOCRATIC-REPUBLICAN candidate for president in 1808. Physically, he didn't look much like a president—or rather, he didn't look the way most people thought a president should look.

Madison was just five feet, four inches tall, and he weighed barely one hundred pounds. His nose was

scarred from frostbite. But Jefferson thought that his secretary of state would make a fine president, and that was good enough for the rest of the party. The Democratic-Republicans nicknamed their candidate the Great Little Madison.

Madison didn't have much opposition. The retirement of John Adams and the death of Alexander Hamilton had so devastated the Federalist party that it didn't even bother to nominate a candidate formally. Instead, the Federalists put up the same ticket they had nominated in 1804, Charles Pinckney and Rufus King. Although Federalist New England went for Pinckney, Madison carried the rest of the country easily.

Between the presidencies of John Adams and his son John Quincy Adams, the Democratic-Republicans held the White House for six consecutive terms covering twenty-four years. This string of presidents is sometimes referred to as the Jefferson Dynasty because both Madison and his successor, James Monroe, considered themselves to be pupils of Jefferson. The period is also called the Virginia Monarchy, because all three men came from Virginia.

JAMES MADISON

4TH PRESIDENT

★

FROM 1809 TO 1817

BORN: March 16, 1751

BIRTHPLACE: Port Conway, Va.

DIED: June 28, 1836

PARTY: Democratic-Republican

VICE PRESIDENTS: George Clinton, Elbridge Gerry

FIRST LADY: Dolley Dandridge Payne Todd

CHILDREN: None

NICKNAME: Father of the Constitution

The first president to wear trousers regularly (instead of knee breeches).

James Madison inherited a country in crisis. The Embargo Act had just been repealed, but its deadening economic effects were still being felt throughout the country. To make matters worse, neither France nor Britain was any closer to respecting U.S. neutrality on the high seas.

Jefferson's solution hadn't worked, and it was now up to his handpicked successor, Madison, to deal with the problem. The Embargo Act had proven that exports were crucial to the U.S. economy, and the only way to export goods to Europe was by ship. Madison's task was to find a way to protect U.S. ships without reducing trade.

WAR HAWKS RISE TO POWER

Frontier Congressmen Take Over Washington

THE MIDTERM ELECTIONS of 1810 brought a new generation of politicians to Washington. Angry with the slow pace of government, the voters had defeated nearly half the members of Congress and replaced them with young men who were very different from their stately elders.

These men took advantage of the public outrage at Britain's harassment of U.S. shipping and campaigned for war. They were nicknamed the War Hawks. Thirty-four-year-old Henry Clay of Kentucky and John Calhoun of South Carolina, who was five years younger, were the leading War Hawks. Both men had been raised on the frontier, and their behavior reflected their upbringing. Clay and Calhoun were both rambunctious, with little of the Old World gentility that had characterized the Founding Fathers.

In addition to demanding war with Britain, the War Hawks wanted to expand the country northward by invading Canada and southward by conquering Florida and taking whatever Indian lands were available.

A DEAL WITH NAPOLEON

Although Madison didn't have many options, he was also something less than a bold leader. He was shy by nature with a quiet speaking voice, and he liked to think matters through a number of times before coming to a decision. His treasury secretary once said that Madison was "slow in taking his ground, but firm when the storm rises."

Madison tried a variety of strategies. The first was to enforce the Non-Intercourse Act of 1809, which had been passed during Jefferson's final days in office. This law represented a new approach to the embargo. It lifted the trade restrictions on every nation except Britain and France and promised to lift the restrictions on these two nations as well if they promised to respect the neutrality of U.S. shipping.

The Non-Intercourse Act didn't work. Britain and France paid no attention, and trade suffered. So Madison tried a somewhat different approach. In 1810, he signed into law Macon's Bill Number Two, which offered a new deal to Britain and France: If one of them would agree to respect U.S. neutrality, trade would be cut off with the other. Napoleon was the first to agree to these terms on behalf of France, so Madison reimposed the trade embargo on Britain.

INDIAN RELATIONS

Meanwhile, things were heating up along the western frontier. Ever since the Battle of Fallen Timbers in 1794, white settlers had been pushing Indians in the Ohio River valley farther and farther into the nation's interior.

Thomas Jefferson had wanted to integrate native peoples into white society by teaching them how to farm

The Early Years

JAMES MADISON WAS RAISED IN A HOUSE BUILT BY HIS grandfather within view of Virginia's Blue Ridge Mountains. As Madison grew up, there were two great traumas in his life. The first was a local smallpox epidemic. The second was the French and Indian War.

When the British general Edward Braddock was defeated by the French and their Indian allies in 1755, many Virginians feared an Indian invasion. That never happened, but the threat of one turned Madison against Indians for the rest of his life.

After serving in the Virginia House of Delegates and the Continental Congress, Madison became a delegate to the Constitutional Convention in 1787. Because of his work there, he would later be known as the Father of the Constitution.

★ **THE FIRST LADY** Known for her charm and intelligence, Dolley Madison stands out as one of the nation's most extraordinary first ladies. During the War of 1812, she also proved that she could be remarkably cool in a crisis.

The first lady was in the middle of planning a dinner party for forty guests when the British closed in on Washington. The president was already safely out of town, and his wife was told to flee. But before she left, Dolley Madison packed up the Declaration of Independence, the national seal, a portrait of George Washington, and her pet parrot, sending them all ahead to safety.

★ **BEAU BRUMMELL** The clothes worn by fashionable American men during the first half of the nineteenth century

were examples of the Regency style that was popular in England. This style was named after its chief patron, George, the prince regent of Britain, who later became King George IV.

At the time, the most fashionable man in the world was Beau Brummell. It usually took Brummell an entire morning to dress in his long jacket, tight breeches, and elaborately ruffled scarf. His look featured country clothes that had been sharpened up for city wear. Meanwhile, fashionable women followed the French style of long, high-waisted dresses with richly embroidered hems.

★**TOM MOLINEAUX** One of the most popular sports during the early nineteenth century was boxing, and the best boxer in the country was a freed slave from Virginia named Tom Molineaux. While he was still in his twenties, Molineaux moved to New York, where he fought informally in amateur matches. In 1809, at the age of twenty-five, he sailed to England to box professionally.

In December 1810, Molineaux became the first American to fight an English champion. He lost to Tom Cribb in the fortieth round. The rematch, which Molineaux lost, drew a record crowd of forty thousand people.

Other popular sports at this time included horse racing, tenpin bowling, rowing, and gouging, which was a frontier sport. The point of gouging was to pluck out an opponent's eyeball. In the Ohio River valley, people grew their thumbnails especially long for this purpose.

★**UNCLE SAM** During the War of 1812, a merchant in Troy, New York, named Samuel Wilson supplied barrels of beef to the U.S. Army. He stamped these barrels "U.S." to show that they were government property. Because Wilson was commonly known as "Uncle Sam," and because the barrels were stamped with these initials, people began referring to the federal government as "Uncle Sam."

Cartoonists began using the symbolic figure of Uncle Sam in the early 1830s. The British humor magazine *Punch* developed the most familiar caricature of a bearded man with a top hat and striped pants. The famous political cartoonist Thomas Nast used Uncle Sam extensively during the 1870s. But the most famous Uncle Sam was drawn by James Montgomery Flagg, whose World War I recruiting poster was captioned "I Want You For the U.S. Army."

in the European fashion and how to make goods they could sell. But most whites had no intention of cooperating with Jefferson's plan, and most Indians had no interest in living as whites did.

Instead, the United States kept taking Indian land either by conquest or deception. Treaties were made and then broken. By 1810, settlers had seized more than one hundred million acres of fertile Indian land.

TECUMSEH'S CONFEDERACY When Tecumseh, a chief of the Shawnee tribe, saw what was happening, he tried to do something about it. His strategy was to form a confederacy of all the frontier tribes from Florida to the Canadian border.

Tecumseh was clever enough to see that many settlers used alcohol to cheat Indians out of their land and control them. He realized that to fight the settlers, the Indians would have to stop drinking the rum and whiskey the settlers offered them.

On November 7, 1811, while Tecumseh was away in the south trying to enlist the Creeks in his confederacy, the U.S. army marched on his village. In the battle of Tippecanoe Creek, General William Henry Harrison beat off a dawn attack and defeated the warriors of Tecumseh's confederacy.

Tecumseh vowed to seek revenge, and he got his chance during the War of 1812. But the result turned out to be another Harrison victory. Tecumseh was killed in that battle, fighting alongside the British in Canada.

THE WAR HAWKS A cautious man, Madison moved slowly with regard to the British. But the rest of the country had little patience for Madison's seemingly endless waiting. During the midterm elections of 1810, nearly half the members of Congress were thrown out of office. Impatient with the pace of Madison's government, the voters wanted change, so they elected a group of much younger politicians. These new congressmen were known as the War Hawks because they promised, if elected, to declare war on Britain.

Madison held firm against the War Hawks for more than a year. But in June 1812, he reluctantly bowed to their pressure and asked Congress for a declaration of war against Great Britain. Madison had few options left.

THE WAR OF 1812 Everyone knew the reasons for war: the impressment of sailors, the lack of respect for U.S. neutrality, and the continuing British agitation of Indian tribes along the northwestern frontier. But the declaration didn't come very quickly. Congress debated the war resolution for seventeen days before approving it in a rather close vote.

The opposition to the war came principally from the Federalists of New England, who were quite vocal in their opposition to what they snidely called "Mr. Madison's War." Despite the aggressive enthusiasm whipped up by the War Hawks, New England merchants wanted nothing to do with a war that would halt trade with their biggest customer, Great Britain.

To protest Madison's policy, most New Englanders boycotted the war and refused to allow their state militias to join in the fighting. Some New England merchants even flirted with treason, as they became fabulously wealthy selling supplies to both sides.

New England's opposition was just the beginning, as Madison soon discovered. As he had feared, the

THE CAMPAIGN OF 1812 WAS THE FIRST EVER HELD during a war. Despite the success of the War Hawks in 1810, opposition to the War of 1812 was strong, especially in New England.

Madison ran for reelection against former New York City mayor DeWitt Clinton, who was also a Democratic-Republican but was running independently of the party. The New England

Federalists chose not to nominate their own candidate, thus ensuring that Clinton would receive their overwhelming support. Clinton also happened to be the nephew of Madison's first vice president, George Clinton, who died in April 1812.

The campaign was most notable for Clinton's outrageous habit of promising different things to different people. To people who supported the war, Clinton promised to continue the fight. To people such as the Federalists who opposed the war, he made speeches blaming the entire mess on Madison and promised to negotiate an immediate peace.

The lack of enthusiasm in the country for Madison's policies gave Clinton a chance, but the president's support in the South and the West was enough to see him through. Clinton won four New England states in addition to Delaware, New York, New Jersey, and five of Maryland's eleven votes. But Madison took the rest, winning 128 electoral votes to Clinton's 89.

24

War of 1812 would be much more difficult to win than it had been to declare.

Things went wrong from the start. For example, when the president called for fifty thousand army volunteers, only five thousand signed up. To make up the difference, the army began enlisting African Americans, both free blacks and slaves. Many slaves fought in the army hoping to win their freedom, but they were generally returned to slavery after the war.

THE INVASION OF CANADA Unwilling to challenge the powerful British navy at sea, Madison instead decided to focus on a land campaign against British-held Canada. The most obvious invasion routes passed through New York and the New England states, but none of these states would permit a federal attack across its border because they opposed the war.

As a result, the first invasion of Canada was launched from Detroit in July 1812. Madison unwisely chose an aging Revolutionary War veteran, General William Hull, to lead the expedition. Hull cautiously crossed the border, but fearing Indian attacks he quickly withdrew to Detroit, which he surrendered to the lesser army of British general Isaac Brock without firing a single shot. Hull was later court-martialed for his actions.

BRITISH BURN CAPITAL

Washington in Flames

WASHINGTON, August 25, 1814—British troops entered the capital yesterday and burned most of the nation's important buildings. The first building the British set on fire was the Capitol, which was still under construction. Then they marched to the president's residence and set it aflame. As night fell, the British relaxed in empty boardinghouses and watched the city burn.

This morning, the British soldiers prepared to destroy the rest of the town, but a storm came up suddenly. The storm accomplished what the U.S. army had been unable to do. It forced the British to retreat.

The route to Washington was laid open to the British after the army failed to stop the invaders in nearby Maryland. President Madison had to flee ahead of his troops after witnessing the brief battle.

By the time the British reached the undefended capital, most of the government officials and residents had left. Only a few women remained behind, packing their belongings. The president's wife, Dolley Madison, stayed long enough to save most of the government's valuable papers.

From this poor start, things got worse. General Brock marched his troops to the Niagara River, where he began making preparations to invade New York. On October 13, 1812, a small federal regiment under Captain James E. Wool attacked Brock's forces on the Canadian side of the river.

At first, the battle went well for the Americans. Brock was killed, and the British scattered. Wool clearly had the advantage, but as he anxiously waited for reinforcements, the British regrouped, and his edge slipped away.

Just before all hope was lost, reinforcements from the New York state militia arrived on the New York side of the river. But they stopped right there. Their orders were clear: defend New York, but do not cross the river into Canada. They watched from the New York side while the British massacred Wool's men.

THE BURNING OF WASHINGTON

As James Madison took the oath of office at his second inaugural in March 1813, the country was in the midst of its greatest crisis since the American Revolution. Madison's invasion of Canada had failed miserably, and now the British were on the offensive.

The Americans enjoyed some success in the Northwest as Captain Oliver Hazard Perry won control of Lake Erie in September 1813 and General William Henry Harrison won the battle of the Thames River in Canada in October. But the British were preparing a much more effective counterpunch. At the end of 1813, they crossed the Canadian border and burned the city of Buffalo, New York. Then, during the summer of 1814, British forces swept past the weak U.S. defenses in the Chesapeake Bay and marched on

★**THE WHITE HOUSE** When the British invaded Washington, they burned the president's house. After the fire, only the walls of the residence remained, and these were blackened by smoke.

To cover the smoke damage, workers painted the outside walls of the reconstructed building white. The result was so eye-catching that people began referring to the president's house as the White House. In 1901, the name of the building was officially changed at the request of President Theodore Roosevelt.

★**GERRYMANDERING** Elbridge Gerry was Madison's second vice president and before that, governor of Massachusetts. During his term as governor, Gerry supported a bill that created a strange-looking voting district in his state. The district was drawn in such an unusual way that some people said it looked like a salamander.

The point of fashioning such an unusual district was to ensure that the Democratic-Republican party would have a voting majority there. Because of the way the district looked, people began calling this tactic "gerrymandering." The term is still used today to describe the practice of redrawing district lines to favor one party or a particular group of voters.

★**FRANCIS SCOTT KEY** When the British attacked Baltimore during the War of 1812, they took an influential lawyer named Francis Scott Key prisoner. Key was held aboard a British ship in the harbor, from which he could see the British bombardment of Fort McHenry.

The British kept firing at Fort McHenry through most of the night. The flashes from their cannon made the scene seem like a nightmare. Then suddenly the firing stopped. At dawn, Key strained to see which flag was flying above the

fort. His joy at seeing the Stars and Stripes inspired him to write "The Star-Spangled Banner." The song became the official national anthem in 1931. It was the only piece of poetry that Key ever wrote.

★**NEW ENGLAND FACTORIES** In the fall of 1810, a wealthy merchant named Francis Cabot Lowell traveled from Boston to England. He told people he was going on a vacation, but Lowell actually wanted to learn more about English textile factories.

When he returned, Lowell hired an engineer named Paul Moody to help him build a new factory. The cloth-making machines that Lowell couldn't buy, he had Moody make.

In 1814, Lowell opened the first fully mechanized textile factory in the United States. He offered good wages and set up clean quarters for his workers, which made work at the factory attractive to local farm girls. The factory provided an example to other business leaders of how profitable manufacturing could be. In this way, Lowell helped change the focus of the New England economy from shipping to manufacturing.

★**MEDICINE** American medical education during the early nineteenth century was not very good. The treatments the doctors used were based more on folk remedies than on science. Sometimes doctors would apply leeches to a patient to suck out a disease. Plants and herbs were also popular medicines, especially in rural areas.

Although many women practiced herbal medicine, most doctors were men. These men kept offices in their homes, but more often they made house calls. When necessary, they even moved in with a patient until he or she was cured.

Many Indian tribes also used herbs to treat diseases, but western Algonquins practiced a different type of therapy. Their medicine men all belonged to the Midewiwin, or Grand Medicine Society. When someone in the tribe was ill, the members of this society would seek a vision, during which spirits would instruct them in ways to cure the patient.

Washington, burning the nation's capital on August 24, 1814.

PEACE TALKS In the meantime, the British minister had informed Madison in January 1814 that his government was prepared to discuss terms for peace. Madison accepted the offer of peace talks immediately. The site would be the town of Ghent in Belgium.

The British believed that they could dictate the terms of the peace. After all, they were winning the war. As far as they were concerned, it should be the Americans who made the concessions.

The British ministers immediately presented a number of demands: They wanted the Americans to stop fishing in the waters off Newfoundland. They also wanted to move the Canadian border to provide access to the Mississippi River. And finally, they wanted to create a territory for their Indian allies in the Ohio River valley between the United States and Canada.

John Quincy Adams, the son of former president John Adams, was one of the U.S. peace commissioners in Ghent. Although he was an experienced diplomat, Adams was shocked by the British demands. He advised his fellow commissioners to return home immediately. But Henry Clay wasn't so quick to leave.

Clay was less experienced in diplomacy than Adams, but he was a better poker player. He thought the British were bluffing and that they would be willing to accept less. The Napoleonic Wars in Europe were winding down, and Great Britain had better things to do than to continue fighting a war an ocean away. Clay convinced the rest of the delegation to stay and press for better terms. The British held firm for months, but eventually they began to reduce their demands.

THE TREATY OF GHENT

When the Treaty of Ghent was finally signed in December 1814, it included none of Britain's original demands. In fact, all it did was end the fighting and restore the status quo ante bellum, which means the state of things before the war.

Neither side gained or lost any territory, and many matters were left unresolved, such as the neutrality rights of U.S. shipping. The War of 1812 did have a lasting effect, however, in that it paved the way for closer relations between the two countries. After the war, Britain showed a great deal more respect for the United States than it had ever shown before.

THE BATTLE OF NEW ORLEANS

While the Treaty of Ghent was being negotiated, however, the fighting continued. Ironically, the last battle of the War of 1812 took place on January 8, 1815, two weeks after the war had formally ended. The battle took place anyway because Ghent was a continent away from New Orleans, and it took a long time in 1815 for even important news to travel that far. Neither side knew yet that the war had ended.

The British army arrived at New Orleans in very late December. Finding the U.S. positions well fortified, they dug a few trenches and began bombarding the town. On January 8, eight thousand British soldiers attacked.

General Andrew Jackson, who led the U.S. troops, fought a brilliant defensive battle. By the end of the bloody day, the British had lost more than two thousand men. Of their four generals, one was dead, one was dying, and another was disabled. The Americans lost only twenty-one men, and Jackson became a national hero.

ONCE HE BECAME THE CANDIDATE OF THE Democratic-Republican party in 1816, Secretary of State James Monroe was practically guaranteed the presidency. Secretary of War William Crawford had a strong following in Congress that might have posed a

threat to Monroe, but Crawford never mounted a serious challenge. He didn't want to risk his place in the new cabinet.

In many ways, Monroe was Madison's natural successor. As secretary of state, he had occupied the same office for Madison that Madison had filled for Jefferson. Indeed, Jefferson had served as secretary of state during the Washington administration. Moreover, Monroe was widely admired for his warm, generous personality.

Meanwhile, the Federalists didn't even bother to nominate a candidate. The failure of the Hartford Convention in 1815 had destroyed what little influence the Federalists still had. At that meeting, Federalist delegates from Connecticut, Massachusetts, and Rhode Island had discussed seceding from the union to form a new Federalist country. Although it never happened, most Americans began thinking of the Federalists as unpatriotic and possibly treasonous.

The best the Federalists could do was support Rufus King of New York, who had run for vice president in 1804 and again in 1808. A dedicated public servant, King had once been George Washington's minister to Great Britain. But King, the last Federalist candidate, was no match for Monroe. The only states that King carried were Connecticut, Delaware, and Massachusetts.

JAMES MONROE

5TH PRESIDENT

★

FROM 1817 TO 1825

BORN: April 28, 1758

BIRTHPLACE: Westmoreland County, Va.

DIED: July 4, 1831

PARTY: Democratic-Republican

VICE PRESIDENT: Daniel D. Tompkins

FIRST LADY: Elizabeth Kortright

CHILDREN: Eliza, Maria

NICKNAME: Last of the Cocked Hats

The last president to have served as an officer in the Revolutionary War.

MARSHALL ISSUES LANDMARK RULINGS

WASHINGTON, December 31, 1819—The year ending today has been a remarkable one for the Supreme Court and its chief justice John Marshall. The court's rulings in two landmark cases will change the government's role in this country.

The first case, *Dartmouth College v. Woodward*, involved the charter of Dartmouth College, which the state of New Hampshire recently tried to change. Dartmouth's charter was originally granted in 1769, when New Hampshire was still a British colony.

As Marshall himself pointed out, the case was really about contracts. The chief justice explained that Dartmouth's charter was actually a contract that no one side had the right to change. The court's decision has made it clear that business contracts will be respected.

In the case of *McCulloch v. Maryland*, Marshall ruled that the state of Maryland could not tax the Second Bank of the United States because the bank was a federal institution. Marshall's ruling stressed that states cannot restrict the federal government's constitutional powers. *McCulloch v. Maryland* also established the constitutionality of the bank itself, thus endorsing Alexander Hamilton's theory of implied powers.

The British burned the president's house so thoroughly during the War of 1812 that years passed before it was completely rebuilt. Even as James Monroe took the oath of office in March 1817, there remained work to be done. Rather than live in temporary housing as the Madisons had done, Monroe decided to take a grand tour of the country until the White House was ready. He wanted to have a close-up look at the country he would be governing.

Beginning his trip in Washington, D.C., Monroe traveled north as far as Portland, Maine. From there, he turned west to Detroit and then southeast back to Washington. The triangular trip took fifteen weeks, and it gave Monroe a better knowledge of the country than any president before him, with the possible exception of George Washington.

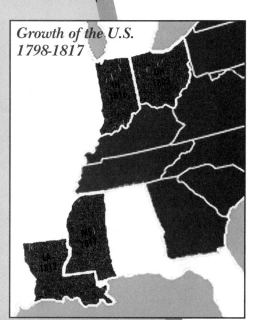

Growth of the U.S. 1798-1817

THE ERA OF GOOD FEELINGS

Everywhere he went, the triumphant president was greeted with cheers from crowds lining the roadways. Even in Federalist New England, the crowds applauded this Democratic-Republican president. The *Boston Columbian Centinel* was moved to describe Monroe's joyful reception as the beginning of an "era of good feelings" for the country.

New England, which had detested James Madison, was quicker to accept Monroe because the region's economy had changed in the years during and after the War of 1812. Before the war, New England had depended almost exclusively on its trade with Great Britain. When the war cut that trade off, New Englanders were forced to find other ways to make a living.

NEW ENGLAND FACTORIES

Pioneering industrialists such as Francis Cabot Lowell opened factories that helped shift the economic focus of New England from shipping to manufacturing. As a result, the region and the country became much more self-sufficient.

Factories such as Lowell's were decent places to work, unlike the grim, dirty factories of industrial England. Although the work force of young men and women typically put in twelve- and fourteen-hour days, they made good wages and were given clean, pleasant quarters in which to live. The evening lectures offered by some factories provided the only schooling most of the factory girls ever had.

But work in factories owned by less charitable people could be harsh and cruel, and soon the conditions in many factories sank to this level. Greedy owners employed entire families to work side by side on the

THE EARLY YEARS

JAMES MONROE'S FATHER DIED WHEN HE WAS ABOUT sixteen years old. The system of inheritance at that time was called primogeniture. Under this system, a man's oldest son inherited all his family's property. Because James was the first-born son of five children, he inherited everything.

About the same time, Monroe enrolled at the College of William and Mary in Williamsburg, Virginia. His mind wasn't on his studies, however. Instead, like most students at William and Mary, he was caught up in the patriotic fever sweeping the colonies. In March 1776, unable to resist any longer, Monroe dropped out of college to enlist in the Continental Army.

★**WEDDING AT THE WHITE HOUSE** In 1818, James Monroe hired Samuel L. Gouverneur as a private secretary. While serving Monroe, the young man fell in love with Monroe's daughter Maria. After a two-year courtship, the couple decided to marry. The date was set for March 9, 1820.

This wedding was the first ever for a president's daughter in the White House. The ceremony was a small, private one. Only forty-two guests were invited. Everyone else had to wait until the reception five days later to congratulate the new couple.

★**JOHN JACOB ASTOR AND THE FUR TRADE**
The fur trade with the Indians was for many years an important part of the North American economy. In colonial times, the most important fur trading centers were on the Great Lakes and in the Ohio River valley.

John Jacob Astor was the poor son of a German butcher. He came to this country at the age of twenty, just after the Revolutionary War. His first employer was a fur trader in New York City. Astor quickly learned the business and soon made a small fortune buying furs upstate and selling them in London.

Beaver furs were particularly valuable because hats made from them were very fashionable in Europe. In fact, so many beaver were being trapped and killed that they were soon in danger of extinction. With his fur trade profits, Astor invested in real estate. Eventually he became the richest man in the country.

★LITERATURE IN AMERICA

The new patriotism encouraged by the Era of Good Feelings helped create America's first national literature. The most important writers of the time were James Fenimore Cooper and Washington Irving.

Cooper wrote a number of stories about the frontier, called the Leatherstocking tales, in which he portrayed Indians as noble savages. His most famous book, *The Last of the Mohicans* (1826), helped popularize the American wilderness.

Irving specialized in short stories. His best known included "The Legend of Sleepy Hollow," featuring schoolmaster Ichabod Crane, and "Rip Van Winkle." Irving was the first American author to win fame in Europe.

★THE MASON AND DIXON LINE

The Missouri Compromise made it clear that there was definitely a political division between North and South. This division was represented on most maps by the Mason and Dixon Line.

Between 1765 and 1768, two Englishmen, Charles Mason and Jeremiah Dixon, surveyed the 233-mile-long border dividing the land grants of Pennsylvania and Maryland. This border had been set by the king of England at latitude 39°43'.

In the years leading up to the Civil War, the Mason and Dixon Line came to symbolize much more than the border between two states. In the minds of most Americans, the Mason and Dixon Line was the line between freedom and slavery.

factory floor. Even the youngest children were used to carry supplies to boys and girls old enough to work the machinery.

Instead of paying cash wages, these factory owners provided their workers with run-down houses and credit at the factory store. Because they had no cash, the workers had to buy what they needed at the factory store. And because the factory store charged very high prices, the workers were always in debt.

As long as the workers owed money, they couldn't leave. And the longer they stayed, the deeper in debt they went. Eventually, they became essentially slaves to the factory owners.

THE AMERICAN SYSTEM

On a more national scale, Congressmen Henry Clay and John Calhoun championed a series of projects designed to improve and update the country's infrastructure—that is, its roads, bridges, and canals. The bills they introduced were part of a larger plan devised by Clay called the American System.

One of these bills imposed a tariff, or tax, on manufactured goods that were imported into the country. The tariff would make European goods more expensive and thus encourage Americans to buy products made in the United States. Also, the money raised by the tariff could be used to build roads and canals in the western territories.

Monroe agreed that Calhoun's public works projects would benefit the nation. But like Madison before him, he worried that these internal improvements were not constitutional. A Jeffersonian at heart, Monroe feared that construction of roads and canals went well beyond the powers granted to the government by the Constitution.

THE CUMBERLAND ROAD

When Congress passed a bill in 1822 to extend the Cumberland Road, Monroe vetoed it because he believed road building was the responsibility of the states. It was the only bill that Monroe ever vetoed in his eight years as president.

During Monroe's administration, the country grew at an amazing rate. Much of its westward expansion took place along the route of the Cumberland Road. Beginning outside Baltimore, the Cumberland Road eventually extended through Pennsylvania, Virginia, Ohio, and Indiana before ending in Illinois. The road made it much easier for people to settle the Northwest Territory.

The first section of the road—from Cumberland, Maryland, to Wheeling in western Virginia—was built between 1811 and 1818. Before the road was extended, settlers could board steamships in Wheeling that would take them farther west along the Ohio River. In the same year that the Cumberland Road reached Wheeling, Illinois became the twenty-first state.

Although roads were less expensive to build, transportation of goods was faster and cheaper by canal. As Monroe took office, the United States had only one hundred miles of canal. By the end of his second term, that distance had jumped to one thousand miles. The canals made it economical for surplus western beef and corn to be sold in New England, where manufacturing was quickly displacing agriculture.

THE GROWTH OF REGIONALISM

Between 1816 and 1821, six new states joined the Union, making a total of twenty-four. Although they were generally welcomed, the admission of these new western and southern

THE ERA OF GOOD FEELINGS MADE JAMES MONROE one of the most popular presidents in the history of the United States. His first term was considered a great success. The peace continued, and profitable new businesses were started every day. Relations with Britain were the best they had ever been, and the Missouri Compromise had resolved the controversy between free and slave states, at least for the time being. As a result, nobody seriously wanted to replace a president who had delivered so much peace and prosperity.

Both Jefferson and Madison had served two terms, so it was expected that Monroe would serve two as well. Because the Democratic-Republicans were so sure that Monroe would be reelected, they didn't even bother to nominate him formally. What little remained of the Federalist party didn't offer any opposition, either. As a result the presidential vote in 1820 was essentially an election without a campaign.

When the electoral college met in 1820, Monroe won all the electoral votes but one. The single contrary vote was cast by New Hampshire governor William Plumer. It has been said that Plumer voted against Monroe so that George Washington would remain the only president ever elected unanimously. According to Plumer's son, however, the New Hampshire governor simply hated Monroe.

President Proclaims Monroe Doctrine

Adams' Speech Sets New Foreign Policy

WASHINGTON, December 2, 1823—President Monroe used the opportunity of his annual message to Congress today to announce a bold new foreign policy. In a speech written by Secretary of State John Quincy Adams, the president warned European nations against trying to establish any more colonies in the Americas.

Monroe also made it clear that his new doctrine does not apply to colonies already in existence.

The speech was prompted by fears that other European powers intended to help Spain recapture its lost colonies in South

America. Highly publicized wars of independence have recently overthrown the Spanish colonial governments in Argentina and Colombia.

In Argentina, the fight for independence was led by José de San Martín. In Colombia, Simón Bolívar led the successful revolution against Spanish rule. Both men have since served as models for others in Central and South America who believe in the principle of self-rule.

---

states was also unsettling for many Americans. Because new regions of the country would of course have their own concerns, those of the original states would necessarily matter less.

Northern factory owners wanted increased tariff protection for their manufactured goods. They also wanted raw materials at a cheap price. Western farmers wanted exactly the opposite. They liked to see high prices for the raw materials they grew and low prices for the manufactured goods they bought. In the South, plantation owners were concerned about a reduction in slave labor, which they thought would hurt their ability to produce cotton at a competitive price.

SLAVERY IN THE NEW STATES Each of these three regions worried about the balance of power in Congress, but the North and South were especially concerned about the issue of slavery. Many northerners wanted to abolish this brutal institution, which the South was equally determined to keep.

Both sides knew that the key votes on slavery would be cast in the West. If the new western states were admitted as slave states, then slavery would likely continue. If they were admitted as "free soil" states, which prohibited human bondage, then slavery would likely pass away in the South as well. Either way, the balance of power would soon shift decisively.

NORTH AMERICA

The United States

ATLANTIC OCEAN

PACIFIC OCEAN

SOUTH AMERICA

THE WESTERN HEMISPHERE

The nation's founders had intentionally passed over the issue of slavery because it was simply too controversial. Had the Constitution tried to resolve the issue, it would never have been ratified. Instead, the fate of the slaves was left to the future.

In the thirty years since the Constitutional Convention, the cotton gin had made the South more dependent than ever on slave labor. To make sure that slavery would continue, southerners began demanding that slavery be extended to the new western states.

THE MISSOURI COMPROMISE

The issue became particularly focused when, in 1819, settlers in Missouri applied for statehood. The question on everyone's mind was: Would Missouri be admitted as a slave state or as a free state? In Washington, Congress debated whether or not the federal government had the power to ban slavery in the new states.

Southerners argued that banning slavery in Missouri would deprive slaveholders of their property—that is, their slaves. Many northerners, however, couldn't bear the thought of slavery spreading to one state and then another. Unable to resolve the issue, Congress adjourned until its next session without reaching a decision.

When Congress met again in 1820, there was a new wrinkle in the debate over Missouri's statehood. Now the territory of Maine also wanted to join the union. Being so far north, it would certainly be a free state.

A compromise was eventually worked out. Maine and Missouri would both be admitted, Maine as a free state and Missouri as a slave state. That way, the number of slave states and free states would remain equal. There would be twelve of each.

★**THE CHEROKEE ALPHABET**

About 1809, when the Cherokee silversmith and warrior Sequoyah was in his forties, he began to work on a writing system for his tribe. The Cherokee had a spoken language but not a written one. Sequoyah believed that the increased knowledge a written language would bring might help his people remain independent of the whites.

At first, he tried using pictographs, as the ancient Egyptians had done. When these didn't work, he began adapting letters from English, Greek, and Hebrew to represent the sounds of the spoken Cherokee language. By 1821, he had created the first Cherokee alphabet.

★**DISCOVERY OF SOUTH PASS** In January 1824, a group of fur trappers found and crossed a wide gap in the Rocky Mountains in present-day Wyoming. Because it was the middle of the winter, the crossing was difficult. The snow was knee-deep, and the explorers had nothing to drink except for the snow they melted by the heat of their hands.

The route they discovered, later called South Pass, turned out to be the easiest way through these difficult mountains. In the 1840s, South Pass became the principal gateway to the West and was used by thousands of settlers traveling the Oregon Trail.

★**EDUCATION** Emma Willard was a pioneer in women's education. In 1819, she presented New York with a plan to improve education for women. The state legislature rejected her plan. Two years later, she founded the Troy Female Seminary in upstate New York.

The seminary was the first enduring college-level school for women in the United States. Few people thought that women needed or could use an advanced education. Other colleges, for example, would admit only men. But Willard wouldn't accept any such limitations, and the Troy Seminary proved she was right.

★**THE AMERICAN COLONIZATION SOCIETY** In 1817, a Presbyterian minister in New Jersey named Robert Finley founded the American Colonization Society. Its goal was to end the practice of slavery.

But Finley's opposition to slavery didn't mean that he thought blacks and whites were compatible. Instead, Finley's group thought that the best solution was to resettle freed black slaves in Africa.

The American Colonization Society established Monrovia on the west coast of Africa in 1822. The colony, which became an independent republic in 1848, was supposed to be a new homeland for freed American slaves. Its name was soon changed to Liberia, but its capital kept the name Monrovia to honor James Monroe.

★**MEDICAL SCIENCE** In the early nineteenth century, medical science progressed slowly. Doctors could only guess at some of the ways the human body worked. The X-ray machine hadn't been invented yet, and there were no other ways to look inside the human body.

In 1822, a remarkable accident gave army surgeon William Beaumont an unusual opportunity. One of his patients, a French-Canadian trapper named Alexis St. Martin, had accidentally shot himself in the stomach. The shotgun blast left St. Martin with a permanent hole there.

Through this hole, Beaumont was able to observe the process of digestion as it took place. Beaumont performed various experiments on his cooperative patient and even published a book on the subject. His studies added much to human knowledge of the digestive system.

What made the deal work, however, was that southerners agreed to a northern demand that slavery be banned in the rest of the Louisiana Territory north of latitude 36°30'.

Monroe seriously considered vetoing the bill. He didn't believe that the federal government had the power to tell a state whether or not it could permit slavery. That was up to the citizens of each state. But Monroe also suspected that a veto would probably start a civil war. After three days of contemplation and consultation with his cabinet, Monroe signed the Missouri Compromise on March 6, 1820.

THE INVASION OF FLORIDA During Monroe's administration, there was little trouble along the western frontier, but the president did face a problem in Georgia, where white settlers and Seminoles were killing each other. Seminole raiding parties that included runaway slaves were burning the farms of whites whom they believed were taking away Indian land.

Most of the Seminoles lived in Florida, which was still a colony of Spain. They made their villages in swampy, jungle-like wetlands that also attracted fugitive slaves because there were so many easy places to hide. Both the Seminoles and the Creeks liked to help escaped slaves because they shared the slaves' hatred of whites. In some villages, the blacks and Indians intermarried and raised families together.

In 1817, Monroe sent Andrew Jackson, the country's most capable general, to punish the raiders. Jackson's hatred of Indians was well known, and when forty of his men were killed in an ambush, he used the attack as an excuse to invade Florida. Jackson burned Seminole villages and hanged many tribal chiefs. Then he captured the Spanish stronghold of Pensacola, which gave him control of northern Florida.

Although Jackson didn't specifically disobey his orders, his decision to invade Florida proved embarrassing to Monroe when the Spanish minister to the United States demanded that Jackson be punished. Secretary of State John Quincy Adams defended Jackson and used Jackson's military presence as a negotiating tool with Spain.

Meeting with the Spanish minister, Adams demanded that Spain either control the inhabitants of Florida, particularly the Seminoles and fugitive slaves, or transfer the territory immediately to the United States. With General Jackson's army already in place, Spain decided to sell. For five million dollars, the United States bought all of Spain's land east of the Mississippi River as well as its claim to territory in Oregon.

THE MONROE DOCTRINE

Now that the United States controlled so much of North America, John Quincy Adams suggested to President Monroe that he use this power to warn European nations against further colonization in the Americas. On December 2, 1823, the president delivered a speech to Congress outlining what soon became known as the Monroe Doctrine.

Neither an executive order nor a law, the Monroe Doctrine was a statement of policy that has guided U.S. actions ever since. Historians have compared its importance to that of George Washington's Farewell Address and John Hay's future Open Door policy with regard to China. For the first time, the United States recognized that it had important national interests outside its geographic borders.

WITH THE PASSING AWAY OF THE FEDERALISTS, there was now just one party left in the country. The next president would surely be a Democratic-Republican. But different party members wanted the job. In the end, the election came down to a four-man race among regional candidates.

Treasury secretary William Crawford of Georgia was the early front-runner, but he suffered a stroke during the campaign that nearly destroyed his candidacy. Secretary of State John Quincy Adams had the solid backing of New England, while Speaker of the House Henry Clay found support in the West. Of the four candidates, only General Andrew Jackson of Tennessee could count on votes from all over the country.

The election of 1824 was particularly notable because it was the first time that the popular vote was considered important enough to be counted. Most of the electors chosen in 1824 were selected by the people instead of by the state legislatures. The right to vote, however, was still restricted to adult white males.

Jackson won more electoral votes than anyone else. But he didn't win a majority, so the election was thrown into the House of Representatives. With Clay's support, Adams was able to win a narrow victory on the first ballot. Adams then made Clay his secretary of state.

John Quincy Adams

6TH PRESIDENT

★

FROM 1825 TO 1829

BORN: July 11, 1767

BIRTHPLACE: Braintree, Mass.

DIED: February 23, 1848

PARTY: Democratic-Republican

VICE PRESIDENT: John C. Calhoun

FIRST LADY: Louisa Catherine Johnson

CHILDREN: George, John, Charles, Louisa

NICKNAME: Old Man Eloquent

The only president to name a son George Washington.

THE RAILROAD IS HERE!

Work Begins on the B&O Line

BALTIMORE, July 4, 1828—Work began today on the United States' first steam-powered railroad, the Baltimore & Ohio. The first B&O line will connect Baltimore and Ellicott's Mills, Maryland, thirteen miles away.

The ceremonial first stone was laid by Charles Carroll, the last surviving signer of the Declaration of Independence, at a formal ceremony held this afternoon.

The work is expected to take about two years. After that, B&O executives plan to extend the railroad to Wheeling in western Virginia within the next twenty-five years.

The Baltimore & Ohio Railroad was chartered last year to help Baltimore compete with other cities for the profitable western trade. The Erie Canal, which opened in 1825, has funneled a great deal of this trade through New York City. Baltimore's merchants are hoping that the B&O line will do as much for their city.

After the House of Representatives chose John Quincy Adams to be the sixth president in February 1825, Adams's friends gave him some advice. They told him to fire all of Monroe's appointees and name his own people to federal office.

Adams's advisors were worried because many holdovers from the Monroe administration had backed Andrew Jackson during the 1824 campaign. The supporters of Andrew Jackson were furious that their candidate had lost to Adams in the House. They believed that Adams had made a corrupt bargain with Henry Clay to steal the election. Many of them vowed revenge, announcing that they would block Adams at every opportunity until Jackson could claim the presidency in 1828.

As it turned out, the advice Adams got was good, but he

refused to heed it. The new president didn't think it would be a good idea, or look right, for him to reward his own followers with powerful political appointments. Instead, his administration remained filled with people who did not wish him well.

THE AMERICAN SYSTEM

Adams was the first president to champion the government's role in making internal improvements for the benefit of trade. Both Madison and Monroe had vetoed government-financed road and canal projects because they believed them to be unconstitutional. Adams, however, wanted the government to take an active role in expanding commerce.

The president had earlier adopted the **American System**, developed by Secretary of State Clay while he was still in the House of Representatives. The point of the American System was to create a self-sufficient national economy. Clay believed that a factory economy in the North could provide markets for southern cotton as well as western grain and beef. In exchange, the South and West would buy northern manufactured goods.

Specifically, Clay proposed high **tariffs** on imported manufactured items, internal improvements, and a strong national bank. The tariffs would protect the New England factory economy, barely a decade old, from competition with cheap European goods. Meanwhile, new roads and canals in the South and West would make it cheaper for farmers to bring their crops to market. Finally, a strong bank could establish a stable national credit system so that trade within the United States could flourish.

The congressmen who fought the American System did so for a number of reasons. Some were merely blocking Adams in order to ensure the election

---

The Early Years

BECAUSE JOHN ADAMS WAS ONE OF THE COUNTRY'S most important diplomats, his eldest son, John Quincy, spent much of his childhood abroad. John Quincy was only ten years old when he traveled to Europe for the first time in 1778. Just three years later, he was sent to Russia with Francis Dana, another American diplomat. Dana wanted John

Quincy along because the boy spoke French fluently. At that time, French was the official language of diplomacy.

In 1797, while in London, Adams met his future wife, Louisa Johnson. Although her father was American, she had been born and raised in London, which made her the only foreign-born woman to become first lady.

★**FREEDOM'S JOURNAL** Founded in 1827, *Freedom's Journal* was the first antislavery newspaper ever published by black people. A New York City pastor, Samuel E. Cornish, edited the journal along with John Russwurm. After Russwurm moved to **Liberia**, Cornish continued to publish the paper under the name *Rights of All*.

★**FACTORY GIRLS** Most early American manufacturers, particularly those in New England, relied on young, unmarried women for their work force. Farmers' daughters were actively recruited to work in clothing

mills, and many jumped at the opportunity to help support their families and make some extra money for themselves.

These factory girls usually worked twelve-hour days. Their pay was about $2.50 a week, which was more than a woman could earn doing any other kind of work.

★**PHOTOGRAPHY** John Quincy Adams was the first president to have his picture taken. The photograph was called a daguerreotype after Louis Daguerre, the Frenchman who perfected the first practical photographic process. Daguerre used a copper plate coated with silver iodide, which he first exposed to light and then to a mercury vapor. The earliest daguerreotypes had to be exposed in bright sunlight for twenty minutes or the pictures wouldn't come out.

★**AFTER THE PRESIDENCY** After John Quincy Adams lost the 1828 election to Andrew Jackson, most people expected him to retire. Instead, in 1830, the sixty-three-year-old Adams ran for a seat in the House of Representatives and won. He thus became the first president to serve in Congress after leaving the White House.

Adams was often in the minority on issues such as the national bank, which he favored, and the annexation of Texas, which he opposed. But he had a great success in 1844, when he helped repeal a congressional rule that suppressed petitions against slavery. To frustrate this "gag rule," Adams spent many hours reading these petitions into the official record.

In February 1848, John Quincy Adams suffered a stroke on the floor of the House. The eighty-year-old former president was carried to a nearby chamber. He died there two days later because doctors considered it too dangerous to move him.

of Jackson in 1828. Others worried that the federal government was becoming too powerful.

Although elected as a Democratic-Republican, Adams didn't share his party's view that the Constitution set very strict limits on the government. Instead, like Alexander Hamilton, he wanted to use government resources actively. In fact, the shift toward a strong federal government was well under way. Ever since the Louisiana Purchase and the War of 1812, the country's growing size and nationalism had made the role of the federal government ever more important.

This development made many states nervous for the same reason Jefferson would have been. They believed that a strong federal government was dangerous because it meant less freedom for the states. Southerners were particularly concerned because they didn't want the federal government to become more involved in the slavery issue.

Because of the opposition Adams faced within his own administration and in Congress, he was able to win passage of only two public works projects. One was an extension of the Cumberland Road into Ohio. The other was the construction of a canal between the Ohio River and the Chesapeake Bay.

THE PANAMA CONGRESS In 1826, the new Latin American republics, which had formerly been Spanish colonies, held a congress to promote friendship within the region and discuss a unified policy toward Spain. Simón Bolívar of Colombia, who organized the event, chose Panama as the meeting place.

Mexican and Colombian ministers asked Secretary of State Clay to send two U.S. delegates. Both Clay and Adams were delighted. Although neither was sure that democratic governments could survive in Latin

America, both were anxious to offer U.S. friendship and trade.

In the Congress, opposition to the mission was strong. Southern congressmen objected because the new Latin American nations had outlawed slavery. With the help of the Jacksonians in Congress, southerners were able to delay the mission. They withheld money and confirmation of the delegates until the Panama meeting was over.

THE TARIFF OF ABOMINATIONS Throughout his presidency, Adams pressed for higher tariffs on imported manufactured goods. His proposals followed Clay's American System, which favored protection for New England manufacturing. During his last year in office, a tariff bill was finally passed by Congress, but it wasn't the bill that Adams had proposed.

In an attempt to embarrass the president, the Jacksonians in Congress had amended Adams's plan so that it raised tariffs on imported raw materials as well. The Jacksonians were sure that New England congressmen, who otherwise supported Adams, would never vote for such a bill because it would raise the prices New England factories paid for their raw materials.

They were wrong. The Tariff of 1828 passed and was signed by the president. It soon became known as the Tariff of Abominations because it was so hated. The new tariff rates dramatically raised the prices of all sorts of goods, which made the public furious.

The new law didn't embarrass Adams, but it did eliminate whatever small chance he might have had at winning reelection. Still, whatever good the Tariff of Abominations did for Andrew Jackson, it also passed along to him a crisis in the making.

GENERAL ANDREW JACKSON STARTED HIS SECOND campaign for the presidency soon after he lost his first. Throughout Adams's term, the shadow of Jackson dogged the president.

As the 1828 election approached, the Democratic-Republican party split into two camps. The Jacksonians called themselves Democrats. The Adams forces called themselves National Republicans.

Because the candidates took similar stands on the issues, the election turned on personal attacks. Adams was hammered for the "corrupt" bargain he allegedly made with Clay to win the 1824 election. Meanwhile, the National Republicans printed handbills that showed a line of coffins and accused the general of executing soldiers for minor offenses during the War of 1812.

The supporters of Adams portrayed Jackson as crude, uneducated, and always ready for a brawl. Although wealthy eastern business leaders found these traits deplorable, ordinary people on the frontier loved

them. In contrast to Jackson, Adams was considered distant and unappealing.

Jackson's nickname was Old Hickory, because he was supposed to be as tough as hickory wood. To publicize his campaign, Jackson's supporters put up hickory poles all over the country. They also sponsored local picnics, parades, and barbecues. Jackson's was the first grass-roots presidential campaign in U.S. history.

Jackson later claimed that his election in 1828 was a victory for the common man. In any case, it was certainly a victory. Adams carried his base in the Northeast and nothing else.

ANDREW JACKSON

7TH PRESIDENT

★

FROM 1829 TO 1837

BORN: March 15, 1767

BIRTHPLACE: Waxhaw, S.C.

DIED: June 8, 1845

PARTY: Democrat

VICE PRESIDENTS: John C. Calhoun, Martin Van Buren

FIRST LADY: Rachel Donelson Robards

CHILDREN: None

NICKNAME: Old Hickory

The first president to ride a train.

Andrew Jackson's victory in 1828 marked a new era in U.S. politics. He was the first common man elected president. All six presidents before him had come from privileged, landed families. But Jackson was a self-made man, a poor orphan who had made a career for himself in the law and the army.

Jackson believed that ordinary Americans—the shopkeepers, farmers, and pioneers—had enough common sense to make political decisions for themselves. This idea was the cornerstone of "Jacksonian democracy," and the public loved him for it.

Jackson used his popular support whenever possible to reinforce his political strength. He also used the "spoils system." Jackson believed in the phrase, "To the victor belongs the spoils." Immediately upon taking office, he fired nearly one thousand of the

WEBSTER, HAYNE DEBATE STATES' RIGHTS

WASHINGTON, January 27, 1830—Senator Daniel Webster of Massachusetts ended his nine-day-long debate today with Senator Robert Y. Hayne of South Carolina. The subject of their exchange was Hayne's claim that a state had the right to "nullify," or choose not to obey, a federal law.

The debate began when Hayne delivered a speech on January 19 asserting the rights of states to be free of federal interference. Hayne insisted that the Tariff of Abominations was responsible for South Carolina's current economic problems. He argued that no state should have to accept a federal law that harmed its interests.

Beginning yesterday, Webster held the attention of the Senate and the country as he delivered his response. According to Webster, no single state has the power to question laws passed by the Congress. Only the Supreme Court can do that.

The Massachusetts senator closed his remarks with the words, "Liberty and Union, now and forever, one and inseparable!"

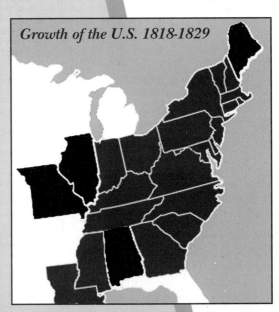

Growth of the U.S. 1818-1829

41

ten thousand people on the federal payroll and replaced them with his own supporters.

Because of his strategic use of the spoils system and his frequent direct appeals to the public for support, Jackson is widely considered to be the first modern president.

Jackson believed the president spoke with the voice of the people because he was the only government official (other than the vice president) elected by all the people. This attitude sometimes brought him into conflict with Congress and the Supreme Court. When that happened, he used his popular support to help him prevail.

AN INAUGURAL MESS

Because Jackson ran as their candidate, the people celebrated his inauguration as no inauguration had been celebrated before. A mob of twenty thousand well-wishers followed Jackson's carriage all the way from the Capitol to the White House. Some of them had traveled hundreds of miles to see Old Hickory, and their exuberance got the best of them.

Many followed Jackson into the White House itself—through the windows as well as the doors. They broke the presidential china, spit tobacco juice on the carpets, and stood on chairs and sofas to get a better view.

Unable to maintain order, Jackson fled through a back window and ran to a nearby hotel. Eventually, waiters drew the crowd out of the residence by serving tubs of punch on the White House lawn.

The damage was costly, but Jackson didn't really mind because the people had been acting out their joy. On the other hand, conservative Washington was scandalized, and it wouldn't be the last time. Soon after the inauguration, another scandal

ANDREW JACKSON'S FATHER DIED BEFORE HE WAS born, and his oldest brother died in 1779 while serving in the Continental Army. The next year, thirteen-year-old Andrew and his remaining brother, Robert, also joined the Continental Army. Andrew served as a colonel's orderly, carrying messages back and forth on horseback.

The Early Years

In April 1781, the brothers were captured and made to march forty miles without food or water to a prisoner-of-war camp. Robert caught smallpox there and died. Andrew's mother died the same year from a disease she caught while caring for wounded soldiers. His mother's death left Andrew alone in the world.

After studying to become a lawyer and serving as Tennessee's first U.S. representative, Jackson headed a volunteer army during the **War of 1812.** General Jackson won a number of victories against Britain's Indian allies before defeating the British themselves at the bloody battle of New Orleans. Jackson's successful invasion of Florida in 1818 helped John Quincy Adams negotiate the purchase of that colony from Spain.

★**THE FIRST LADY** When Andrew Jackson first wed Rachel Donelson in 1791, she was actually still married to her first husband. Both she and Jackson believed that her divorce had been finalized, but it wasn't formally granted until 1793. A few months later, Andrew and Rachel married again, this time legally.

The mistake haunted them during the 1828 campaign, when the National Republicans accused Jackson of adultery because he and Rachel had technically lived together before being legally married. The general tried to shield his wife, but Rachel eventually found out that she was being smeared in the national press.

She quickly fell ill, at least in part because of her heartache, and died less than two months after the election. She was buried in the dress that she had bought to wear at her husband's inauguration.

★ TOM THUMB

America's first steam-powered railroad locomotive was built by a wealthy inventor named Peter Cooper. He nicknamed the locomotive "Tom Thumb" because it was only twenty feet long.

Cooper demonstrated his new invention for the first time in 1830, when the Baltimore & Ohio opened its first railroad line. The locomotive reached a peak speed of fifteen miles per hour during the thirteen-mile trip and proved that train travel was practical along hilly routes.

On the return trip, Cooper and his passengers came upon a horse. A race was suggested. At first, the horse galloped into the lead. Then Tom Thumb caught up and pulled ahead. It seemed as though the locomotive would win easily, but the engine suddenly broke down, and the horse won the race.

★ UTOPIAN COMMUNITIES

One response to the horrible conditions in many U.S. factories was the cooperative community. The first of these was founded in 1825 by Robert Owen, who was already famous for pioneering labor reform at his factory in Scotland.

Owen was concerned by the wide gap between the rich and the poor. The community he founded in New Harmony, Indiana, was supposed to be a utopia, or perfect society, where all the residents worked together for the benefit of the group. Instead, many lazy and unprincipled people joined the community because they thought they could get a free ride. New Harmony failed after two years.

★ THE LIBERATOR

In 1831, William Lloyd Garrison began publishing *The Liberator*, which would soon become the most important and hardest hitting of the abolitionist newspapers. It described the horrors of slavery in great detail and helped spark enormous growth in the northern antislavery movement.

Congressmen in Washington debated whether or not slavery should be extended to the new western states, but Garrison and his followers wanted slavery abolished everywhere, including the South, on moral grounds.

broke. This one involved Jackson's new secretary of war, John Eaton.

THE PEGGY EATON AFFAIR

While he represented Tennessee in the Senate, Eaton had lived in a boardinghouse run by a woman named Peggy Timberlake, whose husband worked for the navy. When John Timberlake went away on long voyages, Eaton would often escort Mrs. Timberlake to social functions. After her husband died in 1829, Eaton married her.

Rumors circulated around town that the relationship between Eaton and his new wife was "improper." People insinuated that the couple had been involved while John Timberlake was still alive. Led by Floride Calhoun, the wife of Vice President John C. Calhoun, the wives of important government officials shunned Peggy Eaton.

Moral rules were very strict during the nineteenth century, especially with regard to women, who were believed to be pure and weak. Peggy Eaton did not fit this image. Nor did her background as a barmaid help her win the approval of Washington society.

Jackson, however, stood by her. Reminded of campaign attacks against his own wife's virtue, the president refused to listen to gossip about Peggy Eaton. Instead, he invited Mrs. Eaton to state dinners and insisted that the wives of his cabinet officers accept her.

Rather than force their wives to receive Mrs. Eaton, most of the members of President Jackson's cabinet decided to hand in their resignations.

Floride Calhoun enraged Jackson by leaving Washington rather than socialize with Peggy Eaton. On the other hand, Secretary of State Martin Van Buren's gracious acceptance of Mrs. Eaton raised his standing with the president as Vice President Calhoun's fell. During the rest of Calhoun's term, he and Jackson would grow further apart.

THE INDIAN REMOVAL ACT

The most important legislation of Jackson's first term was the Indian Removal Act of 1830. For a number of years, the state of Georgia had been trying to confiscate and sell land belonging to the Cherokee Indians. The Cherokee were among five "civilized" tribes that had adopted the ways of white society in order to live peacefully among whites.

To become acceptable to whites, the Cherokee had taken up European-style farming, developed a written language, and even adopted their own constitution. But neither the government of Georgia nor President Jackson cared.

Old Hickory was well known as an Indian fighter, not as an Indian lover. The Indian Removal Act gave him the power to remove Indians from the South to lands west of the Mississippi River. During the next few years, Jackson used federal troops to force the Cherokee, Chickasaw, Choctaw, Seminole, and Creek tribes to abandon one hundred million acres of fertile land and resettle in the West.

The Cherokee asked the Supreme Court for help, arguing that the tribe was essentially a foreign nation. Chief Justice John Marshall denied their petition. Marshall did point out, however, that only the federal government had sovereignty over the Cherokee. Therefore, the state laws of Georgia did not apply to them, and no whites could settle Cherokee land without Cherokee permission. But Georgia ignored the decision, and Jackson refused to enforce it, so the forced removals continued.

THE FIRST MAJOR NATIONAL PARTY CONVENTIONS were held in 1832. Until that time, presidential candidates were generally nominated either by a group of congressmen belonging to the same party or by a state legislature.

The Democratic party met in Baltimore in May to renominate Jackson. Because of the president's fights with him, John C. Calhoun was dropped from the ticket and replaced with Martin Van Buren. Jackson clearly intended to groom Van Buren to succeed him as president.

To oppose Jackson, the National Republicans nominated Henry Clay, who attacked Jackson for his tyrannical attitudes and his use of the spoils system. National Republican cartoons portrayed the president as King Andrew I.

The most important campaign issue was Jackson's policy toward the Second Bank of the United States. The president did not try to hide his contempt for the bank. When Congress passed a bill that summer granting the national bank a new charter, Jackson vetoed it. As a temporarily bedridden Jackson told his loyal aide, "The bank, Mr. Van Buren, is trying to kill me, but I will kill it."

Jackson claimed that the bank favored the interests of the wealthy, while Clay argued that closing the bank would hurt small borrowers as well. Clay polled well in the North, but Jackson carried the South and West again and won comfortably.

REMEMBER THE ALAMO!
183 Texans Die After 13-Day Siege

SAN ANTONIO, March 6, 1836—The thirteen-day siege of the Alamo ended today when the forces of Mexican general Santa Anna stormed the outer walls of the mission. Three thousand Mexicans killed the 183 defenders of the Alamo, sparing only fifteen women and children and one black slave.

The Texan dead included colonels James Bowie and William B. Travis as well as the famous frontiersman Davy Crockett. Estimates of Mexican dead and wounded range from one thousand to sixteen hundred men.

The Texans first captured the town of San Antonio in December of last year, beginning their ongoing war for independence. After Santa Anna's army arrived from the south on February 23, Texan general Sam Houston told the defenders of the Alamo to retreat. Writing from inside the Alamo, Travis replied, "I shall never surrender or retreat.... VICTORY OR DEATH."

THE NULLIFICATION CONTROVERSY

Although President Jackson hated the Tariff of Abominations as much as the public did, John Calhoun hated it even more. As president, Jackson worked with Congress to reduce the tariff rates, but he also took seriously his obligation to enforce the law of the land.

Calhoun thought the tariff was unconstitutional because it placed a cruel and unusual burden on his home state of South Carolina. He argued that states could "nullify," or choose not to obey, federal laws that were not in their own best interests. Calhoun's theory thus extended the **states' rights** theories of Jefferson.

The chief spokesman for nullification in Congress was South Carolina senator Robert Y. Hayne, who faced Daniel Webster in an important 1830 Senate debate. Afterward, people waited anxiously for Jackson to announce his position on nullification.

In April 1830, at a dinner celebrating Jefferson's birthday, Jackson made the first toast: "Our Union—it must be preserved!" Calhoun's toast was, "The Union—next to our liberty, the most dear." Obviously, Calhoun had not softened his position.

In 1832, Congress finally passed a new law reducing tariff rates, but Calhoun wasn't satisfied. Instead, he resigned the vice presidency and accepted a seat in the Senate.

45

Meanwhile, South Carolina decided to nullify both the 1828 and 1832 tariffs. State legislators warned that if federal troops were used to collect the tariffs, South Carolina would secede from the Union.

When Congress met again in 1833 following Jackson's comfortable reelection, nullification was the hottest issue. In nullifying the tariffs, South Carolina had brought into question the very issue of federal superiority that had been settled militarily during the **Whiskey Rebellion** and in the courts by the case of *McCulloch v. Maryland*.

Jackson was not about to stand for such behavior, and with the Senate's approval, he sent federal troops to the South Carolina border. In the meantime, Henry Clay shepherded a compromise tariff through Congress. Faced with the choice of a federal invasion or Clay's compromise, South Carolina backed down and began collecting the new tariff fees.

THE SECOND BANK

Having resolved the nullification crisis, Jackson now turned his attention to the Second Bank of the United States. The future of the bank had been the most important issue during his 1832 campaign against Clay.

Jackson had always hated banks, and the Second Bank in particular. Like many westerners, he blamed the conservative policies of the national bank for tightening credit and thereby slowing the economic development of the West.

The Second Bank was based in Philadelphia with branches all over the country. Its charter was due to expire in 1836, and another act of Congress would be required to keep the bank open beyond that time. But Jackson wanted to close the Second Bank even sooner. He reached out to

★ THE BLACK HAWK WAR

While the Cherokee tried to use the Supreme Court to stop the state of Georgia from taking their land, the Sac and Fox tribes in Illinois tried a different approach. They fought. The Black Hawk War, named after the Sac and Fox tribal leader, ended three generations of resistance to white settlement along the old Northwest frontier.

In 1832, the Illinois militia, including twenty-three-year-old Captain Abraham Lincoln, chased Black Hawk's band of warriors and their families into Wisconsin. The soldiers caught up with the Indians on the Bad Axe River. Although Black Hawk raised a white flag, the militiamen attacked anyway, shooting the women and children as well as the men.

★ NAT TURNER'S REBELLION

In 1831, Nat Turner began the most important, and bloodiest, slave revolt in U.S. history. A deeply religious man, he thought that a solar eclipse was a sign from God that he should free his people.

On the night of August 21, Turner killed his masters in their sleep, the first of at least fifty-one whites who would die. Then he set off with seventy-five fellow slaves

for the seat of Southampton County, Virginia, where he planned to capture the armory and arm his new recruits.

But Turner's band was not nearly strong enough to face the three thousand militiamen waiting for them. Although Turner escaped, six weeks later he was captured and hanged.

Turner's rebellion terrified white southerners. Many had believed the myth that slaves were contented with their bondage and would not stage an armed revolt. Southern states quickly passed new laws to restrict the education of slaves as well as their ability to travel and gather in groups.

★**DAVY CROCKETT** Davy Crockett was born into a pioneer family in Tennessee. He grew up living in the wilderness of the western frontier and spent less than a hundred days in school. While in his twenties, he made a name for himself as an Indian fighter and "b'ar hunter."

Crockett served off and on in Congress from 1827 until 1835. During that time, he charmed eastern journalists with his frontier mannerisms. Soon, these men began to write books and articles about Crockett, casting him as a frontier folk hero in a coonskin cap. Some said he could leap the Ohio River and wrestle wildcats. After his death at the Alamo, Crockett lived on in dozens of books, songs, television shows, and movies.

★**AMERICAN COOKING** In colonial America, most cooking in the North was based on British recipes. But the food people ate was also influenced by the availability of local ingredients and by Indian cooking techniques. Pumpkin pie was one popular dish that resulted from a combination of the two cuisines.

This type of cultural exchange also took place in Texas, where local Mexicans taught white settlers how to cook with corn. In the South, cooking was influenced by West Indian and African styles brought over by the slaves. Black-eyed peas, peanuts, okra, and rice were all staples of West African cooking before they became favorites in the South.

★**KITCHEN CABINET** Since the administration of George Washington, presidents had met regularly with their cabinets to discuss and decide matters of government policy. But Jackson didn't like his cabinet officers very much to begin with, and he liked them even less after the Peggy Eaton Affair.

Jackson cut down the number of cabinet meetings until he stopped them altogether. Instead, he discussed politics almost every night with his closest friends at meetings held in the White House kitchen. These men—including Martin Van Buren, John Eaton, newspaper editor Amos Kendall, and William B. Lewis—came to be known as the Kitchen Cabinet.

the people and asked for their support in destroying the "monster bank."

Jackson ordered Treasury Secretary Louis McLane to withdraw all the federal deposits from the Second Bank and place them instead in state banks. When McLane refused, Jackson dismissed him and appointed William Duane, who also refused and was fired.

After a frustrating search, Jackson finally found someone who would follow his orders, Attorney General Roger B. Taney, whom Jackson would later appoint to the Supreme Court. In September 1833, Taney ordered the withdrawal of the deposits.

In response to Jackson's move, Nicholas Biddle, the president of the Second Bank, called in his bank's outstanding loans. In part this was a sensible business decision. If the Second Bank were to close, it would have to settle its affairs.

But Biddle also wanted to pressure Jackson to change his mind. By calling in the Second Bank's loans, Biddle limited the availability of credit and brought the country to the brink of a financial panic.

The pressure mounted on Jackson. But each time someone complained, the president said, "Go to Nicholas Biddle." In the end, Biddle relented, and the near-panic turned into a land boom. The state banks began lending money from the new federal deposits at bargain rates, and this in turn led to a new round of land speculation in the West.

TEXAN INDEPENDENCE During his last year in office, Jackson's attention also turned west, to Texas, which was still Mexican territory. While he longed to add Texas to the Union, he also felt bound to honor Mexico's sovereignty and was concerned that the admission of Texas as a slave state would disturb the precarious balance between North and South.

ANDREW JACKSON 1829-1837

47

In December 1835, however, white settlers in Texas revolted against the new Mexican government of General Antonio López de Santa Anna, principally because Santa Anna had recently outlawed slavery. Raising an army, they captured the town of San Antonio, alarming Santa Anna and leading to the Mexican siege of the Alamo.

Santa Anna's victory there was short-lived, however. Six weeks later, on April 21, 1836, an army of Texans under the command of Sam Houston won both the battle of San Jacinto and independence for Texas. The Texans' battle cry was "Remember the Alamo!" On July 4, Congress agreed to recognize the new Republic of Texas, taking the first step toward making Texas part of the Union.

THE SPECIE CIRCULAR One of Jackson's last actions before leaving office was to issue the Specie Circular in July 1836. The Specie Circular declared that buyers could no longer use paper money to purchase federal land. Instead, they would have to use gold or silver. (Coins made out of precious metals were known as "specie.")

Jackson instituted this policy because of the land boom touched off by his successful campaign against the Second Bank. He was worried that all the new credit offered by the state banks was making the economy unstable. He was also concerned that speculators were buying too much land with devalued paper money instead of with hard cash.

Jackson's drastic policy reversal, from easy credit to no credit, sent land prices plunging, which in turn led to bankruptcies. By the time Jackson left office, businesses all over the country were closing their doors, and with the government still refusing paper money, the panic spread.

OBEYING JACKSON'S ORDERS, THE DEMOCRATIC party nominated Vice President Martin Van Buren as its presidential candidate in 1836. Van Buren's opposition came from the Whig party, formed by Jackson's political enemies in 1834.

The Whigs were unable to decide on a single candidate, in part because they had little in common beyond their hatred of Jackson. So the party members decided to run three regional candidates. They hoped to deny Van Buren an electoral majority. If that happened, the election would be thrown into the House of Representatives.

The Whigs ran the war hero William Henry Harrison in the West, Daniel Webster in the North, and Hugh Lawson White of Tennessee in the South. Only Harrison was regarded as a serious national candidate.

Jackson's endorsement was a mixed blessing for Van Buren. The president was still personally popular, but his controversial policies, especially regarding the Second Bank, posed some problems for Van Buren.

Whenever possible, Van Buren tried to avoid the issues, especially slavery. His success depended on a coalition of Democrats from the North and South, and he didn't want to upset any of them.

Van Buren won with just over half the popular vote and a solid electoral majority. But it would be 152 years before another vice president was elected to follow the president he served.

DEMOCRATIC TICKET.

FOR PRESIDENT,
MARTIN VAN BUREN.
FOR VICE PRESIDENT,
RICHARD M. JOHNSON.

OHIO ELECTORS.
John M. Goodenow,
Othniel Looker,
Jacob Felter,
James B. Cameron,
David S. Davis,
James Fife,
John J. Higgins,
Joseph Morris,
James Sharp,
John McElvain,
William Trevitt,
David Robb,
Hugh McComb,
Robert Mitchell,
James Mathews,
Joshua Seney,
Stephen N. Sargent,
Thomas J. McLain,
Noah Frederick,
Jacob Ihrig,
James Means.

MARTIN VAN BUREN

8TH PRESIDENT

★

FROM 1837 TO 1841

BORN: December 5, 1782

BIRTHPLACE: Kinderhook, N.Y.

DIED: July 24, 1862

PARTY: Democrat

VICE PRESIDENT: Richard M. Johnson

FIRST LADY: Hannah Hoes

CHILDREN: Abraham, John, Martin, Smith

NICKNAME: Little Magician

The first president not born a British subject.

Just two months after Martin Van Buren took office, the United States was hit by one of the worst depressions in the nation's history. The economic crisis that began during the summer of 1837 lasted nearly a decade. These hard times dominated Van Buren's presidency and eventually cost him reelection in 1840.

Although Van Buren received much of the blame, the crisis was largely the fault of Andrew Jackson. Jackson's policies, designed to destroy the Second Bank of the United States, had at the same time weakened the economy.

In trying to crush the Second Bank, Jackson had ordered that government funds be withdrawn from the national bank and deposited instead in state banks. These state banks, however, often used the money to make unwise loans. Their loose banking

THOUSANDS OF CHEROKEE DIE ALONG THE TRAIL OF TEARS

During 1838 and 1839, fifteen thousand Cherokee were forced to leave their homeland in Georgia and march west to government reservations in Oklahoma. This journey, during which more than one-fourth of the Cherokee died, has been called the Trail of Tears.

The Cherokee were escorted by federal troops under the command of General Winfield Scott. Along the way, government officials took what little money the Cherokee had. In return, the government provided inadequate supplies for the trip.

Despite the shortages of food and other necessities, General Scott refused to slow the pace of the march. Even the sick and the elderly were forced to keep up. This policy caused many of the deaths.

One observer wrote at the time that "such a denial of justice, and such deafness to screams for mercy, were never heard of in time of peace...since the earth was made."

practices led to a period of inflation during which prices soared.

During his last months in office, Jackson issued the Specie Circular, an executive order intended to curb this inflation and control land speculation in the West. The Specie Circular stated that paper money could no longer be used to purchase government land. Instead, buyers would have to pay for the land with specie.

During the nineteenth century, paper money was "backed" by precious metals such as gold and silver. Coins made from these valuable metals were known as "specie." Under this banking system, a one-dollar bill could be exchanged at any time for a dollar's worth of specie.

The Specie Circular forced buyers of land to exchange their paper money for gold or silver. But this created a demand for specie that the banks could not meet. Because of the inflation and the bad loans the banks had made, there was no longer enough gold and silver to back all the paper money in circulation. As a result, the value of the paper money fell.

THE PANIC OF 1837 The Panic of 1837 began when a number of banks in New York City stopped converting paper money into gold and silver. Loans also became harder to get. As a result, speculators who were denied credit stopped buying land, and land prices fell sharply.

Nearly one thousand banks around the country failed. When they did, work on the internal improvement projects the banks had been financing also stopped, throwing many people out of work. In some cities, hungry people rioted for food. Meanwhile in Washington, Van Buren wore expensive, tailored clothes, which hurt his popularity.

The Early Years

ALTHOUGH HE LATER BECAME KNOWN FOR HIS expensive tastes, Martin Van Buren did not grow up wealthy. His father was a poor farmer and tavern keeper in Kinderhook, New York, a small Dutch village on the Hudson River. The Van Burens spoke Dutch at home, and Little Mat was raised according to European customs.

After school he often helped his father in the tavern where famous politicians, including Alexander Hamilton and Aaron Burr, often stopped on their way to Albany. Young Martin loved to listen to their arguments, and he quickly developed an interest in politics that would last his entire life. He became such a crafty politician himself that he was nicknamed the Little Magician and the Red Fox of Kinderhook.

★**A DANDY PRESIDENT** A small, dapper, and refined man, Van Buren was both respected and criticized for the way he behaved and dressed. He wore a coat with a velvet collar and tight-fitting gloves made from very soft leather. He traveled through the muddy and smelly streets of Washington in a luxurious green coach driven by men in fancy uniforms. People often complained that their president behaved more like a king than a Democrat.

★**TRANSCENDENTALISM** During the 1830s, a group of writers including Ralph Waldo Emerson and Henry David Thoreau developed the philosophy of transcendentalism. Transcendentalists believed that, because people are basically good, human society can be perfected through experimentation and reform. The most important transcendentalist journal was *The Dial*, founded in 1840 and first edited by Margaret Fuller.

The transcendentalists particularly influenced American literature, but they also were active in social reform movements. Among the causes they championed were women's suffrage, public education, and better working conditions in factories.

★ FRONTIER WOMEN

The first white people to move out west were almost exclusively men. Some were cowboys, others were miners, but they were all fortune seekers who wandered through the wilderness and rarely put down roots. Not until women began moving west were the first farms settled, the first churches built, and the first towns established.

When they did arrive, women found freedom on the frontier that they could never have experienced in the established cities of the East. Life in the West was hard, and frontier women had to be tough and capable. But they did receive a certain measure of equality in return.

★ THE TELEGRAPH

Portrait painter Samuel Morse first got the idea for the telegraph in 1832. Five years later, he displayed the first working model, which introduced an electric current in a wire. Morse Code was later developed to translate letters of the alphabet into groups of long and short pulses. The telegraph provided the first means of communicating instantly over long distances.

To convince the government to fund the development of the telegraph, Morse arranged a demonstration. He had telegraph wire strung between Baltimore and Washington. Then, using equipment set up in the Supreme Court, he transmitted the message "What hath God wrought!" and received an immediate reply. Morse's device was probably more shocking to people in its time than any other invention, including the automobile, the radio, and the computer.

At first, Congress did little more than debate the country's problems. But Van Buren had a plan. He wanted to set up an independent treasury, run by the government. He felt that an independent treasury was the only way to protect federal money from irresponsible loans.

A number of congressmen opposed the president's plan because they didn't want government funds removed from the banks in their home states. It was not until 1840, the last year of Van Buren's term, that Congress finally passed the Independent Treasury Act.

THE TEXAS QUESTION In 1837, the year that Martin Van Buren became president, Washington was still a swampy, malaria-ridden town. Open sewers wound through the unpaved streets of the nation's capital. Pigs and chickens scurried about. In busy markets, slaves were bought and sold.

At his inauguration, the new president spoke directly to the issue of slavery, which he had carefully avoided during the 1836 campaign. Now Van Buren declared that he would fight attempts to abolish slavery in the South. He said that the southern states had the right to decide the matter for themselves.

What Van Buren really wanted was for the issue to go away, but it wouldn't. The president was forced to confront slavery again when Texas applied for admission to the Union shortly after winning its independence from Mexico.

If Texas were to be admitted, it would be as a slave state. There was no doubt about that. It was the Mexican government's attempt to abolish slavery in Texas that had started the rebellion there in the first place.

Admitting Texas as a slave state, however, would upset the delicate balance between slave and free states preserved by the **Missouri Compromise**. Despite the president's strong support of slavery in general, he decided to oppose the admission of Texas because he feared the political consequences. Van Buren worried that admitting Texas as a slave state would reopen the slavery debate.

The president's stand was unpopular in the South, of course, but it was also attacked by many others who wanted to expand the territory of the country no matter what the cost.

THE CAROLINE AFFAIR

Meanwhile, as Congress argued about Texas and the economy, the threat of war returned along the nation's northern border. The trouble began early in 1837 when Canadian rebels attacked Toronto in an effort to end British colonial rule there. When the attempt failed, the rebels retreated to Navy Island in the Niagara River, which separates the United States from Canada.

Americans supporting the Canadian rebels began ferrying them supplies from New York using the steamship *Caroline*. That December, the enraged British ordered loyal Canadian militia to attack the *Caroline* as it lay anchored off the New York shore. During the successful raid, the *Caroline* was set afire and sent over Niagara Falls. One American was killed and several injured.

Van Buren called the attack an "outrage" and sent troops to the U.S.-Canadian border. Many congressmen urged him to declare war on Britain, but Van Buren resisted the pressure and instead declared U.S. neutrality with regard to the Canadian rebellion. Despite this declaration, relations with Britain remained strained for several years.

THE 1840 ELECTION WAS DOMINATED BY THE economic depression that followed the Panic of 1837. Many people blamed Van Buren and wanted a change. To oppose the president, the Whigs put up General William Henry Harrison again.

Although Harrison's supporters assured voters that the general would end the depression, they didn't

say how. Instead, they concentrated on hoopla. The Whigs' focus on staged events, campaign advertising, and campaign souvenirs, such as decorated hairbrushes and tobacco tins, made this the first modern presidential election.

The Whig campaign took on a great deal of momentum when a Democratic newspaper mocked Harrison as a bumpkin who would enjoy nothing more than a barrel of hard, or alcoholic, cider and a log cabin in which to drink it. Although Harrison actually lived in a twenty-two-room mansion, the Whigs cleverly saw the opportunity to portray him as a man of the people. To encourage this image, they used log cabins for their campaign headquarters and served hard cider in cabin-shaped mugs.

On the other extreme, rumors were spread that Van Buren was such a dandy that he ate with a golden spoon and bathed in a tub of cologne. Actually, Harrison was far wealthier than Van Buren.

The campaign was so exciting that an astounding eighty percent of eligible voters cast ballots. Van Buren kept the popular vote respectably close, but he lost the electoral vote by a wide margin, including his home state of New York.

WILLIAM HENRY HARRISON

9TH PRESIDENT
★
1841

BORN: February 9, 1773

BIRTHPLACE: Charles City County, Va.

DIED: April 4, 1841

PARTY: Whig

VICE PRESIDENT: John Tyler

FIRST LADY: Anna Tuthill Symmes

CHILDREN: Elizabeth, John Cleves, Lucy, William, John Scott, Benjamin, Mary, Carter, Anna, James

NICKNAME: Old Tippecanoe

The first president to die in office.

PNEUMONIA KILLS HARRISON AFTER ONE MONTH IN OFFICE

WASHINGTON, April 4, 1841—President William Henry Harrison died last night of pneumonia. A messenger has been dispatched to the home of Vice President John Tyler in Williamsburg, Virginia, to inform him of the news.

Just one month ago, the sixty-eight-year-old president gave the longest inaugural address in history, lasting nearly two hours. He delivered the speech while standing outdoors in a cold wind wearing neither a hat nor an overcoat.

Later, the president went out walking and got caught in a rainstorm. He came back to the White House drenched. The cold he caught that day later developed into the pneumonia.

Doctors applied heated suction cups to the president's skin, hoping to draw out the disease. When this and other modern treatments failed, the doctors turned in desperation to traditional Indian cures, including one therapy involving snakes.

In times of crisis, people often turn—sometimes foolishly, sometimes not—to war heroes for leadership. George Washington was such a hero. So was Andrew Jackson.

General William Henry Harrison was born on a large Virginia plantation just before the outbreak of the American Revolution. His father, Benjamin, signed the Declaration of Independence. Harrison's first career choice was medicine, but his money ran out soon after his father's death in 1791. When that happened, Harrison left medical school and joined the army as a professional soldier.

Harrison saw his first action in the Northwest Territory during the Indian wars of the 1790s. He was commended for his bravery at the Battle of Fallen Timbers in 1794.

While serving as the governor of the Indiana Territory in 1811, Harrison led an army of professional soldiers and militiamen against the village of Shawnee chief Tecumseh. His victory at Tippecanoe Creek earned him national fame and the nickname Old Tippecanoe. His 1840 campaign slogan was "Tippecanoe and Tyler, Too."

JOHN TYLER

10TH PRESIDENT
★
FROM 1841 TO 1845

BORN: March 29, 1790

BIRTHPLACE: Charles City County, Va.

DIED: January 18, 1862

PARTY: Whig

VICE PRESIDENT: None

FIRST LADIES: Letitia Christian, Julia Gardiner

CHILDREN: Mary, Robert, John, Letitia, Elizabeth, Anne, Alice, Tazewell, David, John Alexander, Julia, Lachlan, Lyon, Robert Fitzgerald, Pearl

NICKNAME: His Accidency

The first president to have a veto overridden.

Because William Henry Harrison was the first president to die in office, his death caused much confusion. Vice President John Tyler's transition to power should have been simple, but it wasn't.

Tyler didn't even know the president was sick. He was shocked when a government clerk awoke him at home in Williamsburg, Virginia, with news of Harrison's death.

Tyler's larger problem was that he had been nominated for vice president simply to balance the Whig ticket. The Whigs needed support in the South, and Tyler was a southerner. He had joined the Whig party because of his hatred for Andrew Jackson and the Democrats. But he had never really accepted the Whigs' nationalist policies. As a result, the Whig party leaders, especially Senator Henry Clay, didn't trust him.

EUROPEAN IMMIGRATION WAVE HITS U.S.

During the 1840s, the United States experienced a massive wave of immigration from Europe. Between 1844 and 1854, nearly three million people made the Atlantic crossing. Of these immigrants, 1,300,000 were Irish and 940,000 were German.

The Irish were escaping a terrible famine in their country caused by a series of potato crop failures. Tens of thousands of people starved, but many more fled to the United States.

Because they were too poor to move farther inland, most Irish immigrants settled in the northeastern port cities in which they landed. Large Irish neighborhoods quickly grew up in New York, Boston, and Philadelphia.

German immigrants, most of whom arrived with a little more money, generally moved to the Midwest. Cities such as Milwaukee became magnets for them as well as for the Scandinavians who followed. By 1860, nearly one-third of the population of Wisconsin was foreign born.

★EDGAR ALLAN POE

In 1841, *Graham's Magazine* published a short story by Edgar Allan Poe entitled "The Murders in the Rue Morgue." *Graham's* regularly printed works by the best known American authors—including James Fenimore Cooper, Nathaniel Hawthorne, and Henry Wadsworth Longfellow.

"The Murders in the Rue Morgue" was the first detective story ever written. It exhibited the ghoulish and gruesome style that later made Poe's work famous. His stories, poems, and essays were widely published at the time, but Poe never made much money. In 1843, his best year, he earned just three hundred dollars from his writing.

★THE OREGON TRAIL

During 1843, "Oregon fever" swept through the Mississippi Valley. A thousand settlers headed west that year to find out whether the Willamette Valley of Oregon was indeed as beautiful and fertile as people said. They followed the two-thousand-mile-long Oregon Trail.

Beginning in Independence, Missouri, the Oregon Trail passed through deserts, over mountains, and across Indian territory. Most families traveled in canvas-covered wagons called "prairie schooners" because the tops of the wagons often looked liked sails in the wind. Schooners were popular sailing ships.

Trains of fifty or so wagons set off each morning about four o'clock and kept going until dusk, stopping only to graze the animals. Even so, the trip to Oregon usually took six months, because the wagons could make only twelve miles a day over the difficult terrain.

Clay was a nationalist, which meant that he wanted to use the federal government to build a strong, unified country. His current program was a revised version of the American System he had originally developed in the years after the War of 1812.

During the month that William Henry Harrison occupied the White House, it seemed to many as though Clay was actually running the country. On most important policy matters, Harrison let the senator decide, which was exactly the way Clay had hoped it would be.

Unlike Clay, Tyler was an advocate of states' rights. He believed, as many southerners did, that strengthening the federal government threatened individual freedom. Southerners worried that a strong national government would attempt to outlaw slavery.

Clay and his followers tried to limit Tyler's power by refusing to recognize him as the new president. They referred to him as the "acting president." Although some people called him His Accidency (a pun on His Excellency, the address used for royalty), Tyler never doubted that he was president. He even returned, unopened, mail that came addressed to "Acting President Tyler."

WHIGS IN TURMOIL Tyler's first public clash with Clay came over the national bank. Clay had wanted to bring back a national bank ever since Jackson had crushed the Second Bank of the United States. Twice Clay pushed bills through Congress to charter a new Third Bank, and twice Tyler angered his own party by vetoing them.

To protest Tyler's vetoes, his entire cabinet, with the exception of Secretary of State Daniel Webster, resigned in September 1841. Webster stayed on because he was in the middle of important treaty negotiations with Britain.

Tyler quickly appointed new cabinet officers who agreed with him, but the loss of Whig support had its consequences. After the president vetoed the bank bill a second time, the Whigs disowned him. Thus, Tyler became the first president to serve without a party.

Although Tyler's domestic policies often met opposition in Congress, he had greater freedom to act when it came to foreign affairs. His administration's first success came in resolving a border fight with Canada. The agreement, negotiated by Daniel Webster and Lord Ashburton of Great Britain, granted the United States slightly more than half the disputed land along the Maine border. The Webster-Ashburton Treaty fixed the U.S.-Canadian border all the way from the Atlantic Ocean to the Rocky Mountains.

THE ANNEXATION OF TEXAS

To the south, Tyler took up the matter of Texan statehood, which had been pending since the Van Buren administration. By 1843, Texans had grown tired of waiting. They began talking with Britain about the possibility of remaining independent under British protection.

Tyler began his own secret talks with Texas, which led to a treaty rejected by the Senate in June 1844. This treaty—written by Tyler's new secretary of state, John C. Calhoun—included a section glorifying slavery that sealed its defeat.

That fall, however, James Knox Polk was elected president because he favored expansion of the nation. Polk's victory convinced Congress that the public wanted Texas to be annexed. Three days before he left office, Tyler signed a joint resolution of Congress admitting Texas to the Union.

H AVING THROWN TYLER OUT OF THE PARTY, THE WHIGS weren't about to nominate him for another term. Instead, the party chose Henry Clay, who had already run for the presidency twice before, in 1824 and again in 1832.

When the Democrats met to choose their candidate, former president Martin Van Buren won a majority of the delegate votes on the first ballot, but he never won the two-thirds necessary for nomination. As Van Buren's support waned, the convention turned to James Knox Polk, a former governor of Tennessee. This dark-horse, or long-shot, candidate was so poorly known compared to Clay that the Whigs made "Who is Polk?" their campaign slogan.

The key issues of the campaign were western expansion and the spread of slavery. Clay opposed the annexation of Texas, while Polk strongly supported that step as well as the annexation of Oregon as far north as 54°40' latitude. The Democratic slogan was "Fifty-four Forty or Fight!"

Clay's stand on Texas cost him support in the South, where voters thought he was trying to stop the spread of slavery. Clay hoped that these losses would be offset by gains in the North. But Clay, like Polk, was himself a slaveholder, which third-party abolitionist candidate James G. Birney often pointed out. Birney didn't win any electoral votes, but he did win enough popular votes in New York to tip the state—and the election—to Polk.

James Knox POLK

11th President
★
From 1845 to 1849

Born: November 2, 1795

Birthplace: Mecklenburg County, N.C.

Died: June 15, 1849

Party: Democrat

Vice President: George M. Dallas

First Lady: Sarah Childress

Children: None

Nickname: Young Hickory

The first president to have his inauguration reported by telegraph.

During the 1840s, Americans were particularly eager to expand the territory of the United States. An almost unknown expansionist candidate, James Polk, proved the strength of this cause by defeating Henry Clay for president. After his election, Polk focused his political program on the nation's "manifest destiny" to rule the North American continent.

The phrase "manifest destiny" was first used by magazine editor John L. O'Sullivan in an 1845 article favoring the annexation of Texas. O'Sullivan used the phrase to refer to the popular belief that it was proper and inevitable for the United States government to control North America.

GOLD RUSH FEVER

Miners Hurry to California

SAN FRANCISCO, February 28, 1849—The first ship carrying prospectors from the East arrived in port today, thirteen months after James W. Marshall discovered gold at Sutter's Fort.

These miners, nicknamed "forty-niners" after the year of their arrival, are the first of forty thousand expected to sail to California this year. As many are expected to come overland. As President Polk has pointed out, "Nearly the whole of the male population of the country [has] gone to the gold districts."

James Marshall made his discovery in January 1848 while building a sawmill for John Sutter on the American River near Sacramento. By August, when the *New York Herald* first printed news of his find in the East, there were already four thousand miners living in primitive huts on the hillside above the river.

"My eye was caught by something shining in the bottom of a ditch," Marshall wrote. "I reached my hand down and picked it up; it made my heart thump, for I was certain it was gold."

57

O'Sullivan wrote that it was "our manifest destiny to overspread the continent allotted by Providence for the free development of our yearly multiplying millions."

Like most of his fellow citizens, President Polk believed that it was the nation's manifest, or obvious, destiny to spread democracy from the Atlantic Ocean to the Pacific. It didn't matter that obstacles stood in the way—rivers, mountains, native peoples—because success was inevitable.

Polk believed that the United States was on a divine mission and that one day the nation would create an "empire for liberty" from New York all the way to California. He used the idea of manifest destiny to justify morally the taking of new territory. His policy was the more, the better.

THE OREGON TREATY The annexation of Texas was completed during Tyler's last days in office, so Polk turned his immediate attention to the Oregon Territory. The southern border of Russian lands in Alaska had been set at 54°40' north latitude. The northern border of Spanish California was 42° north latitude, also known as the Forty-second Parallel. Between these two borders, from the Rocky Mountains to the Pacific, was Oregon.

Both the United States and Great Britain had longtime claims to the Oregon Territory. At first, Polk refused to negotiate with the British. After all, the Democrats' slogan during the 1844 election had been "Fifty-four Forty or Fight!"

As president, however, Polk soon agreed to a compromise. A new boundary was set at the Forty-ninth Parallel, granting to the United States present-day Oregon and Washington. Polk thus became the first president to govern a United

THE OLDEST OF TEN CHILDREN, JIMMY POLK WAS born on his family's farm in North Carolina. When he was ten years old, the Polks moved to central Tennessee, traveling more than five hundred miles over rough ground in a covered wagon. The family prospered there, eventually owning thousands of acres worked by more than fifty slaves.

Jimmy Polk was a sickly child, who did poorly in the rough-and-tumble games favored by boys on the

The Early Years

frontier. He was particularly troubled by stones in his gallbladder. When he was seventeen, Polk underwent a dangerous and exceedingly painful operation to remove them. The surgeon gave him only liquor to ease the pain. It was not until the time of Polk's presidency that a doctor in Boston first used ether to put a patient to sleep during an operation.

★**THE FIRST LADY** Sarah Childress Polk was an exceptionally popular hostess in Washington because of her charm, liveliness, and intelligence. As first lady, she hosted the first Thanksgiving dinner at the White House and, being a devout Presbyterian, banned dancing and liquor at all White House events. For a woman of her time, she was unusually well educated, having attended the exclusive Moravian Female Academy in North Carolina. The president often consulted with her on policy matters.

★**AMELIA'S BLOOMERS** Women's clothing during the middle of the nineteenth century could be so confining that it sometimes felt like a cage. Underneath wide hoop skirts and stiff blouses, women wore tightly laced corsets that squeezed their waistlines down to an unnatural twenty inches. These corsets often did permanent damage to the liver and kidneys.

In 1851, a women's rights activist named Amelia Bloomer introduced a new, comfortable style of dress that featured loose-fitting trousers worn underneath a knee-length skirt. The pants quickly became known as "bloomers." Despite their practicality, bloomers so scandalized the public that women did not begin wearing trousers regularly for another century.

★THE SENECA FALLS CONVENTION

The Seneca Falls Convention Many female leaders of the abolitionist movement also wanted to end the "domestic slavery" of women in the United States. In July 1848, a group of these pioneering feminists met in Seneca Falls, New York, where they founded the women's rights movement.

The delegates to the Seneca Falls convention prepared a list of ways in which women suffered discrimination and agreed to a number of resolutions for change. One of these resolutions declared that women deserved to vote, a right that nearly all nineteenth-century women were denied. Only four western states gave women the right to vote before 1900, the first of these being Wyoming in 1869.

★FREDERICK DOUGLASS

At the age of twenty, Frederick Douglass escaped slavery in Maryland. Seven years later, in 1845, he wrote an autobiography, which became one of the most important works of the anti-slavery movement. His *Narrative of the Life of Frederick Douglass, an American Slave* inspired thousands of abolitionists with its detailed description of the horrors of slavery. Later, during the Civil War, Douglass recruited blacks to serve in the Union army and advised President Abraham Lincoln on issues relating to African Americans.

States that extended from ocean to ocean.

After settling the dispute in the West, Polk's attention turned to Mexican territory in the Southwest and California, which became the focus of his expansionist policies. Polk would soon become the first president to act militarily in support of the cause of "manifest destiny."

THE MEXICAN WAR Although Texas formally joined the Union in 1845, the United States and Mexico continued to fight over Texas's southern border. Congress insisted on the Rio Grande, while the Mexicans refused to recognize Texas south of the Nueces River.

At first, Polk tried to bargain. He offered to pay Mexico for the disputed land and expressed his willingness to buy New Mexico and California as well. When the Mexicans, still angry over the annexation of Texas, refused him, Polk sent troops under General Zachary Taylor to the Rio Grande.

On April 25, 1846, Mexican troops engaged U.S. soldiers in a skirmish. In his message to Congress, Polk asked for a declaration of war because Mexican soldiers had "shed American blood upon the American soil." He got what he wanted. The vote was 40-2 in the Senate and 174-14 in the House.

The Mexican War became the central political event of the Polk presidency. His party rallied behind him, while the Whigs were divided. Those from the South and West favored the war, while northern abolitionists such as Representative Abraham Lincoln of Illinois believed the war was part of a secret plan to expand slavery into the Southwest.

The Mexican army vastly outnumbered U.S. forces in the area, but superior U.S. technology and strategy overcame this disadvantage. The revolver, invented in 1835 by Samuel Colt, proved to be a powerful weapon.

Although Colt's own business had failed in 1842, the success of his revolver during the Mexican War led to a large government contract. Colt used the money to build the world's largest private armory, where he made significant advances in the use of interchangeable parts.

The Mexican War ended in February 1848 with the signing of the Treaty of Guadalupe Hidalgo. Under its terms, Mexico ceded to the United States more than five hundred thousand square miles of territory, including New Mexico and California. In return, the U.S. paid Mexico fifteen million dollars and agreed to allow Mexicans living on the land to remain if they so chose. The Mexican Cession was the nation's largest acquisition of land since the Louisiana Purchase

RETIREMENT

During the 1844 campaign, Polk had promised that, if elected, he would serve only one term as president. Although he was widely popular and could easily have won a second term, President Polk decided to keep his word. He announced that he would retire in 1849.

"I feel exceedingly relieved that I am now free from all public cares," Polk wrote in his diary on the last day of his term. "I am sure I shall be a happier man in my retirement...."

Although Polk expected to enjoy a peaceful retirement in Nashville, he fell ill during a goodwill tour of the South. Polk's condition grew progressively worse until he died just three months after the inauguration of his successor, Zachary Taylor.

BECAUSE OF POLK'S RETIREMENT, THE DEMOCRATS turned to Senator Lewis Cass of Michigan, who had sought the nomination four years earlier. The Whigs drafted General Zachary Taylor, a hero of the Mexican War.

Although the election of William Henry Harrison in 1840 had shown again that generals made popular

candidates, Taylor was somewhat reluctant to accept the nomination. He had neither run for office before nor even voted in a presidential election. In the end, however, the general agreed to run and to accept the Whig platform.

The main issue of the campaign was the extension of slavery. Of particular concern was the Wilmot Proviso, a congressional bill that would have banned slavery in the territories acquired during the Mexican War. The Wilmot Proviso twice passed the House only to be defeated in the Senate.

Taylor refused to comment on the bill, but his ownership of more than one hundred slaves made his position appear clear. Cass openly opposed the

measure, arguing that the decision should be left to the citizens of the territories.

Former president Martin Van Buren ran again as the candidate of the Free-Soil party. Although they were not yet willing to abolish slavery, the Free-Soilers opposed its spread and endorsed the Wilmot Proviso. Van Buren did well enough in his home state of New York to swing a very close election to Taylor, who won with less than half the popular vote. The presidential election of 1848 was the first in which the voting in every state took place on the same day.

ZACHARY TAYLOR

12TH PRESIDENT
★
FROM 1849 TO 1850

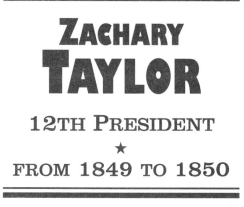

BORN: November 24, 1784

BIRTHPLACE: Orange County, Va.

DIED: July 9, 1850

PARTY: Whig

VICE PRESIDENT: Millard Fillmore

FIRST LADY: Margaret Mackall Smith

CHILDREN: Anne, Sarah, Octavia, Margaret, Mary, Richard

NICKNAME: Old Rough and Ready

Rode his horse sidesaddle into battle.

PRESIDENT TAYLOR DIES IN OFFICE

WASHINGTON, July 9, 1850—President Zachary Taylor died this evening in the White House from a digestive illness. During the last few days, the president's doctors had tried numerous cures, including the drug opium, but Taylor's condition steadily worsened.

Just before the end, the president said, "I am about to die. I expect the summons very soon. I have tried to discharge my duties faithfully. I regret nothing, but I am sorry that I am about to leave my friends."

Taylor began to feel sick five days ago when he spent Independence Day at the unfinished Washington Monument listening to hours of patriotic speeches in the July sun.

Returning to the White House, the president ate a bowl of cherries and drank a pitcher of milk. Later, he developed severe intestinal cramps. Taylor's doctors believe that either the cherries or the milk was contaminated with cholera, a stomach ailment caused by poor sanitation.

The most important issue confronting President Zachary Taylor when he took office was the extension of slavery to the territories of the Mexican Cession Southerners continued to see any limitation on slavery as a threat, while northern abolitionists refused to tolerate the spread of human bondage to any new states.

Taylor had been careful not to reveal his opinion during the campaign. Instead, he let people assume that, because he owned many slaves, he must support slavery. These same people were shocked to find out after the election that the new president intended to oppose the extension of slavery into the new territories.

Instead, Taylor proposed to Congress that two-thirds of the Mexican Cession be set aside for huge new states, New Mexico and California, and that both these states be free.

Southerners who had supported Taylor were furious at what seemed to be a change of heart. People in South Carolina were so upset that they again threatened to secede from the Union, as they had during the nullification controversy of 1833.

There was no simple solution, but statehood for California became a pressing matter once gold was found there. Because of the Gold Rush, the population of California grew from ten thousand to one hundred thousand in just a few years as a wilderness suddenly became one of the richest territories in the nation.

Moderates called for a compromise. Otherwise, the fighting over slavery might soon lead to civil war. To avoid this fearsome possibility, Senator Henry Clay proposed a set of resolutions in January 1850 that he hoped would satisfy both sides. His plan earned him the nickname The Great Compromiser.

Clay's compromise called for the admission of California as a free state, leaving the issue of slavery in the rest of the Mexican Cession to the people who lived there. Most northerners were happy to accept these points, but southerners needed a strong enticement if they were to agree.

FUGITIVE SLAVE ACT

The enticement Clay offered was the Fugitive Slave Act. This notorious bill, the most controversial element of Clay's package, made it the responsibility of the federal government to return runaway slaves to their masters. At the time, escaped slaves were allowed to remain free if they could successfully reach the North.

Abolitionists were outraged by the Fugitive Slave Act. It gave southerners the right to pursue runaway slaves into the North, kidnap them, and take them back to the South without having to go through any legal process whatsoever.

While he lived, President Taylor opposed the Compromise of 1850 and made it known that he planned to veto any bill that would result in the spread of slavery. After his death, however, that decision passed to his vice president, Millard Fillmore.

The Early Years

ZACHARY TAYLOR WAS RAISED IN KENTUCKY WHILE THAT state was still at the edge of the western frontier. He grew up living under the constant threat of an Indian attack. Living in the wilderness, Taylor received only the most basic schooling, and he remained a poor speller all his life.

At the age of twenty-four, Taylor decided to make his career in the military. During his forty years as an army officer, he survived the War of 1812, the Black Hawk War, and the Mexican War. His victory over a much stronger Mexican army at Buena Vista in 1847 made him a national hero and an attractive candidate for president.

★**POSTAGE DUE** During the nineteenth century, presidential candidates never attended party conventions. Instead, they stayed at home and awaited the results. To notify Taylor of his nomination, the president of the Whig convention sent the general a letter. But he didn't put any postage on the envelope.

Sending mail without postage was a common practice then because it forced the recipient to pay the postage due. Taylor, however, received so many postage-due letters from admirers that he told his local post office to stop delivering them. As a result, the first notice of his nomination never arrived. Weeks later, the Whigs realized what had happened and sent another letter, postage paid.

★*UNCLE TOM'S CABIN* In 1852, Harriet Beecher Stowe published *Uncle Tom's Cabin*. Ten thousand copies of this antislavery novel were sold in the first week, and three hundred thousand were sold in the first year after its publication.

The book helped to convince many people that slavery was indeed a terrible institution. It encouraged disobedience of the Fugitive Slave Act and stiffened opposition to the spread of slavery. But most northerners were still unwilling to abolish slavery in the South, where it was most entrenched.

Many years later, during the Civil War, President Abraham Lincoln invited Mrs. Stowe to the White House. Shaking her hand, Lincoln reportedly said, "So this is the little lady who made this big war!"

MILLARD FILLMORE

13TH PRESIDENT
★
FROM 1850 TO 1853

BORN: January 7, 1800

BIRTHPLACE: Cayuga County, N.Y.

DIED: March 8, 1874

PARTY: Whig

VICE PRESIDENT: None

FIRST LADY: Abigail Powers

CHILDREN: Millard, Mary

NICKNAME: Last of the Whigs

Established the first permanent library in the White House.

PERRY OPENS JAPAN TO U.S. TRADE

EDO BAY, Japan, July 8, 1853 — Commodore Matthew C. Perry sailed into Edo Bay today with two navy warships. Perry's mission is to force Japan, which has been isolated for two centuries, to establish diplomatic and trade relations with the United States.

The Japanese immediately ordered Perry to leave, but the commodore refused. He told the Japanese government that it must appoint a suitable official to receive the diplomatic letters he carried. Otherwise, he would deliver them by force.

Perry believes that the Japanese defenses are no match for U.S. naval power. He has long argued that only a strong show of force and a "resolute attitude" can win concessions from the Japanese.

Perry's expedition was first ordered by President Fillmore in March 1852. Since then, it has been publicized around the world. Officials in the State Department expect that, once Perry compels Japan to accept trade with the United States, other Western powers will force their way into Japanese ports.

Millard Fillmore was chosen as the Whigs' vice-presidential candidate in 1848 because of his loyalty. Fillmore helped found the Whig party in western New York in the early 1830s. Later, as a congressman from the Buffalo area, he tried to prevent the split between President Tyler and the congressional Whigs. When the split came, however, Fillmore sided with the party.

Although Fillmore had a reputation for being a dull speaker and a mediocre leader, he was also known as an honorable man. He never smoked or drank, and he only gambled once in his life. At the age of fifteen, he had entered and won a turkey raffle at a New Year's Day party.

During the 1848 campaign, Fillmore was largely ignored. He didn't meet Zachary Taylor until after the election, and he was excluded from any role in shaping the cabinet.

Taylor might have found Fillmore useful in helping to promote his programs in Congress. But the president kept Fillmore so far from power that he even denied his vice president the courtesy of making political appointments in New York, Fillmore's home state. All that changed, of course, when Taylor died.

THE COMPROMISE OF 1850

President Taylor had strongly opposed the Compromise of 1850, especially those measures designed to appease the South. President Fillmore, however, supported the compromise. He thought it was the only way the nation could avoid civil war.

In September 1850, Fillmore signed the five separate bills written by Senator Henry Clay of Kentucky that together formed the compromise. By far the most controversial of these bills was the Fugitive Slave Act.

Most northerners resented this law, which gave slave owners the right to come north, kidnap blacks accused of being runaways, and take them back south without a trial or even a hearing. Abolitionist newspapers wrote often about cases of free blacks being enslaved by mistake or by unscrupulous slave hunters.

Antislavery activists tried to obstruct the law whenever possible. They offered free legal advice to escaped slaves and posted notices warning blacks of the kidnappers.

Fillmore thought that backing the Compromise of 1850 would improve his political position and perhaps earn him the 1852 Whig nomination for president. But he miscalculated. Northern Whigs refused to accept him because he had signed the Fugitive Slave Act. Denied the nomination, Fillmore retired.

BEFORE HE WAS MADE THE DEMOCRATIC NOMINEE, Franklin Pierce had no intention of becoming president. The office, he had said, was "utterly repugnant to my tastes and wishes." Having retired from the Senate ten years earlier, neither he nor his wife had any desire to return to Washington, which they considered an unpleasant city.

The Democratic convention, which had been deadlocked, made Pierce its compromise choice on the

forty-ninth ballot, rejecting four other candidates including Lewis Cass, James Buchanan, and Stephen Douglas. Although Pierce's name was not even mentioned before the thirty-fifth ballot, the party quickly rallied around him. "We Polked you in 1844; we'll Pierce you in 1852," the Democrats warned the Whigs.

Although Millard Fillmore was an incumbent president, he faced a tough battle for the nomination of his party. Because of his support for the Fugitive Slave Act, northern Whigs sided with yet another general, Mexican War hero and antislavery candidate Winfield Scott. Scott was nicknamed Old Fuss and Feathers because he always insisted that subordinates strictly follow military regulations.

Although Fillmore received the backing of the southern "cotton" Whigs, the northern "conscience" Whigs were able to gain the nomination for Scott on the fifty-third ballot. This division within the party, however, proved difficult for Scott to overcome during the campaign. With the backing of a united Democratic party, Pierce easily won the general election.

FRANKLIN PIERCE

14TH PRESIDENT
★
FROM 1853 TO 1857

BORN: November 23, 1804

BIRTHPLACE: Hillsborough, N.H.

DIED: October 8, 1869

PARTY: Democrat

VICE PRESIDENT: William R. King

FIRST LADY: Jane Means Appleton

CHILDREN: Franklin, Frank Robert, Benjamin

NICKNAME: Handsome Frank

Always insisted that grace be said before a meal.

TUBMAN LEADS PARENTS TO FREEDOM ALONG UNDERGROUND RAILROAD

DORCHESTER COUNTY, Maryland, June 1857—The runaway slave Harriet Tubman returned to Maryland this month to free her parents, who had remained slaves after their daughter's escape in 1849.

Tubman's journey was one of nineteen she has made to help slaves escape to the North. She has been one of the "conductors" along the Underground Railroad. The "stations" on this railroad are worked by sympathetic whites, many of them Quakers. Almost all of the conductors are black, however.

The escaped slaves move from station to station at night under the cloak of darkness. It has been estimated that more than fifty thousand slaves have traveled to freedom along the Underground Railroad. Tubman has personally led as many as three hundred people to safety.

She has been called the Moses of Her People, after the Hebrew leader who led the Jews out of bondage in ancient Egypt. Rewards for Tubman's capture have reached as high as forty thousand dollars.

Franklin Pierce was famous throughout his native New Hampshire as a brilliant courtroom lawyer. People from all over would flock to the courthouse to hear his trial speeches. Pierce was such an experienced speaker that he was able to deliver his inaugural address from memory.

In this address, Pierce stated his belief that owning slaves was a legal right guaranteed by the Constitution. However, he feared that fanatics on both sides, the proslavery South and the antislavery, abolitionist North, threatened the Union.

At his inauguration, Pierce's tone was mournful. Two months earlier, his only surviving son, Bennie, had been killed in a railroad accident. The Pierces never recovered from the loss. Two full years passed before First

Lady Jane Pierce felt comfortable appearing in public, and the White House remained a gloomy place throughout Pierce's term.

Pierce was careful to balance northern and southern interests in his cabinet. For secretary of state, the president appointed William Marcy of New York. For secretary of war, he picked a senator from Mississippi, Jefferson Davis. Pierce was so successful in his selections that he became the first president to complete his term in office without making a single change in his cabinet.

THE GADSDEN PURCHASE During Pierce's administration, the United States continued to expand. In 1853, the U.S. minister to Mexico, James Gadsden, negotiated the ten-million-dollar purchase of land that is now in Arizona and New Mexico. The land lay in the path of a proposed new transcontinental railroad. With the addition of these 29,644 square miles, mapmakers could now draw a map of the United States showing the modern outline of the forty-eight continental states.

Pierce also wanted to acquire Cuba, the Spanish island about one hundred miles south of Florida. Secretary of State Marcy instructed the U.S. minister to Spain, Pierre Soulé, to open negotiations for the purchase of Cuba. In the meantime, at Marcy's suggestion, Soulé met in Ostend, Belgium, with the U.S. ministers to Britain and France to plan a negotiating strategy.

The result was the secret Ostend Manifesto of 1854. This document proposed offering up to $120 million for Cuba. If the Spanish refused to sell even at that price, the ministers recommended taking the island by force.

When the Ostend Manifesto was printed in the *New York Herald,* the fact that Pierce was even considering

FRANKLIN PIERCE GREW UP IN HILLSBOROUGH, New Hampshire, during the **War of 1812**. As a boy, he loved to listen to the stories of battle told by his older brothers who were serving in the army. These stories inspired Pierce to become a soldier himself.

When the **Mexican War** broke out in 1846, Pierce had already served a number of terms in the House and Senate. Yet despite his background, he enlisted as a private in the army's volunteer corps. Within a year, he was given a commission as a colonel in the regular army. And a month after that, he was promoted to brigadier general.

THE GADSDEN PURCHASE

★LEVI'S In 1850, a German immigrant named Levi Strauss traveled to San Francisco aboard a ship filled with fortune-seekers. They were just a few of the hundred thousand people drawn to California by the **Gold Rush**.

Strauss, who planned to open a dry goods store, brought with him a supply of blue canvas called denim. He planned to sell the material for tents, but when he got to San Francisco he found that what the miners really needed were sturdy work clothes. Strauss promptly stitched his denim into pants that later became famous as blue jeans.

★**RAILROADS** The 1850s were a boom time for railroad building in the United States. Workers laid more than twenty-one thousand miles of track. These new lines opened up the western wilderness and made the railroads the country's first billion-dollar industry.

Americans were thrilled by this display of power, speed, and national ingenuity. Writers and poets wrote in awe of the "iron horse" that snorted steam and smoke. "Railroad iron is a magician's rod," wrote Ralph Waldo Emerson. Not everyone appreciated the railroads, however. "I will not have my eyes put out and my ears spoiled by its smoke and steam and hissing," snarled Henry David Thoreau.

★**SLAVE SONGS** Slaves in the South often sang work songs and spirituals to help them get through the day. Slave owners liked to pretend that the slaves sang because they were happy.

In their songs, slaves combined elements of African and American folk songs. Some songs like "Nobody Knows the Trouble I've Seen" told the story of the slaves' difficult lives, while others told of happier times ahead. Runaway slaves often sang "Steal Away" and "O Freedom, O Freedom, O Freedom Over Me!" as they made their way north. The origins of jazz and blues lie in these moving songs.

★**WHALING** Herman Melville's *Moby Dick* told the story of an epic hunt for a great white whale. The novel was published in 1851, when the whaling industry was at its height. Whale fat, called blubber, was particularly prized for its many industrial uses.

According to the whalers, who sailed out of southern New England, the most dangerous part of the hunt was

the "Nantucket sleigh ride." During this final operation, crewmen in a small boat would tie their craft to the struggling whale while a mate closed in with his harpoon for the kill.

war over Cuba caused an uproar. Northern congressmen in particular suspected that the president's hidden interest in Cuba was its slaves. Having been exposed, Pierce and Marcy were forced to abandon the Ostend Manifesto and give up their plans for Cuba.

THE KANSAS-NEBRASKA ACT At the same time, the federal government was considering plans to build the first transcontinental railroad. Senator Stephen Douglas of Illinois was working hard to make sure that the railroad took a northerly route through his home state. He knew that wherever the railroad went, business and success would follow.

Southerners, of course, wanted the railroad to pass through their region, but they were outnumbered in Congress. To gain some more power, members of Congress from the southern states announced that they would not support a railroad through any territory that did not allow slavery.

Anxious to see the northern railroad approved, Stephen Douglas suggested a compromise that became the Kansas-Nebraska Act. Douglas's bill proposed the division of the Nebraska Territory through which the railroad would run. The residents of the two resulting territories, Kansas and Nebraska, would then decide for themselves whether or not to permit slavery.

Douglas's plan was controversial for many reasons. For one, it went against the **Missouri Compromise** of 1820, which had outlawed slavery north of latitude 36°30'. Both Kansas and Nebraska were north of that line. And while it was clear that Nebraska would prohibit slavery, Kansas, which bordered on slaveholding Missouri, seemed up for grabs.

BLEEDING KANSAS

With Pierce's backing, the Kansas-Nebraska Act passed Congress, but it caused more problems than it solved. Fanatical abolitionists from New England poured into Kansas, hoping to win control of the territorial government. At the same time, gangs of proslavery thugs called Border Ruffians moved up from Missouri to challenge them.

During March 1855, about four thousand Missourians crossed the border and voted illegally in Kansas, electing a proslavery government. The territorial governor tried to disqualify some of the people who were elected, but President Pierce quickly ordered him back to Washington.

Feeling they had been denied a fair vote, the Free-Soilers turned to violence, and civil war broke out in Kansas. More than two hundred people were killed in the territory that became known as Bleeding Kansas.

Nor was the violence of 1856 limited to Kansas. That May, Charles Sumner of Massachusetts was attacked on the Senate floor by Representative Preston Brooks of South Carolina. Senator Sumner had earlier delivered a nasty, dramatic speech directed against supporters of slavery. When Brooks heard about the speech, he rushed onto the Senate floor and beat Sumner with a cane. Sumner collapsed on the floor, his head split open and bleeding. It took Sumner more than three years to recover.

Two days after Senator Sumner's beating, a radical abolitionist named John Brown organized a raid against his proslavery neighbors near Pottawatomie Creek, Kansas. The attack was brutal. Leading a group of seven fanatics, including his four sons, Brown broke into a number of cabins and hacked five men to death.

B Y THE TIME THE 1856 ELECTION CAME AROUND, THE country had lost confidence in Franklin Pierce. His handling of Bleeding Kansas made it clear that he could not win reelection, and Pierce himself had no interest in staying on. To replace Pierce, the Democrats chose James Buchanan. As the president's minister to Great Britain, Buchanan had avoided the many controversies that plagued Pierce's administration.

Buchanan thought slavery was immoral and even acted against it privately, but he remained acceptable to southern Democrats because he opposed interfering in the affairs of the South. His position was important because slavery wasn't simply one campaign issue. It was the only campaign issue.

Running against Buchanan was John C. Frémont of California, the first presidential candidate of the new Republican party. The Republicans had specifically come together to oppose the spread of slavery. Frémont was known as the Pathfinder of the West, because he had led surveying expeditions that helped map the growing nation.

T he Republican slogan was "Free Speech, Free Press, Free Soil, Free Men, Frémont, and Victory!" The party warned that compromising with southern slaveholders increased the chances of civil war. The Democrats responded that the Republicans were too radical. They claimed that a vote for Buchanan was a vote for national stability. Although Frémont carried much of the North, the Democrats' broad national support gave Buchanan the victory.

HUNKERS, ATTEND!
FIRE AWAY!!

The above is a true likeness of "ten cent Jimmy" Buchanan, the "Damed-Black-Rat's" candidate for President.

OLD BUCK'S SONG.
Old Jimmy Buck goes in for to win,
But we go in for to beat him,
We'll hit him on the head
With a chunk of cold lead
And land him on tudder side of Jordan.

FREMONT'S SONG
Ye friends of Freedom rally now
And push the cause along,
We have a glorious candidate,
A platform broad and strong.

P. S. "Jimmy" you cannot win!

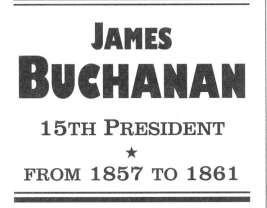

JAMES BUCHANAN

15TH PRESIDENT

★

FROM 1857 TO 1861

BORN: April 23, 1791

BIRTHPLACE: Cove Gap, Pa.

DIED: June 1, 1868

PARTY: Democrat

VICE PRESIDENT: John C. Breckinridge

FIRST LADY: None

CHILDREN: None

NICKNAME: Ten-Cent Jimmy

The first and only bachelor president.

SUPREME COURT RULES IN DRED SCOTT CASE

WASHINGTON, March 6, 1857—In a 7-2 decision handed down today, the Supreme Court ruled that the slave Dred Scott cannot sue for his freedom because he is property and not a citizen. Chief Justice Roger B. Taney wrote in his opinion that Scott had "no rights which any white man was bound to respect."

The court also ruled that the Missouri Compromise of 1820 was unconstitutional, because Congress had no power to outlaw slavery in the territories. Only a state can exclude slavery from its midst, the court ruled.

People in the South were delighted by the decision, while antislavery forces in the North were outraged. "If the people obey this decision, they disobey God," one abolitionist newspaper editor wrote.

Dred Scott was a slave from Missouri who moved with his master's family to Illinois, a free state. His case, which was argued by leading antislavery lawyers, claimed that living in a free state made him free.

James Buchanan won the election of 1856 by carrying the South and taking a few key northern states. Although he was a northerner and personally opposed slavery, Buchanan nevertheless favored the interests of the South.

As Buchanan took office in 1857, the most important task facing him was the prevention of civil war. People considered the new president to be one of the most capable and experienced politicians in the country, so there was great anticipation. Everyone wondered what the Buchanan administration would do to resolve the issue of slavery, particularly with regard to its extension into the new territories.

After devouring twelve hundred gallons of ice cream, guests at Buchanan's inauguration settled down to listen to the inaugural address.

Buchanan stood up to his six-foot height, spread his broad shoulders apart, and announced his belief that the conflict over slavery had a clear and simple solution.

Buchanan, trained as a lawyer, was known for his devotion to reason and the law. The argument he made in his speech was both legal and logical. He pointed out that few Americans disputed the constitutionality of slavery in the southern states, where it had always existed. If these states could legally permit slavery within their borders, Buchanan reasoned, how could the federal government deny new states the same privilege? Letting new territories decide the slavery issue for themselves was therefore the proper and most reasonable course.

Just two days after Buchanan took office, the Supreme Court handed down its decision in the Dred Scott case, ruling that slaves were legally property and not citizens. The court thus confirmed Buchanan's legal view that ownership of slaves was a constitutional right that the federal government could not limit or deny.

Buchanan's argument made legal sense, but it tragically underestimated the growing opposition to slavery on moral grounds. Abolitionists believed slavery was always wrong and deserved to be outlawed everywhere.

THE KANSAS QUESTION Meanwhile, the nation's attention remained focused on Bleeding Kansas, which was still seeking statehood. One of Buchanan's early actions as president was to appoint Robert Walker of Mississippi as the territorial governor there. Walker put the weight of the territorial government behind the proslavery forces.

At a state constitutional convention held in Lecompton in October 1857, proslavery delegates

JAMES BUCHANAN WAS BORN IN A LOG CABIN A FEW miles outside Mercersburg, Pennsylvania. When he was five years old, his family moved into the town of Mercersburg, where his father, an Irish immigrant, made a living as a merchant and farmer.

The Early Years

Buchanan attended Dickinson College, where he was considered a discipline problem. After graduation, he became a lawyer. When his fiancée died in 1819, he entered politics in earnest. Buchanan served in Congress for ten years, first as a Federalist, then as a Jacksonian Democrat. Later he became James Polk's secretary of state and Franklin Pierce's minister to Great Britain, during which time he helped write the **Ostend Manifesto.**

★**BACHELOR PRESIDENT** Buchanan was the only president to remain unmarried his entire life. Once, when he was twenty-eight, Buchanan had been engaged to Anne Coleman, whose father was one of the wealthiest men in Pennsylvania. After a fight, however, she broke off the engagement, and a few months later she died, possibly of suicide.

Rumors circulated that she broke off the engagement because she thought Buchanan was after her money. But Buchanan was doing quite well then as a lawyer and had about three hundred thousand dollars.

Buchanan never considered marrying again. During his term as president, his orphaned niece, Harriet Lane, served as the official White House hostess.

★**THE MODERN KITCHEN** Throughout her life, Catharine Esther Beecher lectured and wrote about the place of women in American society. She believed strongly that a woman's place was in the home. Along with her famous sister, Harriet Beecher Stowe, she wrote *The American Woman's Home.*

This manual of household advice described the sisters' design for a new type of kitchen. Their "modern" kitchen included separate areas for the sink and the stove as well as two windows for proper ventilation. The Beechers also came up with the idea for built-in cabinets and drawers. Some of their innovations are still used in kitchens today.

70

★ SOJOURNER TRUTH

In 1843, the former slave Isabella Van Wagener changed her name to Sojourner Truth and began traveling across the country. She spoke about the cause of freedom wherever she could, often in churches and on village streets.

Sojourner Truth's passionate and persuasive speeches against slavery and for the rights of women inspired thousands to give their support to these causes. In 1864, President Lincoln received her at the White House. She told Lincoln that he was the best president the country ever had but admitted that she had not heard of him before he was nominated. "I had heard of you many times before that," Lincoln told her.

★ THE PONY EXPRESS

Freight-hauler William H. Russell wanted to prove that mail could be carried promptly and profitably across the as-yet-unsettled American West. The Pony Express service that he began in April 1860 showed at least that mail could be delivered promptly.

Russell developed a relay system using lightweight teenage boys. Riding the fastest horses available, they raced from station to station. The boys changed horses six to eight times each before passing on the mail to the next rider. Using this system, Russell was able to deliver mail from St. Joseph, Missouri, to San Francisco—a distance of nearly two thousand miles—in just ten days. The Pony Express lost a huge amount of money, however, and was put out of business by the completion of the first transcontinental telegraph in October 1861.

approved a proslavery constitution for Kansas. Abolitionists boycotted the proceedings because they charged that the election for delegates had been rigged.

Ignoring the boycott, Buchanan supported the Lecompton Constitution and urged Congress to admit Kansas as a slave state. Stephen Douglas of Illinois led the opposition to Buchanan in the Senate. Douglas insisted that the people of Kansas be allowed to vote up or down on the Lecompton Constitution before the Congress accepted it.

In 1858, Kansans voted in a statewide referendum and rejected the proslavery constitution by a wide margin. Buchanan didn't give up. He convinced Congress to order a second referendum. But the results were the same. By the time Kansas was finally admitted to the Union as a free state in January 1861, the nation was on the brink of civil war.

THE LINCOLN-DOUGLAS DEBATES

In 1858, Abraham Lincoln of Illinois ran for the U.S. Senate as a Republican. His opponent was the short but feisty Democratic incumbent, Stephen A. Douglas, whose nickname was the Little Giant.

Their Senate campaign, covered by the national press, featured seven eloquent debates. During one of these debates, Lincoln forced Douglas to admit that he believed a territory could outlaw slavery within its borders. This position contradicted the *Dred Scott* decision, which held that owning slaves was a constitutional right.

Douglas's answer didn't stop him from defeating Lincoln in Illinois, but it did hurt his popularity in the South. Losing southern support made it nearly impossible for him to win the Democratic nomination for president in 1860.

Despite his loss in the Senate race, Lincoln's performance in the debates earned him national fame. "A house divided against itself cannot stand," Lincoln said, using a well-known phrase from the Bible to describe the conflict between North and South over slavery.

Events in Kansas had shown that Americans on both sides were willing to shed blood over slavery. In 1859, the fanatical white abolitionist John Brown developed a daring plan. Leading a small group of raiders, he would seize the federal arsenal at Harpers Ferry, Virginia, and use the weapons he captured there to start a slave rebellion.

On October 16, 1859, Brown and twenty-one of his followers captured the arsenal but were unable to escape. The townspeople of Harpers Ferry bottled up the raiders until a company of marines led by Colonel Robert E. Lee arrived two days later. The marines captured Brown and put him on trial for treason. He was hanged on December 2.

SECESSION During the last frantic months of his failed presidency, Buchanan tried to remain friendly to the South while preserving the Union. He knew that secession, or withdrawal from the Union, was illegal, but he also feared that resisting the South would surely lead to civil war. In the end, he did nothing to stop the inevitable flow of events.

Southern states considered Lincoln's victory in the election of 1860 to be an outrage. Before Buchanan left office, seven of their number seceded from the Union. Alabama, Georgia, Florida, Louisiana, Mississippi, South Carolina, and Texas formed the Confederate States of America, electing Jefferson Davis as their president in February 1861.

THE PRESIDENTIAL CAMPAIGN OF 1860 WAS THE most fateful in U.S. history. John Brown's 1859 attempt to start a slave revolt at Harpers Ferry had brought tensions to the breaking point. The result of the upcoming election might mean the difference between war and reconciliation.

Meeting in Charleston, South Carolina, the governing Democratic party finally split over the issue of slavery. Southern Democrats were so outraged by front-runner Stephen Douglas's refusal to include a proslavery plank in the party platform that they walked out of the convention. Two months later, they held their own convention and nominated Vice President John C. Breckinridge of Kentucky to represent their views. The northern Democrats stuck with Douglas.

The young Republican party chose Abraham Lincoln over William H. Seward of New York because of Lincoln's strength in the hotly contested states of Pennsylvania and Indiana. Although the Republicans objected to the expansion of slavery, they were willing to permit slavery where it already existed. Still, the prospect of a Republican president scared southerners. They threatened to secede if Lincoln won the election.

In the South, Breckinridge competed for votes with the nominee of the new Constitutional Union party, John Bell, a moderate from Tennessee. Meanwhile, in the North, Lincoln and Douglas were the only serious candidates. When all the votes were counted, Lincoln won the presidency with nearly two-thirds of the electoral vote but only forty percent of the popular vote.

ABRAHAM LINCOLN

16TH PRESIDENT

★

FROM 1861 TO 1865

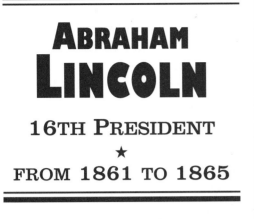

BORN: February 12, 1809

BIRTHPLACE: Hardin County, Ky.

DIED: April 15, 1865

PARTY: Republican

VICE PRESIDENTS: Hannibal Hamlin, Andrew Johnson

FIRST LADY: Mary Todd

CHILDREN: Robert, Edward, William, Thomas (Tad)

NICKNAME: Honest Abe

The first president to wear a beard while in office.

CIVIL WAR!

REBELS TAKE FORT SUMTER

CHARLESTON, S.C., April 13, 1861—Major Robert Anderson, commander of the federal troops stationed in Charleston harbor, surrendered Fort Sumter today after a thirty-four-hour bombardment by Confederate artillery. Anderson waited until he was out of ammunition and the fort was in flames before running down the U.S. flag. Remarkably, no one died during the attack, which began at 4:30 A.M. yesterday.

After taking office a month ago, President Lincoln informed the Confederacy that he intended to resupply Fort Sumter peacefully with food only. This decision placed the burden of whether or not to begin a war on the Confederate authorities. If the rebels attacked a peaceful mission bringing food, the responsibility for firing the first shot would be theirs.

As Lincoln prepared for his March inaugural, events were already overtaking him. In the four months since his election, seven states had seceded and formed the Confederate States of America.

Before he took office, Lincoln said there would be "no bloodshed unless it is forced upon the government." But he also announced that he intended to keep control of all federal property in the South. He made it clear that his primary concern was the preservation of the Union, not the abolition of slavery.

The president responded to the Confederate attack on Fort Sumter by ordering the navy to blockade southern ports. The point of the blockade was to halt the exportation of cotton, the South's cash crop. The blockade also prevented the agricultural South from importing manufactured

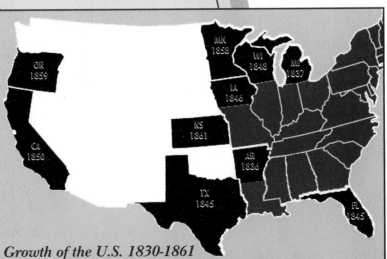

Growth of the U.S. 1830-1861

items such as guns and clothing, which it could not produce for itself. Meanwhile, the beginning of the war caused four more reluctant states to join the Confederacy.

Because they expected a speedy victory, most northerners supported Lincoln's war effort enthusiastically. The song "We are Coming, Father Abraham" was sung at Union army rallies that attracted thousands of recruits. At first, blacks were excluded from the army. But as the years passed, and the war took an unexpected turn for the worse, two hundred thousand blacks were eventually allowed to join the fight.

The Confederacy was no less successful in raising an army. Regional pride was particularly strong south of the Mason and Dixon Line, and volunteers flocked to enlist in the rebel army.

Fathers and sons went off to battle together as women on both sides took over family farms and businesses. Other women raised money, recruited soldiers, and served as nurses, spies, and scouts.

BULL RUN AND ANTIETAM   The first real battle of the Civil War was fought in July 1861 on the banks of a creek called Bull Run in northeastern Virginia, not far from Washington, D.C.

Because the battlefield was so close to the capital, a number of congressmen rode out to Bull Run in carriages to see for themselves the defeat of the Confederacy and the end of the rebellion. Many brought picnic lunches with them.

They lost their appetites when Confederate general Thomas "Stonewall" Jackson broke the Union attack and sent the federal troops scurrying back to Washington. The battle of Bull Run taught the Union that victory would not come as easily as many people thought.

L INCOLN WAS BORN IN A LOG CABIN IN KENTUCKY. The cabin's one room had a dirt floor. When Abe was seven, his family moved farther west to Indiana.

The Early Years   About Indiana, Lincoln later wrote, "It was a wild region, with many bears and other wild animals still in the woods."

Living on what was then the frontier, Lincoln had barely a year of schoolhouse education. Unlike his father, however, he did learn to read and write. Among his favorite books was Parson Weems's often-mythical biography of George Washington.

Lincoln worked as a rail-splitter turning logs into fence rails, a ferryboat captain, a clerk in a general store, and a postmaster before becoming one of the best trial lawyers in Illinois. He never lost his strong frontier accent, however. Speaking in a high voice, Lincoln would pronounce *get* as *git* and *there* as *thar*.

★**THE FIRST LADY**   Mary Lincoln was not well-liked in Washington. Although she had been charming and witty as a young woman, her mental health, which had always been fragile, was placed under severe stress by events in the White House.

Because she came from a southern family, four of her brothers joined the Confederate army, and some congressmen accused her of being a Confederate spy. The charge upset her, but it was the death of her twelve-year-old son Willie in 1862 that finally crushed Mary Lincoln. She became noticeably disturbed and went on wild shopping sprees, buying three hundred pairs of gloves in one four-month period. Her husband's assassination sickened her further, and she was eventually admitted to an insane asylum.

★ MATHEW BRADY

Mathew Brady was the most famous photographer in the country. He specialized in portraits of famous people, especially presidents. His photographs of Lincoln are among the most memorable images of the nineteenth century.

To document the Civil War, Brady hired twenty photographers and sent them all over the country, especially to the battlefields. When pictures of the dead at Antietam first arrived at Brady's New York studio, *The New York Times* reported that "Mr. Brady has done something to bring home to us the terrible reality and earnestness of war. If he has not brought bodies and laid them on our dooryards and along the streets, he has done something very like it...."

★ HOMESTEADING

From the time of Washington, government officials assumed that public lands should be sold off to raise money. During the 1830s, however, the homesteading movement arose to demand that public lands in the West be given free to Americans willing to farm them.

In 1862, President Lincoln signed the Homestead Act, which granted 160 acres of public land free to anybody willing to farm it for at least five years. During the next forty years, homesteaders claimed more than eighty million acres of public land in the West.

Lincoln responded quickly to Bull Run. Making the first of several changes in command, he appointed George B. McClellan as commander-in-chief of the Army of the Potomac.

McClellan was a cautious general. His army was stronger and better supplied than the Confederates, but he moved slowly. During the campaign of 1861, the Confederates boldly outmaneuvered him and beat him on several occasions. In January 1862, Lincoln became worried that "delay is killing us."

During the summer of 1862, McClellan led the Peninsular Campaign against the Confederate capital of Richmond. Once again the general had a superior force, but his constant hesitation allowed Robert E. Lee to beat him back. Lee won a second victory at Bull Run in August and then marched north, crossing the border into the Union state of Maryland.

One witness called Lee's poorly supplied invasion force "the dirtiest men I ever saw, a most ragged, lean, and hungry set of wolves." At the battle of Antietam, McClellan and Lee fought to a standstill. More than twenty thousand soldiers were killed or wounded in the single day of fighting, the bloodiest day of the war. Afterward, Lee retreated back across the Potomac River. McClellan pursued the Confederates, but not quickly enough to catch them.

THE EMANCIPATION PROCLAMATION

Antietam, which could only loosely be called a Union victory, gave President Lincoln the opportunity he needed to announce his Emancipation Proclamation. This executive order formally freed the slaves in areas of rebellion—but not those in Union slave states, such as Maryland, or in areas recaptured by the Union. It also changed the government's war aim from preservation of the Union to the abolition of slavery.

After Antietam, Lincoln dismissed McClellan and replaced him with Ambrose Burnside, who protested his own appointment. Burnside turned out to be right. A month after taking command of the Union army, he suffered a disastrous defeat at Fredericksburg that prompted Lincoln to replace him immediately with Joseph Hooker.

Hooker, too, performed poorly and resigned soon after losing the battle of Chancellorsville in May 1863. Lincoln replaced Hooker with General George Meade. Meanwhile, Lee's army was marching north again, this time into Pennsylvania.

Just three days after Meade's appointment—on July 1, 1863—he and Lee met at Gettysburg. For the next seventy-two hours, their armies fought with the outcome of the war hanging in the balance. On July 3, the failure of George Pickett's charge against Union-held Cemetery Ridge sealed the Union victory. By the time Lee retreated south, he had lost more than twenty thousand men, almost a third of his entire command. The Union dead and wounded numbered twenty-three thousand.

THE GETTYSBURG ADDRESS
On November 19, Lincoln traveled to Gettysburg for the dedication of a battlefield cemetery there. The speech he gave, which became known as the Gettysburg Address, was just 272 words long. It didn't mention slavery, the battle, or even the Union army. But its remarkable language captured the reasons why the war was being fought. After Lincoln finished, the crowd burst into applause.

In March 1864, Lincoln turned over command of the Union forces to General Ulysses S. Grant. During

AS THE CAMPAIGN OF 1864 GOT UNDER WAY, LINCOLN was in serious political trouble. The end of the Civil War was not yet in sight, and fear about how it would turn out hurt the president's chances for reelection. Although he was renominated without opposition, a number of Republican party leaders said publicly that he could not win the general election.

Lincoln ran in 1864 as the candidate of the National Union party. The Republicans had temporarily adopted that name in order to include within their party southern Democrats who had remained loyal to the Union. To emphasize this political marriage, Lincoln dropped Vice President Hannibal Hamlin from the ticket and replaced him with Andrew Johnson, the military governor of Tennessee and one of the leading spokesmen for the Homestead Movement.

To oppose Lincoln, the northern Democrats nominated General George B. McClellan, whom Lincoln had dismissed as commander of the Union army in 1862. McClellan blamed Lincoln for the poor performance of Union troops and called for both an immediate cease-fire and a negotiated peace treaty with the South.

In July and August, McClellan appeared to be leading the race. But Sherman's capture of Atlanta in September demonstrated that the war was now going very well for the Union. McClellan tried to back away from his call for a cease-fire, but the public's renewed confidence in Lincoln carried the president to an easy victory.

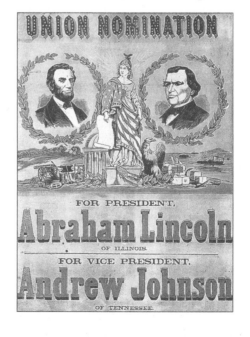

UNION NOMINATION
FOR PRESIDENT.
Abraham Lincoln
OF ILLINOIS.
FOR VICE PRESIDENT.
Andrew Johnson
OF TENNESSEE.

President Lincoln with his son Tad.

LINCOLN ASSASSINATED

WASHINGTON, April 15, 1865—President Lincoln died this morning after being shot last night during a performance of the comedy *Our American Cousin* at Ford's Theater. His assassin, the actor John Wilkes Booth, escaped and is still at large.

A fanatical Confederate sympathizer, Booth arrived at the empty theater about 6:00 P.M. when he tampered with the door to the presidential box. He returned during the play's third act and, finding the president unguarded, shot him through the back of the head.

After firing his single-shot Derringer, Booth jumped down to the stage and landed awkwardly, breaking his leg. Although hobbled, he was still able to reach his horse in the alley and escape.

The dying president was carried to the bedroom of a boardinghouse across the street. Because of his six-foot, four-inch height, Lincoln was placed diagonally across the bed. When the president died just after seven o'clock this morning, Secretary of War Edwin Stanton said, "Now he belongs to the ages."

1862 and 1863, Grant had captured important Confederate forts in Tennessee and led Union troops in the successful siege of Vicksburg, Mississippi. Now he turned his attention to Lee and Richmond. Grant's victories had been costly, bloody ones, but Lincoln was willing to tolerate the high casualty rates. "I cannot spare this man," Lincoln said of Grant. "He fights."

THE END OF THE CIVIL WAR

Meanwhile, General William Tecumseh Sherman began his March to the Sea through Georgia. Along the way, Sherman's unstoppable army of sixty thousand soldiers destroyed the South's ability to wage war. Sherman systematically smashed railroads, factories, and plantations. Atlanta was burned.

In early 1865, Sherman's army turned north to join Grant's forces surrounding Richmond, which fell on April 3. Six days later, Robert E. Lee surrendered to Grant at Appomattox Court House, Virginia. Disease, desertion, and the Union's relentless attacks had finally brought the proud Confederacy to its knees.

BORN: December 29, 1808

BIRTHPLACE: Raleigh, N.C.

DIED: July 31, 1875

PARTY: National Union

VICE PRESIDENT: None

FIRST LADY: Eliza McCardle

CHILDREN: Martha, Charles, Mary, Robert, Andrew

NICKNAME: Tennessee Tailor

ANDREW JOHNSON

17TH PRESIDENT
★
FROM 1865 TO 1869

His wife taught him to read and write.

The news of Abraham Lincoln's assassination shocked every American, none more so than Andrew Johnson. Less than three hours after the president's death, the one-time tailor's apprentice was sworn in as Lincoln's successor. He had been vice president for only forty-one days.

Lincoln had won the Civil War for the Union. Now it was Johnson's turn to tackle the equally enormous task of making the peace. Johnson would have to reunite a land in which neighbor had fought against neighbor, friend against friend, and brother against brother.

Johnson shared Lincoln's view that the country should forgive, forget, and welcome back the rebels. His plan was a simple one. Under the direction of temporary federal governors, each Confederate state would draft a new constitution abolishing slavery and renouncing secession. After that, the states would be free to govern themselves as before. Johnson

JOHNSON ESCAPES CONVICTION IN IMPEACHMENT TRIAL

WASHINGTON, May 16, 1868—The Senate voted today on the first of the eleven articles of impeachment brought by the House of Representatives against President Andrew Johnson. The final count was 35-19, one vote short of the two-thirds majority necessary for conviction.

President Johnson owes his acquittal to seven moderate Republican senators who chose to ignore party loyalty and instead voted with the twelve Democrats.

The House approved the impeachment articles against President Johnson on February 24. The principal charges were related to the president's dismissal of Secretary of War Edwin Stanton. Stanton's firing violated the Tenure of Office Act, which had been passed over Johnson's veto.

The House vote of 126-47 made Johnson the first president ever to suffer the indignity of impeachment. According to the Constitution, a president impeached by the House is then tried before the Senate. If convicted by the Senate, the president is removed from office.

LIKE LINCOLN, JOHNSON BEGAN HIS LIFE AS ONE OF the frontier poor. His father, Jacob, died when Andy was just three years old. Growing up without a father meant that Johnson had to work from a very early age.

The Early Years

When he was twelve years old, he and his brother were apprenticed to a tailor named Selby, becoming what were then known as "bound boys." They worked for room and board while they learned the trade of tailoring. Andrew Johnson received his first schooling while working for Selby, who paid people to read aloud to the apprentices as they sewed.

★**SEWARD'S FOLLY** In 1867, Secretary of State William Seward arranged for the United States to buy Alaska from the Russians. Seward's political rivals thought he was mad to pay $7.2 million for the huge, unexplored territory, which was then an unknown quantity. For many years, while the deal still appeared foolish, people referred to Alaska as Seward's Folly. But when miners taking part in the Klondike Gold Rush found gold on Alaskan beaches, the shrewdness and foresight of Seward's purchase became clear.

★**KU KLUX KLAN** Dismayed by the loss of the Civil War, and made defiant by the humiliations of Reconstruction, many white southerners formed violent vigilante groups to prevent freedmen from voting and thereby electing black candidates to public office. The most widespread of these hate groups was the Ku Klux Klan, founded in 1866 in Pulaski,

Tennessee. Its members were Confederate veterans who believed that the white race was superior to all others. Often dressed in white robes and pointed hoods, klansmen rode through the night, terrorizing former slaves who tried to own property or vote.

also proposed that the citizenship of southerners be restored once they took a simple oath of allegiance to the federal government.

Johnson's plan didn't get very far. So-called Radical Republicans in the Congress wanted to punish the South for seceding. They were also worried that the Democratic party might rise again in the southern states. They still remembered the Democratic coalition that governed the country before Lincoln's election in 1860.

THE BLACK CODES The Civil War had ruined the southern economy and brought poverty to every level of southern society. The four million newly liberated slaves, now known as "freedmen," were the hardest hit, because they had started with the least.

The Thirteenth Amendment, ratified in December 1865, abolished slavery and liberated all those slaves not already freed by the Emancipation Proclamation. But what were the freedmen to do with their new freedom? Most owned little more than the clothes on their back. Although Congress established the Freedmen's Bureau to help former slaves find jobs and go to school, southern whites did everything they could to keep the freedmen poor and powerless.

The Black Codes were a series of measures adopted by southern states to deny African Americans the basic rights of citizenship, such as the right to vote. Radical Republicans responded by passing the Civil Rights Act of 1866, which spelled out the rights to which all Americans were entitled, regardless of the color of their skin.

Because he didn't want to anger his fellow southerners any further, Johnson vetoed the bill. But the Radical Republicans had enough votes to override Johnson's veto, and the bill became law despite the president's opposition.

During the next two years, Congress passed more laws over Johnson's veto, reorganizing the state governments of the South and forcing them to grant blacks the right to vote. Although racism continued, African Americans were able to enjoy a number of political successes.

In 1870, Hiram K. Revels of Mississippi became the first black elected to the Senate when he won the seat once occupied by Jefferson Davis. All together, between 1869 and the end of Reconstruction in 1877, sixteen blacks were elected to Congress from southern states.

IMPEACHMENT

The conflict between Johnson and the Radical Republicans reached a crisis when the president fired Secretary of War Edwin M. Stanton. Like the rest of Johnson's cabinet, Stanton was a holdover from the Lincoln administration. He was also a leader of the Radical Republicans and had been working actively to undermine the tolerant Reconstruction policies of his president.

The House of Representatives responded to Johnson's dismissal of Stanton by voting to impeach the president for violating the Tenure of Office Act. This law, passed over Johnson's veto in 1867, blocked the president from removing certain government officials without the consent of the Senate.

Johnson hadn't really committed any crime, other than opposing congressmen who were determined to control the direction of Reconstruction.

Although the president survived his trial in the Senate, his political career seemed over. Denied renomination, he retired to Greenville, Tennessee.

THE NATIONAL UNION PARTY TICKET ON WHICH Lincoln and Johnson had run in 1864 didn't survive the Civil War. For the election of 1868, President Johnson returned to the Democratic party, and the Republicans took their old name back.

Having only narrowly survived impeachment, Johnson was given little chance of winning election in his own right. At the Democratic convention in July, Johnson faded early as the balloting swung to former governor Horatio Seymour of New York.

At the Republican convention, Civil War hero Ulysses S. Grant was nominated unanimously on the first ballot. Grant seemed to be the perfect choice for president. Voters naturally assumed that the brilliance and daring he had shown on southern battlefields would be easily transferred to the political battlefields of Washington. Grant's campaign theme, "Let us have peace," caught the mood of a country tired of war and the turmoil of Reconstruction.

Reconstruction was, of course, the main issue of the campaign. The Republicans planned to continue the program they had passed over Johnson's vetoes, while the Democrats favored a more lenient approach to reunification with the South.

White southerners supported Seymour overwhelmingly, but many were unable to vote, having lost their citizenship because they once swore allegiance to the Confederacy. Their former slaves could vote, however, thanks to Radical Republican

laws, and these freedmen voted in huge numbers for Grant. The popular vote was close, but the general won the electoral vote by a wide margin.

ULYSSES S. GRANT

18TH PRESIDENT

★

FROM 1869 TO 1877

BORN: April 27, 1822

BIRTHPLACE: Point Pleasant, Ohio

DIED: July 23, 1885

PARTY: Republican

VICE PRESIDENTS: Schuyler Colfax, Henry Wilson

FIRST LADY: Julia Boggs Dent

CHILDREN: Frederick, Ulysses, Ellen, Jesse

NICKNAME: Uncle Sam

The only president to get a speeding ticket while driving a horse.

From Andrew Johnson, Grant inherited Reconstruction, an issue that dominated his first term as president. Grant also inherited a Congress with its own ideas on the subject. Because of laws enacted by the Radical Republicans, federal troops controlled nearly every aspect of civilian life in the South.

Grant understood the desire of Radical Republicans to ensure justice for blacks. But he also believed that the federal government could not force white southerners to accept a way of life they despised. These conflicting ideas put Grant in a difficult, if not impossible, position.

GOLDEN SPIKE COMPLETES TRANSCONTINENTAL RAILROAD

PROMONTORY POINT, Utah, May 10, 1869—Workers today drove a golden spike to join symbolically the Union Pacific and Central Pacific railroads into the nation's first transcontinental line. The ceremony was attended by a large number of public officials anxious to take credit for this remarkable achievement.

Congress first authorized the construction of a transcontinental railroad in 1862. Subsidies and land grants were given to two companies, the Union Pacific and the Central Pacific. The Union Pacific began laying track westward from Omaha, Nebraska, while the Central Pacific worked east from Sacramento, California.

The difficult terrain caused long delays, but the construction crews persevered. The Union Pacific, which laid 1,086 miles of track to reach Promontory Point, used crews made up mostly of Civil War veterans and Irish immigrants. The Central Pacific, which laid 689 miles of track, used primarily Chinese immigrants.

What the voters expected when they elected Grant was a decisive leader, but they didn't get one. Instead, the bold and stern general turned out to be an unsure president. Grant tended to let others make difficult policy decisions for him, and these people quickly took advantage of his gullibility and lack of leadership.

Grant himself was personally incorruptible, but many of the officials he appointed were less than honorable. As a result, Grant's administration was rocked early and often by corruption scandals.

THE GILDED AGE The dishonesty in Washington was no worse than that in the rest of the country. Ruthless people everywhere exploited a society still weakened by the upheaval of the Civil War. Most notorious among these scoundrels were the northerners who went south and used political connections to prey on the defeated Confederacy. These men were called "carpetbaggers" because of the carpet-covered suitcases they carried. Their southern accomplices were known as "scalawags."

In the North, political "machines," such as the Tweed Ring in New York City, enriched themselves at the taxpayers' expense by corruptly dominating large groups of immigrant voters.

Simultaneously, the country's most successful industrialists made their money exploiting workers and consumers alike. These men—including Cornelius Vanderbilt, John D. Rockefeller, and Andrew Carnegie—were called "robber barons." Like Boss Tweed, they manipulated laws and lawmakers to increase their own wealth and power. Mark Twain called this period of matchless corruption, greed, and splendor the Gilded Age, and the name stuck.

GRANT WAS BORN IN THE OHIO COUNTRYSIDE, WHERE his father, Jesse, owned a successful leather tanning business. Jesse Grant's personality was gruff and combative, but his son was shy and sensitive. Because the boy was particularly good at handling horses, most of his chores involved their care.

When Grant was seventeen, he received an appointment to the military academy at West Point, where he was an average student. Later in his army career, he developed a drinking problem, which forced him to resign in 1854. He tried farming, real estate, and peddling firewood, but nothing worked. By Christmas 1860, he was so broke that he had to pawn his watch in order to buy presents for his family.

Grant was working at his father's leather goods store when the Civil War broke out. Because of the urgent need for experienced officers, Grant was recommissioned as a colonel and then promoted to brigadier general two months later.

The Early Years

★**PROFESSIONAL BASEBALL** On March 15, 1869, Harry Wright and George Ellard organized the first professional baseball team. They called their club the Cincinnati Red Stockings. Baseball had become quite popular during the Civil War, leading Wright and Ellard to believe they could make a living off the game. The ballplayers they hired barnstormed around the country, challenging local amateur clubs to games for which an admission price was charged. The success of the Red Stockings—they went undefeated during the 1869 season—paved the way for professional baseball.

★BELL'S TELEPHONE

Speech specialist Alexander Graham Bell first got the idea that sound could be transmitted electrically over telegraph wires in the early 1870s. Working at night with a repair mechanic named Thomas Watson, Bell turned his idea into the telephone, for which he received U.S. Patent Number 174,465 in March 1876.

Although most people considered Bell's invention to be something of a joke, the huge Western Union Telegraph Company quickly saw its commercial possibilities and backed a rival patent. The battle over Bell's patent was the most complicated in U.S. legal history. Bell's case was so good, however, that Western Union was forced to settle.

★U.S. GRANT

Jesse Grant originally named his oldest son Hiram Ulysses Grant, but young Grant hated his initials, which spelled H.U.G., so he began signing his name as Ulysses Hiram Grant. A clerical error listed him on the West Point rolls as Ulysses Simpson Grant, which Grant saw no reason to change. His West Point classmates joked that his initials stood for "Uncle Sam," and Grant was called Sam by his close friends for the rest of his life. During the Civil War, soldiers in his command took to calling him "Unconditional Surrender" Grant because of the terms he forced on his Confederate foes.

★SUSAN B. ANTHONY

After the Civil War, Susan B. Anthony became an important leader in the growing women's suffrage movement. Beginning in 1868, she published a newspaper called *Revolution* in New York City. This radical weekly, edited by Elizabeth Cady Stanton, campaigned for many women's issues, including equal pay for equal work and more liberal divorce laws.

When Anthony tried to cast a ballot in the 1872 presidential election, she was arrested, convicted, and fined for voting illegally. She refused to pay the fine, but the matter was dropped. This prevented her from appealing her case all the way to the Supreme Court, which had been her plan.

BLACK FRIDAY

The first of the Grant administration scandals broke in September 1869. The president had been in office a little over six months. At that time, two of the wealthiest robber barons, James Fisk and Jay Gould, tried to corner the gold market. That is, they tried to buy up enough gold to control its supply and therefore raise its price.

Their plan had one shortcoming, which was that the federal government controlled the largest supply of gold in the country. If the scheme was to work, Fisk and Gould would have to keep the government's gold off the market. They paid Grant's brother-in-law, Abel Corbin, to use his influence to do just that.

When Grant realized what was happening, he ordered Treasury Secretary George Boutwell to sell four million dollars' worth of gold from the government's reserves. The sale—which took place on September 24, 1869—ruined Fisk and Gould's plan, but it also sent the price of gold plummeting. When the fall in gold prices triggered a financial panic, Grant's reputation suffered. The day of the gold crash came to be known as Black Friday.

RECONSTRUCTION

Grant tried to shake off the scandal by returning the focus of his administration to Reconstruction. Beginning in 1870, he won passage of a number of bills in Congress that gave him the power to enforce civil rights laws in the South. He used the Force Act of 1870 and the Ku Klux Klan Act of 1871 to threaten southern states with federal military action unless they stopped terrorizing blacks and denying them the right to vote. In South Carolina, for example, where the **Ku Klux Klan** was particularly active, Grant declared martial law and ordered mass arrests.

Until the passage of these enforcement laws, the federal government had to rely on local authorities to control the Klan. This system didn't work too well because many local policemen were themselves Klan members. Grant's enforcement of the civil rights laws temporarily broke the power of the Klan, but this period of relative safety for African Americans lasted only as long as federal troops remained in the South.

Just as the campaign of 1872 was getting under way, another scandal broke. This one involved the Union Pacific Railroad.

THE CRÉDIT MOBILIER SCANDAL By 1872, national investment in the railroads had reached nearly three billion dollars. Guaranteed federal loans and subsidies paid for much of the track work in the West, particularly along the route of the transcontinental Union Pacific Railroad.

Major stockholders in the Union Pacific formed a second company, called Crédit Mobilier of America, which they used to steal some of the federal money for themselves. They even bribed congressmen by selling them shares of stock in Crédit Mobilier at half the market price.

When the *New York Sun* broke the story of the scandal, Congress appointed a committee to investigate. Among those implicated were Vice President Schuyler Colfax and Representative James Garfield. The committee found no evidence that President Grant was involved, but many people felt the scandal was the result of his negligence.

Grant's bad fortune continued during his second term when the nation suffered one of its worst depressions. For several years, the U.S. economy had been sickly. The government was still paying off its

GRANT DIDN'T HAVE MUCH TO SHOW FOR HIS FIRST term in office. The Radical Republicans still controlled Reconstruction, and little progress had been made on economic issues. Worse still, the corruption scandals had stained his reputation. The Crédit Mobilier scandal, in particular, caused his vice president, Schuyler Colfax, to be dropped from the ticket.

Despite these problems, Grant was renominated without much of a fuss. His opponents within the party, the Liberal Republicans, didn't even bother to show up. Instead, they held their own convention and nominated New York newspaperman Horace Greeley to run against him. The disorganized Democrats also supported Greeley's candidacy because it was their only chance to oust Grant.

GREELEY had made a name for himself as the editor of the *New York Tribune*. In the editorial columns of the *Tribune*, he promoted the causes of working people and denounced big business. His often-quoted advice was to "Go West, young man, and grow up with the country."

Many people considered Greeley a crackpot because of the many contradictory positions he had taken over the

years. In fact, he had supported Grant in 1868 but was now critical of Grant's first term. Greeley called for an end to the corruption, reform of the civil service, full amnesty for the Confederate rebels, and the end of federal rule in the South.

Because Greeley's campaign never posed much of a threat, Grant's political backers were able to convince voters that the president was really an honest man and that the scandals were not his fault. Grant won a convincing majority in the popular vote, and Greeley died just a few weeks after the election, even before the electoral vote had been counted.

President Grant with an official of the Chinese government.

Civil War debt, while massive railroad construction projects and the 1871 Chicago Fire had drained private financial resources.

THE PANIC OF 1873

When the banking house of Jay Cooke and Company failed in September 1873, the stock market collapsed along with it. The Panic of 1873 lasted five years, put three million people out of work, and forced thousands of small companies out of business.

While the country was still reeling from the depression, Treasury Secretary William Richardson became the focus of the next Grant administration scandal. After taking over for George Boutwell in 1873, Richardson appointed his friend John D. Sanborn as special agent in charge of collecting overdue taxes.

Normally, this was a difficult and unrewarding job. But Richardson made an astonishing and illegal deal with Sanborn, allowing Sanborn to keep half the money he collected. By the time Congress got around to investigating Sanborn in 1874, he had already pocketed two hundred thousand dollars. Richardson was forced to resign, and Grant was embarrassed again.

Grant scarcely caught his breath before the next scandal broke.

CUSTER'S LAST STAND

Seventh Cavalry Massacred at Little Big Horn

MONTANA TERRITORY, June 25, 1876—General George Armstrong Custer and the men under his immediate command were all killed today when they attacked a huge Indian village on the banks of the Little Big Horn River.

Seventh Cavalry units under Major Marcus Reno and Captain Frederick Benteen survived only by retreating to a line of bluffs above the river.

Custer had been sent on a scouting mission to locate bands of hostile Sioux and Cheyenne who had left their reservations. He disobeyed orders by attacking the village, which held many thousands of Indians, including the powerful war chiefs Sitting Bull and Crazy Horse.

During the Civil War, the twenty-three-year-old Custer became the youngest general in the Union army. Afterward, like many other Civil War veterans, he continued his military career fighting Indians in the West. The Sioux called him Son of the Morning Star because of his long blond hair.

85

In 1875, Richardson's replacement as treasury secretary, Benjamin Bristow, uncovered a conspiracy that had been cheating the government for years. Federal officials who were supposed to be collecting liquor taxes were instead dividing the money among themselves and the distillers.

Frustrated by the unending scandals, Grant demanded quick action. He instructed the government prosecutors to arrest everyone involved. "Let no guilty man escape," Grant said. But when his own personal secretary, Orville Babcock, was implicated, the president shielded him.

While these federal officials were using their positions to get richer, the depression continued. For those who still had jobs, wages declined. In large cities, tens of thousands of homeless men and women crowded police stations for shelter. Eventually, the poor demanded a change. In the mid-1870s, thousands of low-salaried and unemployed workers staged protests in Pittsburgh, New York, Baltimore, and other cities. Often, the police and the National Guard turned out to beat the demonstrators with guns and clubs.

THE CIVIL RIGHTS ACT OF 1875 In between scandal investigations, Congress passed the Civil Rights Act of 1875. This was the last major piece of Radical Republican legislation passed during Reconstruction. It guaranteed blacks the civil rights being denied them in the South. The new law integrated hotels, theaters, and restaurants. Under its terms, owners could no longer keep African Americans out or segregate them into back rooms. The act was poorly enforced, however, and eventually declared unconstitutional by the Supreme Court in 1883.

★**THE BUTCHER OF GALENA**
So many of Grant's Civil War victories were bloody ones that soldiers began calling him the Butcher of Galena. (The name referred to his hometown of Galena, Illinois.)

Yet Grant himself was highly squeamish. He became physically sick at the sight of blood and refused to eat any meat unless it was cooked until dry. Even the hint of blood in meat juices was too much for him.

The responsibility for sending tens of thousands of men to their deaths also sickened the general, who suffered regularly from severe migraine headaches. After particularly horrible battles, he would often retire to his tent and cry.

★**MARK TWAIN** Samuel Clemens grew up in Hannibal, Missouri, on the banks of the Mississippi, where he fell in love with the romance and mystery of river life. He was fascinated by the con men, thieves, and gamblers who populated the paddleboats traveling to and from New Orleans.

In 1863, Clemens began writing under the pen name Mark Twain. He borrowed it from a riverman's term for water that was barely safe for navigation.

By the time he published *The Adventures of Tom Sawyer* in 1876, Twain was already famous as a humorist and lecturer. Tom Sawyer relived many of Clemens's own adventures as a child in Hannibal.

★**MAIL-ORDER CATALOGS** In August 1872, Aaron Montgomery Ward founded the first mail-order business in the United States. His first "catalog" was a single sheet of paper listing approximately 150 items. Ward's main customers were farmers in the countryside who were unable to make regular trips into town. By 1888, when Sears Roebuck began its own catalog, Montgomery Ward's sales had already topped one million dollars a year. Ward was also the originator of the money-back guarantee.

★BOOKER T. WASHINGTON

Booker T. Washington was the leading African-American spokesman of the late nineteenth century and also one of the country's foremost educators. Born into slavery in Virginia, Washington was just nine years old when the Civil War ended and he was freed. Dirt poor but determined to get an education, he enrolled in 1872 at the Hampton Institute, one of the first schools for blacks in the South. He worked as a janitor there to pay his expenses.

From an early age, Washington believed that the only way for blacks to gain equality in American society was through education and economic success. In 1881, he took over a small black school in Tuskegee, Alabama, and turned it into the internationally respected Tuskegee Institute.

★THE GREAT CHICAGO FIRE For three days beginning on October 8, 1871, the city of Chicago burned. When the blaze was finally brought under control on October 10, nearly four square miles of the city, including the downtown business district, lay in ruins. The Great Fire left ninety thousand people homeless and caused two hundred million dollars' worth of damage. Legend has it that the blaze was started when a cow owned by a Mrs. O'Leary knocked over a lantern in its stall.

The final Grant administration scandal broke in 1876, when Secretary of War William Belknap was found to be taking kickbacks from traders at Indian reservations. Cheating the Indians was a long-standing government practice, but rarely did it reach as high as the president's cabinet. Belknap resigned before a Senate trial could remove him from office. A weary Grant told Congress, "Failures have been errors of judgment, not of intent."

Despite the scandals that marred his time in office, many people still wanted Grant to run for a third term. No president had ever done that before, and Grant wasn't about to become the first. He felt he had been president long enough.

The qualities that had served him so well during wartime—resolution, independence, and daring—deserted him as president. Grant entered the White House a well-meaning man pledged to peace, honesty, and civil rights. But as president, he neither resolved the key issues of Reconstruction nor set high standards for the officials he appointed.

AN INDUSTRIAL NATION In 1803, Thomas Jefferson looked to the future and saw a nation of farmers. As late as the start of the Civil War, Jefferson's vision still held true. In 1860, the United States was still a chiefly agricultural nation. Most Americans were farmers, and farming was the nation's biggest business.

The Civil War changed all that. The need to supply a huge army with clothing, arms, and equipment sent the industrial economy of the North into high gear. When the war ended, the factories just kept going. By the end of Grant's second term, the United States had become one of the greatest industrial nations in the world. It dug more coal and iron ore, made more steel, drilled for more oil, laid more railroad track, and built more factories than any other nation on earth.

This enormous change in the country's economy had profound effects. Vast numbers of immigrants came to the United States to work in the booming cities, and the country's ethnic makeup changed dramatically. From a people of largely northern European descent, the United States became a nation of many nationalities. People began to call it a "melting pot."

Industrialization also brought a change in the nation's identity abroad. Once a distant republic, the United States now had the makings of a world power.

RETIREMENT Grant left office in 1877. After a trip around the world, he settled in Manhattan, where he invested all his money in a brokerage firm founded by his son Ulysses, Jr. Perhaps not surprisingly, this venture ended in scandal, too. Their partner, Ferdinand Ward, embezzled the firm's money, bankrupting the company and the Grants. About the same time, the former president learned that he had an advanced case of throat cancer.

Determined to provide for his family before he died, Grant set to work on his memoirs. A month before he died, he moved to Mount McGregor in the Adirondacks. Unable to speak or eat regularly, he sat on the front porch of his cottage, racing to finish his book.

Grant completed the manuscript on July 16. A week later, he died. The memoirs, published by his friend Mark Twain, sold five hundred thousand copies and restored his family's financial security.

THE ELECTION OF 1876 WAS BY FAR THE MOST controversial in U.S. history. The Republican candidate, Governor Rutherford B. Hayes of Ohio, was known as a trustworthy and reform-minded administrator. His Democratic opponent, Governor Samuel J. Tilden of New York, was even more famous as a reformer, having helped break the notorious Tweed Ring in New York City. Both men pledged to end the corruption that still plagued the Grant administration.

Because of his national reputation, the backlash against Grant, and the revival of southern Democrats, Tilden was the early favorite. But the Republicans were still the stronger national party, and Hayes made the race a close one. When the popular vote was counted, Tilden appeared to have won the election. But twenty electoral votes were in doubt.

Tilden needed only one of those votes to win the presidency. But a special election commission made up of ten congressmen and five Supreme Court justices voted 8-7 along party lines to give all the disputed votes to Hayes, who won 185-184.

Southern Democrats, believing that the election had been stolen from them, threatened to secede once again. But Tilden gracefully restrained them, and Hayes agreed to the Compromise of 1877. In order to end the crisis, Hayes promised to withdraw federal troops from

the South, ending Reconstruction. He also agreed to rebuild railroads and industry there and include at least one southern Democrat in his cabinet. This remarkable back-room bargain brought some calm to U.S. politics, but it also created enormous problems for the new president.

RUTHERFORD BIRCHARD HAYES

19TH PRESIDENT
★
FROM 1877 TO 1881

BORN: October 4, 1822

BIRTHPLACE: Delaware, Ohio

DIED: January 17, 1893

PARTY: Republican

VICE PRESIDENT: William A. Wheeler

FIRST LADY: Lucy Ware Webb

CHILDREN: Sardis, James, Rutherford, Joseph, George, Frances, Scott, Manning

NICKNAME: His Fraudulency

The first president to use a telephone in the White House.

EDISON DOES IT AGAIN!

Wizard of Menlo Park Invents Light Bulb

MENLO PARK, N.J., October 21, 1879—Thomas Edison demonstrated his newest invention today at his laboratory in Menlo Park. He calls it the light bulb.

The device consists of a vacuum-sealed glass bulb with a filament inside. When electricity passes through the filament, it glows, producing light. Edison's breakthrough came when he found the right material for the filament: scorched cotton thread.

Edison, who invented the phonograph in 1877, first became interested in electric light last year when he saw an exhibit of electric street lamps.

His announcement last fall that he would attempt to develop a cheap and practical form of electric light caused gas company stocks to tumble on Wall Street. It now seems likely that inexpensive electric light will soon replace the gas lamps used in most homes.

Rutherford Hayes began his term under difficult circumstances. The Compromise of 1877 that confirmed his election as president also robbed him of the authority that usually came with the job.

Because his victory was won in the cloakrooms of Congress rather than at the polls, newspapers referred to Hayes as Rutherfraud and His Fraudulency. Out in the country, most people thought the election had been rigged. Hayes had always been an honorable and decent public servant, but he was never quite able to overcome the concessions he made in accepting the compromise.

Southern Democrats, shut out of power since the Buchanan administration, were particularly eager to embarrass Hayes. Since the Civil War, the Republicans had run "bloody shirt" campaigns against the southern Democrats.

"Waving the bloody shirt" meant reminding voters that the Democrats had been the party of secession and therefore deserved the blame for the bloody war that followed.

As part of the price for accepting Hayes as president, the southern Democrats demanded that Reconstruction end immediately. They wanted the Republican carpetbaggers out of the South along with the federal troops who supported the freedmen.

Having little choice, Hayes agreed. One of his first acts as president was to remove the last federal troops from the South, ending a decade of Radical Republican rule over the defeated Confederacy.

Although southern whites were overjoyed, their former slaves were not. The end of Reconstruction meant that political power in the South would return to those people who believed in the superiority of the white race.

By withdrawing the troops, Hayes left southern blacks at the mercy of these white supremacists. Without federal soldiers to enforce the civil rights laws, blacks were once again denied their legal right to vote. And without troops to control the Ku Klux Klan, its members resumed their nighttime missions of terror and death.

RAILROAD STRIKES Meanwhile in the North, the economy was still suffering from the lasting effects of the Panic of 1873. The railroads were in particularly bad shape. The cutthroat nature of the business, in which labor was the biggest expense, led to a series of wage cuts for railroad employees. The pay cuts announced in the spring of 1877 were the last straw for many workers.

The first spontaneous strike came in Baltimore, where firemen on the B&O Railroad walked off the job on July 16. The labor revolt then spread to Pittsburgh, where local militia called out to break the strike instead sided with the workers. Hayes finally

RUTHERFORD HAYES WAS BORN AT HIS FAMILY'S HOME in Delaware, Ohio. The doctor's fee for the delivery was $3.50. Because his father died before he was born, Rutherford was raised by his mother, Sophia, and her bachelor brother, Sardis Birchard.

From his earliest days, Hayes dreamed of holding public office. He did well in school, graduating from Kenyon College and Harvard Law School. In 1852, at the age of thirty, Hayes married Lucy Ware Webb, a fervent abolitionist who convinced him to leave the Whigs and join the new Republican party. Beginning in 1853, Hayes devoted some of his time to defending runaway slaves.

★LEMONADE LUCY
A devout Methodist and a passionate believer in temperance, First Lady Lucy Hayes had an immediate impact on the White House when she banned all liquor from state functions. Because she often

served lemonade instead, her critics dubbed her Lemonade Lucy. She is also remembered for conducting group hymns with the cabinet and for hosting the first White House Easter egg roll. At this annual spring event, children roll painted Easter eggs up and down the White House lawn.

★JESSE JAMES AND THE JAMES GANG Jesse James and his brother Frank were born on a farm near Centerville, Missouri. During the Civil War, they both joined bands of Confederate raiders. These rough outfits preyed on Union supply trains, especially those carrying payrolls. After the war, the James brothers took to robbing banks and civilian trains instead.

The James Gang soon became well known in the East, where stories of western adventure always sold well. Magazines filled their pages with romanticized versions of the brothers' criminal exploits. Jesse and Frank were usually portrayed as heroes who became outlaws because federal lawmen hated all former Confederates.

★THE INDIAN WARS

The Civil War years were generally peaceful ones for Indian tribes on the Great Plains. Because the U.S. government thought one war was enough for the time being, federal officials negotiated a number of peace treaties with the Sioux and the Cheyenne.

One treaty signed in 1868 guaranteed the Sioux all rights to their sacred Black Hills in the Dakota Territory. General George Custer violated this treaty in 1874 when he escorted a survey team into the Black Hills looking for gold, which the expedition found. The horde of miners that followed Custer into the Black Hills provoked the Sioux to go on the warpath.

Even though the Sioux and Cheyenne were able to defeat Custer at the battle of the Little Big Horn, the Indians were no match for the U.S. army. Most were forced to return to government reservations, although a few hundred, led by Sitting Bull, escaped to Canada.

★P.T. BARNUM

Phineas Taylor Barnum was probably America's greatest showman. His most famous acts were the twenty-five-inch-tall midget, General Tom Thumb, and singer Jenny Lind, whom Barnum billed as the Swedish Nightingale.

Barnum was already sixty years old when he started his first circus during the early 1870s. In 1881, he teamed up with James A. Bailey. Until that time, circuses were one-ring affairs that usually played small towns. The Barnum & Bailey Circus, however, reflected Barnum's legendary sense of spectacle. It had three rings, toured major cities, and featured nationally known acts such as the elephant Jumbo. Barnum called it "The Greatest Show on Earth."

RUTHERFORD BIRCHARD HAYES 1877-1881

had to send in federal troops to restore order. By August 2, after hundreds of deaths and thousands of injuries, railroad service was restored by force on all lines.

CHINESE IMMIGRATION

Hayes also confronted violence born of economic despair in California, where gangs of Irish Americans were attacking Chinese immigrants.

The Chinese had come to work in California's gold mines and on its railroad construction crews. The jobs they took were the most difficult and usually paid the least—jobs that other Californians wouldn't take. By 1877, Chinese immigrants made up nearly ten percent of the state's population.

Trouble began when the gold mines went bust, railroad building tapered off, and the Chinese began competing with Irish Americans for the same jobs. The Chinese often got the jobs because they were willing to work for less. This angered the Irish, who believed they were entitled to the jobs because they had come to this country first.

The conflict came to a head in San Francisco, where Irish gangs attacked (and sometimes killed) Chinese on the street. Congress's response was to pass a law banning Chinese immigration. Hayes vetoed the bill and instead had Secretary of State William Evarts negotiate the Treaty of 1880, which limited immigration in a manner acceptable to the Chinese government.

The great success of Hayes's term was his "hard money" policy. To help finance the Civil War, the government had issued paper money called "greenbacks." The greenbacks were "soft" or "easy" money because they weren't backed by gold. That is, they could not be redeemed for gold coins, or specie.

During the Grant administration, Congress had passed the Resumption of Specie Act, which called for the government to take the greenbacks out of circulation and start redeeming paper money with gold again.

Farmers who held mortgages and other long-term debtors wanted an easy money policy that would encourage inflation. With more money in circulation, each dollar would be worth less, and their debts would be cheaper to pay off. Hayes stood firm, however, and the government resumed specie payments on schedule.

CIVIL SERVICE REFORM

Hayes's other great cause was civil service reform. Civil servants are the government's civilian employees: the bureaucrats who run everything from the mint to the post office. Under the spoils system made famous by Andrew Jackson, many of these jobs went to people whose only qualifications were their political connections.

Because he believed that government jobs shouldn't be used as political rewards, Hayes issued an executive order in June 1877 barring civil servants from taking part in political activities. He also supported the efforts of Interior Secretary Carl Schurz to develop competitive exams for hiring and promotion. But he couldn't convince Congress to act on large-scale reform.

Hayes was able to take some limited action himself. He removed a number of federal officials, including the heads of the post office in St. Louis and the customhouse in New York. Hayes said these men were misusing their public offices for political gain. One of them later became president: Chester A. Arthur, then collector of duties for the Port of New York.

WHEN HE ACCEPTED THE REPUBLICAN nomination in 1876, Hayes said he would serve only one term. Four years later, he hadn't changed his mind. Hayes's retirement left the race wide open. The surprise front-runner among the Republicans was former president Grant, who had decided to try for a third term after all. Opposing him were James G. Blaine of Maine and Hayes's treasury secretary, John Sherman.

Grant held the lead at the convention for thirty-five ballots, but he remained about seventy votes short of victory. On the thirty-fourth ballot, Wisconsin cast sixteen votes for a compromise candidate, Representative James Garfield of Ohio, the man who had nominated Sherman.

Garfield remained loyal to Sherman, jumping out of his seat and shouting, "I won't permit it." But two ballots later, the Blaine and Sherman forces joined together to draft him. As a gesture to the conservative Republicans, known as Stalwarts, who had supported Grant, the convention chose Chester Arthur of New York as Garfield's running mate.

To oppose Garfield, the Democrats nominated General Winfield Hancock, a Union hero and military governor during Reconstruction. The election was remarkably close. Garfield won the popular vote by just ten thousand ballots out of nine million cast. However, he got those votes where he needed them, winning the electoral college, 214-155.

Garfield had made a deal, known as the Treaty of Fifth Avenue, with New York party boss Roscoe Conkling. In exchange for Conkling's Stalwart support, Garfield agreed to consult Conkling when making federal civil service appointments in New York. As a result, the state, its thirty-five electoral votes, and the election all went to Garfield.

JAMES ABRAM GARFIELD

20TH PRESIDENT
★
1881

BORN: November 19, 1831

BIRTHPLACE: Orange, Ohio

DIED: September 19, 1881

PARTY: Republican

VICE PRESIDENT: Chester A. Arthur

FIRST LADY: Lucretia Rudolph

CHILDREN: Eliza, Harry, James, Mary, Irvin, Abram, Edward

NICKNAME: Preacher President

Juggled clubs to build up his muscles.

PRESIDENT GARFIELD DIES TEN WEEKS AFTER SHOOTING

ELBERON, N.J., September 19, 1881—President James Garfield died tonight, ten weeks after being shot by Charles Guiteau, a mentally ill office-seeker. Guiteau shot Garfield July 2 as the president walked through a Washington railroad station.

Guiteau was an obscure New York Stalwart who broke with the local party to support Garfield. After the election, he expected as a reward to be made a minister to Europe. When the State Department refused him, Guiteau decided that Garfield had to die.

At first, Garfield was treated in the White House. But once his condition stabilized, he was taken by train to the New Jersey coast, where he could escape the heat of the Washington summer. The track along his route was lined with straw to make the journey easier.

The immediate cause of Garfield's death appears to have been blood poisoning brought on by the doctors who treated him. They often failed to wash their hands and, in examining the president's gunshot wounds, used unsterile instruments, which reinfected him.

Most people didn't expect much from Garfield as president. His involvement in the Crédit Mobilier scandal and his campaign deal-making led many people to believe that his administration would be just as scandal-ridden as Grant's.

But Garfield proved them wrong during his very first week in office. When the new postmaster general uncovered evidence of wrongdoing in the post office, Garfield ordered him to pursue the investigation, no matter where it led.

Garfield also decided to take on Roscoe Conkling. Although he had promised the Republican party boss a say in appointments to government jobs, when it came time to make them Garfield ignored Conkling's wishes and made the appointments on merit alone.

During the long weeks after Garfield was shot, the president's popularity rose nearly every day. Each morning, the country waited nervously for news of his condition. A number of times it improved, but the poor state of medical science at the time eventually killed the president.

93

BORN: October 5, 1829

BIRTHPLACE: Fairfield, Vt.

DIED: November 18, 1886

PARTY: Republican

VICE PRESIDENT: None

FIRST LADY: Ellen Lewis Herndon

CHILDREN: William; Chester, Jr.; Ellen

NICKNAME: Elegant Arthur

Owned eighty pairs of pants, which he changed several times daily.

CHESTER ALAN ARTHUR

21ST PRESIDENT
★
FROM 1881 TO 1885

Americans hadn't expected much from James Garfield when he took office, and they expected even less from Chester Arthur when he became president upon Garfield's death. Garfield had surprised people with his turnaround on the civil service issue, but no one believed Arthur had much to offer.

Arthur had been chosen as Garfield's running mate simply to appease Roscoe Conkling and the conservative Stalwarts. No one seriously believed that Arthur would, or should, be president.

Arthur had been an important cog in Conkling's political machine. As the collector of duties for the Port of New York, he had regularly forced his employees to contribute money to Republican campaigns. Because of this practice, President Hayes had removed him from office in 1878.

Yet, in a transformation even more remarkable than Garfield's, President Arthur worked for genuine reform. When his cronies came to Washington looking for jobs, Arthur turned them

EARPS WIN GUNFIGHT AT O.K. CORRAL

TOMBSTONE, Arizona Territory, October 26, 1881—The long-standing battle between the Earps and Clantons for control of Tombstone was settled today at the O.K. Corral. The Earps killed Billy Clanton and Tom and Frank McLaury in a shootout there. Only Ike Clanton, leader of the Clanton gang, and Billy Claiborne escaped. At stake was control of the rich silver trade, which has driven Tombstone's recent boom.

Town marshal Virgil Earp was backed up in the fight by his two brothers, Wyatt and Morgan, and also by Doc Holliday. Wyatt has been working as a gambler and guard at the Oriental Saloon. Holliday is also a gambler and gunman, who occasionally practices dentistry.

Virgil Earp insisted that he and his brothers were just enforcing the law. But townspeople, who believe the gunfight was more likely murder, are planning to fire Earp and hire a new marshal to replace him.

CHESTER ARTHUR'S FATHER WAS THE Reverend William Arthur, a fiery Baptist minister who served eleven different parishes in Vermont and upstate New York during his career. Because Chester moved around with his father, he didn't really settle down until he entered Union College in 1845. As a student there, Arthur took part in his share of pranks, once dumping the school bell into the Erie Canal.

The Early Years

Soon after moving to New York City and becoming a lawyer in 1854, Arthur agreed to represent a black woman, Lizzie Jennings, who wanted to sue a streetcar company because she had been forced to leave a whites-only car. Arthur won the case, which ended racial segregation of public transportation in New York City.

★**HOT DOGS** German immigrant Anton Feuchtwanger made his living as a sausage vendor in St. Louis. At first, he served his sausages plain. For his customers' convenience, he loaned them white gloves so that they could keep their fingers clean while they ate. The problem was that too many customers kept the white gloves instead of returning them. In 1880, Feuchtwanger decided to solve this problem by asking his brother-in-law, a baker, to make special rolls that could hold the sausages. The result was the first hot dog.

★**BUFFALO BILL** William Cody took a job as a rider for the Pony Express when he was just fourteen years old. He got his nickname eight

I AM COMING

years later in 1868, when he hunted buffalo to feed railroad crews laying track for the Union Pacific. In just eight months, he killed 4,280 buffalo.

While serving as a scout during the Indian Wars, Buffalo Bill began to realize the commercial possibilities of his frontier adventures. In 1883, he organized the first of his hugely successful Wild West shows. These traveling entertainments featured real cowboys and Indians as well as reenactments of a buffalo hunt, a stagecoach robbery, and a Pony Express ride. Cody's stars included the famous sharpshooter Annie Oakley and the legendary Sioux chief Sitting Bull.

away. "For the vice presidency, I am indebted to Mr. Conkling," Arthur once said, "but for the presidency of the United States my debt is to the Almighty." In other words, there would be no payoffs.

In 1882, Arthur proved that he meant what he said by vetoing the Rivers and Harbors Act. This bill authorized nineteen million dollars in spending for construction projects around the country.

It was an obvious example of "pork barrel" legislation, composed of unnecessary projects designed to benefit the districts of powerful congressmen. Although the veto was overridden, Arthur won praise for his attempt to stop wasteful spending.

CHINESE IMMIGRATION Arthur also vetoed a bill banning Chinese immigration for twenty years. He did, however, sign the compromise Chinese Exclusion Act of 1882, which halted immigration for ten years and kept Chinese already in the United States from becoming citizens.

This law placed the first significant restrictions on immigration to the United States. It also broke the Treaty of 1880 with China. This treaty allowed restrictions on immigration but not an outright ban. The Chinese Exclusion Act was renewed twice before being repealed in 1943.

CIVIL SERVICE REFORM In 1883, Arthur signed the most important legislation of his administration, the Pendleton Act, which reformed the civil service. Civil service reform had been an important political issue since the scandals of the Grant years. It was widely believed that the civil service was filled with politically connected people who did little or no work.

Strangely, it was President Garfield's assassination that made real reform possible. Because Charles Guiteau had been looking for a government job when he shot the president, the public got the mistaken impression that Garfield's assassination was somehow linked to civil service corruption. Although Guiteau's motives were altogether different, people demanded immediate reform of the civil service. To everyone's surprise, Arthur enthusiastically supported the cause.

THE PENDLETON ACT

The Pendleton Act created competitive exams for government jobs. It also set up a Civil Service Commission to oversee the new merit system and banned the practice of demanding campaign contributions from federal employees.

In reforming the civil service, however, the Pendleton Act also changed the way political parties were funded—not necessarily for the better. No longer able to rely on civil service workers for income, political parties had to look elsewhere for money to run their campaigns.

Big business was the most likely source. Companies such as John D. Rockefeller's Standard Oil and Andrew Carnegie's U.S. Steel were eager to find ways to influence lawmakers. Both political parties were happy to accept their money.

By 1884, many of Arthur's critics had been won over by his handling of the presidency. But others couldn't understand his change of heart. Why, they wondered, did Arthur keep turning his back on the politicians who once bossed him around?

The answer may have been a secret known only to Arthur and his doctors. Arthur had Bright's disease, a then-fatal kidney illness. Perhaps knowing that he might die soon gave Arthur the courage he needed to do things he believed to be right.

THE DEMOCRATS HAD BEEN OUT OF POWER FOR twenty-eight years when they met in 1884 to select a presidential candidate. Desperate for a winner, the convention chose Governor Grover Cleveland of New York. Cleveland had made a name for himself by standing up to Tammany Hall, the corrupt political organization that controlled Democratic politics in New York City.

The Republicans picked James G. Blaine, who had served briefly as Garfield's secretary of state. Blaine had tried for the Republican nomination in 1876 and again in 1880 but failed both times. Arthur gave him some opposition at the convention, but the president's about-face on civil service reform had cost him his Stalwart allies without convincing reform Republicans that he could be trusted.

The campaign turned on personal attacks. The Democrats talked up the Mulligan Letters, which suggested that Blaine had taken bribes from railroads while serving in Congress. Blaine's cause was further hurt when he was seen having dinner with John Jacob Astor, Jay Gould, and other robber barons.

For their part, the Republicans unearthed the story that Cleveland, still a bachelor, had fathered a son out of wedlock ten years before. Cleveland admitted fathering the child, and the voters didn't hold it against him. To the Republican chant, "Ma, ma, where's my pa?" the Democrats replied, "Gone to the White House, ha, ha, ha!"

The election turned in New York, which Blaine lost by just a thousand votes. His close association with Protestants there cost him the support of New York's numerous Irish Catholics—and with it, the electoral votes he needed to beat Cleveland.

GROVER CLEVELAND

22ND PRESIDENT

★

FROM 1885 TO 1889

BORN: March 18, 1837

BIRTHPLACE: Caldwell, N.J.

DIED: June 24, 1908

PARTY: Democrat

VICE PRESIDENT: Thomas A. Hendricks

FIRST LADY: Frances Folsom

CHILDREN: Ruth, Esther, Marion, Richard, Francis

NICKNAME: Uncle Jumbo

The first Democrat elected president after the Civil War.

By an extremely close vote, Grover Cleveland became the first Democratic president since the Civil War. But his tiny margin of victory wasn't his only handicap. Cleveland was also little known around the country. Even in Washington, he was a stranger. His trip to the capital for the March 4, 1885, inauguration was only his second to the city. The crowd that gathered to hear him speak that day was the largest he had ever seen.

A lesser person might have been overwhelmed by the presidency, but Grover Cleveland was a man of conviction, which gave him strength. He had come to Washington to do a job, and he intended to see that job get done.

At first, Cleveland tried to do everything himself. During his

LABOR RIOT IN HAYMARKET SQUARE

CHICAGO, May 4, 1886—A workers' meeting in Haymarket Square tonight exploded into a riot when a bomb went off, killing seven policemen. The bomb thrower has not been identified.

The mass meeting had been called to protest yesterday's trouble at the McCormick Harvester Works, where police fired into a crowd of striking workers, killing four and wounding many more.

Tonight's Haymarket demonstration was organized in part by political radicals in the labor movement. "When you ask [your boss] to lessen your bur-dens, he sends his blood-hounds out to shoot you," one of their pamphlets read. "To arms, we call you, to arms!"

Eight radicals have been arrested for inciting murder, although only one of them was actually present in the Haymarket tonight.

Moderate union leaders are concerned that factory bosses will use popular hatred of these radicals, who are mostly foreigners, to undermine the fight for the eight-hour workday.

97

first months in office, he went without a secretary, even answering the White House telephone himself on occasion.

Because of his hard work and attention to detail, Cleveland usually knew more about the issues of the day than his opponents. He always did his homework. But sometimes he got so caught up in the specifics of an issue that he lost the big picture.

"HANDS-OFF" GOVERNMENT The new president was blunt and somewhat hot-tempered. He made few friends in Washington and many enemies. But he knew what he wanted, and that was a "hands-off" government. Cleveland believed that the people should support the government and not the other way around.

In 1887, for example, a severe drought hit Texas, causing terrible crop failures. The Congress passed a bill to distribute free seed there so farmers could replant. Although the bill was extremely popular, Cleveland vetoed it. He believed that people should be suspicious of government rather than look to it for handouts.

THE INTERSTATE COMMERCE ACT Because of his attitude toward government, Cleveland played almost no role in the shaping of legislation. He either signed bills or he vetoed them. One of the most important bills he signed was the Interstate Commerce Act.

For many years, railroads had been free to charge passengers and shippers whatever they liked. Often, the rates were outrageously high, and usually there was favoritism. Railroads used such practices as rebates to favor big corporations over small companies.

The Interstate Commerce Act was passed to ensure that the railroads

GROVER CLEVELAND WAS A BIG, STRONG BOY WHO loved fishing. In school, he was not outstanding, but he worked hard. He planned to go on to college, but his father's death in 1853 forced the sixteen-year-old Cleveland to find a job. After working for a year in New York City, he was offered a full scholarship to college if he agreed to become a Presbyterian minister, as his father had been.

Although Cleveland yearned for a formal education, he turned down the offer and decided to head west. He got as far as Buffalo, where his uncle arranged for him to study law. He eventually entered politics. His remarkable success as a reform mayor of Buffalo led to his election as governor of New York State in 1882.

★**A WHITE HOUSE MARRIAGE**
Grover Cleveland became the first president to be married in the White House when he wed twenty-one-year-old Frances Folsom on June 2, 1886. Frances, the youngest first lady ever, was the daughter of the president's longtime friend and law partner Oscar Folsom. Cleveland, who was forty-nine when he married, had known Frances since her birth, but they didn't become romantically involved until she was in college.

The couple kept their engagement secret for nearly a year and revealed it just five days before their wedding. John Philip Sousa and his Marine Band played at the ceremony, which was made the focus of much attention by the press. Although the couple took a five-day honeymoon, President Cleveland worked as usual on his wedding day.

★**THE AMERICAN FEDERATION OF LABOR** In 1886, Samuel Gompers organized the American Federation of Labor. The AFL was a new kind of union because its members were not workers but other unions. Until that time, organizations such as the Knights of Labor tried to win better conditions for workers through political activity. But Gompers thought political reform was a waste of time. He believed a union's strength lay in its bargaining power with big business. A strong union could force a company to pay better wages and improve working conditions. The point of the AFL, one union official explained, was "not to assist men to lift themselves out of their class, as if they were ashamed of it…but to raise the class itself in physical well-being and self-estimation."

★GERONIMO SURRENDERS With the flight of Sitting Bull to Canada and the death of **Crazy Horse** in 1877, Indian resistance to whites ended on the Great Plains. Only the Chiricahua Apaches of Arizona fought on under the leadership of the war chief Geronimo.

When Geronimo surrendered to General Nelson "Bearcat" Miles on September 4, 1886, it was the third time he had been captured by the U.S. army. Twice before, he had escaped when he feared that the soldiers planned to kill him. This time, Miles promised Geronimo that he would be able to return to his Arizona homeland after a temporary exile in Florida. But the government didn't keep its promise. Geronimo never saw Arizona again.

★COCA-COLA An Atlanta druggist named John Pemberton invented Coca-Cola in 1886. At first, he promoted the drink as a health tonic, but it soon became popular as a soft drink. The name Coca-Cola was chosen by Pemberton's bookkeeper, Frank Robinson, who borrowed it from the syrup's active ingredients: coca leaf and kola nut extracts.

In 1891, Pemberton sold out to Asa G. Candler, who took the drink nationwide, building bottling plants in Dallas, Philadelphia, and Los Angeles. Under Candler's leadership, sales of Coca-Cola syrup rose from 9,000 gallons in 1890 to more than 370,000 gallons in 1900. Candler, who paid Pemberton $2,300 for Coca-Cola, sold out himself in 1919 for $25,000,000.

charged "reasonable and just" rates. The Interstate Commerce Commission that it created to oversee the railroads was the first regulatory agency ever created by Congress.

INDIAN AFFAIRS In 1881, Helen Hunt Jackson published *A Century of Dishonor*. This widely read book described the federal government's cruel treatment of Indians on the frontier, and it generated an enormous emotional response. Groups devoted to defending the rights of Indians sprang up all over the country.

The goal of these groups was to help reservation Indians adopt white culture so they could be integrated into white society. Because of their prodding, Congress passed the Dawes Severalty Act in 1887. This law granted citizenship to Indians willing to renounce membership in a tribe. If they did so, they were given a small parcel of reservation land to homestead.

Although the reformers meant well, the Dawes Act was misguided because it failed to take into account the Indians' native culture. Because Indians were used to sharing their hunting grounds with others, they didn't value the concept of private property. Because they didn't understand the white meaning of ownership, they often sold their plots for a fraction of their market value. As a result, the Dawes Act did more harm than good.

PENSION BILLS Cleveland exercised his veto power often when it came to bills that he considered raids on the Treasury. Chief among these were bills introduced by congressmen to provide pensions for particular veterans of the Union army.

Cleveland believed that the government was obligated to provide pension benefits for soldiers injured in battle. But he worried that the prospect of "easy" pension money was leading to a great deal of fraud.

Corrupt lawyers often filed false claims on behalf of Union veterans who were perfectly healthy. Sometimes the Pension Bureau accepted these claims without any investigation. And even if the Pension Bureau did reject a claim, individual veterans could still request that their congressman introduce private bills forcing the Pension Bureau to pay them benefits.

In this manner, pensions were fraudulently granted to deserters, to criminals, and even to men who had never served in the army. Although his actions infuriated the veterans lobby, Cleveland read each and every one of these bills—there were hundreds—and he vetoed nearly all of them.

TARIFF REFORM Near the end of his first term, Cleveland challenged Congress to reduce U.S. tariff rates. Ever since the Lincoln administration, when rates were raised to pay for the Civil War, tariffs had been extraordinarily high. After the war, the high rates had protected developing U.S. industries, but they had also pushed up prices and created a large surplus in the Treasury.

Congressmen were eager to spend the extra money on **pork barrel** projects in their home states, but Cleveland wouldn't allow it. Instead, the president demanded that Congress lower tariff rates.

Reaction to Cleveland's proposal was strong. Big business enjoyed the protection from foreign competition, and labor organizations believed that high tariffs kept wages high. In fact, reaction to Cleveland's repeated call for tariff reform was so strong that his position probably cost him reelection in 1888.

By THE TIME THE REPUBLICANS MET IN JUNE 1888 TO nominate a presidential candidate, the united party was determined to unseat Grover Cleveland. James G. Blaine, the 1884 nominee, had stepped aside so that the party could rally behind a single candidate.

After eight ballots, the delegates nominated Benjamin Harrison, a former senator from Indiana and the grandson of President William Henry Harrison. Besides having a well-known name, Harrison came from a state whose electoral votes were considered crucial to a Republican victory. Harrison's campaign slogan was "Grandfather's Hat Fits!"

Cleveland and Harrison were both rather dull, honorable men whose campaigns matched their personalities. Cleveland made only one public appearance, while Harrison, acting under the advice of his campaign manager, stayed at home in Indianapolis, where he confined his remarks to prepared speeches before groups of people who had come to visit him.

The party platforms were remarkably similar. Both favored lower taxes, a larger navy, and statehood for the western territories. The only real difference between them had to do with tariff reform. Cleveland's insistence that tariff rates be lowered was very unpopular, and the Republicans—who favored high, protective tariffs—used the issue to hurt him.

For the fourth time in a row, the election was very close. Cleveland won the popular vote by one hundred thousand ballots but lost the electoral vote by sixty-five. Again, New York's thirty-six electoral votes, the most of any state, made the difference. Cleveland's enemies in **Tammany Hall** torpedoed his campaign there. Had the former governor carried New York, he would have won reelection by seven electoral votes.

BENJAMIN HARRISON

23RD PRESIDENT
★
FROM 1889 TO 1893

BORN: August 20, 1833

BIRTHPLACE: North Bend, Ohio

DIED: March 13, 1901

PARTY: Republican

VICE PRESIDENT: Levi P. Morton

FIRST LADY: Caroline Lavinia Scott

CHILDREN: Russell, Mary, Elizabeth

NICKNAME: Little Ben

The first president to use electricity in the White House.

INDIANS MASSACRED AT WOUNDED KNEE

WOUNDED KNEE CREEK, S.D., December 29, 1890— The Seventh Cavalry today massacred more than two hundred Sioux men, women, and children who only last night had surrendered peacefully.

This morning, after the Sioux were nearly disarmed, a fight broke out over a young brave's new rifle. A shot went off, which prompted the soldiers to fire wildly into the crowd.

The Indians' clubs and knives were no match for the machine guns of General Custer's former outfit. It has been suggested that the troopers' murderous ferocity can be traced back to the regiment's defeat at the Little Big Horn.

These Sioux were the last followers of Wovoka, the holy man whose Ghost Dance religion had inspired the recent revival among the Indians. Wovoka preached that the Ghost Dance he taught would make the white man's bullets bounce off Indian warriors and bring Indian ancestors back from the dead.

B24.12

Unlike Grover Cleveland, who could be pleasant and jovial, Benjamin Harrison was uncomfortable with people. He was highly formal, and his personality lacked warmth. Some people called him the "human iceberg."

But Harrison shared a number of important traits with Cleveland, including an attention to detail and a determined work ethic. Harrison was also personally incorruptible, which was more than could be said for his campaign manager, Matt Quay of Pennsylvania.

After winning the election, President-elect Harrison declared that "Providence has given us the victory."

Upon hearing Harrison's remark, Quay laughed, "Think of the man! He ought to know that Providence hadn't a damn thing to do with it." It was likely, Quay continued, that Harrison "would never know how close a number of men were compelled to approach the gates of the penitentiary to make him president." Quay's handling of the campaign left Harrison with a debt to big business that would have to be repaid sooner or later.

THE SHERMAN ANTI-TRUST ACT

During the Gilded Age, the country's largest corporations had created near-monopolies in a number of industries. In 1882, for example, John D. Rockefeller had formed the Standard Oil trust to corner the oil market legally.

In his inaugural address, Harrison warned the trusts to play by the rules of free trade or else face government discipline. When the trusts ignored his warning, Congress passed the first antitrust law in 1890.

The Sherman Anti-Trust Act, sponsored by Ohio senator John Sherman, made it a crime to restrict trade by "combination in the form of a trust or otherwise." This meant that men such as Rockefeller could no longer control, or combine, several companies in order to monopolize a particular industry.

There were a number of ways around the law, however, which were soon upheld in court. "What looks like a stone wall to a layman is a triumphal arch to a corporation lawyer," political humorist Finley Peter Dunne joked at the time.

FOREIGN POLICY

Under the leadership of Navy Secretary Benjamin F. Tracy, the Harrison administration continued the huge shipbuilding program begun during Cleveland's first term. The modernization of the navy fit in well with Harrison's plan to expand U.S. influence in Latin America and the Pacific.

Harrison favored an aggressive foreign policy and backed the first

The Early Years

BENJAMIN HARRISON WAS BORN AT THE NORTH BEND, Ohio, home of General William Henry Harrison. When he was seven, his grandfather was elected president. Benjamin's childhood was typical for a farm boy at that time. He fetched wood and water, fed the horses and cattle on the family's six-hundred-acre farm, hunted, fished, and swam.

In July 1862, after becoming a leading Republican lawyer in Indianapolis, Harrison went off to fight in the Civil War, joining the Seventieth Indiana Infantry as a second lieutenant. Rising eventually to the rank of brigadier general, Harrison fought bravely in Kentucky, Tennessee, Alabama, and Georgia.

★OLD WHISKERS

President Harrison was an animal lover who always made sure his grandchildren had plenty of pets. The Harrisons had dogs, horses, and even an opossum. Their favorite pet was Old Whiskers, a goat. One day, as Old Whiskers pulled the children around the White House lawn in a cart, the gates were opened to allow the president's carriage to leave. Seizing his opportunity, Old Whiskers dashed for freedom. He took off through the gate with the children still in tow. The president couldn't believe his eyes. Nor could the residents of Washington, who watched the president of the United States race down the street, waving his cane and chasing a goat.

★POPULISM   The populist movement of the 1890s had its roots in farmers' alliances such as the Grange movement of the 1870s. Granges were initially organized in the West to relieve the boredom of rural life. At first, they sponsored social activities. But they soon came to represent the farmers' political views as well.

In 1892, a number of populist groups met in St. Louis, where they formed the People's Party. Its members, mostly farmers, believed that big business had too much say in the way government was run. Wanting to reorganize things drastically, the populists called for government ownership of the railroads, an eight-hour workday, and a federal income tax.

★**ELLIS ISLAND** By the 1890s, huge numbers of immigrants from Eastern and Central Europe were arriving in New York City every day. Overwhelmed port officials were in desperate need of a place to hold all these people until their papers could be processed.

On January 1, 1892, the federal government opened a new processing station on Ellis Island in Upper New York Bay within sight of the Statue of Liberty. For the next half-century, the red brick buildings on Ellis Island provided the first glimpse millions of immigrants, particularly Jews and Italians, got of their new home in the United States.

★**CARRY A. NATION** By 1890, alcoholism was becoming an increasingly severe problem in the United States. Drunkenness led to the abuse of women and children in the home as well as to absenteeism at work, not to mention frequent brawls in saloons. Women and church groups had for many years worked together unsuccessfully in the temperance movement. Their goal was to ban the sale of liquor.

The most zealous of the new wave of temperance crusaders was Carry A. Nation, who believed that her name was literally her destiny. An imposing woman who stood six feet tall and weighed 175 pounds, Nation became famous for using a hatchet to demolish saloons in Kansas. She was jailed often, but she always paid her fines using money raised from speaking tours and the sale of souvenir hatchets.

Pan-American Conference. Chaired by Secretary of State James G. Blaine, this conference increased the U.S. presence in Latin America and reduced that of Great Britain. Harrison's specific goal was to control the narrow strip of land called the Isthmus of Panama across which the United States hoped to build a canal.

Meanwhile in the Pacific, U.S. minister to Hawaii John L. Stevens landed troops to protect white business leaders who had recently rebelled against Queen Liliuokalani. After overthrowing her native government and setting up their own, the whites, mostly sugar growers, asked for immediate annexation to the United States. The president negotiated a treaty of annexation during his final weeks in office, but it was still pending before the Senate when Harrison's term ended.

THE TREASURY SURPLUS One of the issues that Harrison faced at home was a huge Treasury surplus carried over from the Cleveland administration. Republicans and Democrats both wanted to get rid of the surplus, but they disagreed on how to do it. The Democrats wanted to lower the tariff rates and thereby take in less money, but Harrison and the Republicans wanted to spend the surplus.

The first big spending bill that Harrison signed was the Dependent and Disability Pensions Act of 1890. Harrison had been a general during the Civil War, and he had great sympathy for his fellow veterans. The Dependent and Disability Pensions Act showered money on them in the form of pensions for all Union veterans who were now unable to work for any reason. That is, their injuries did not have to be battle-related.

Meanwhile, new silver discoveries in Arizona and Nevada had created a host of boom towns. However, the more silver the miners dug up, the less valuable the metal became, because the market could only absorb so much. To keep the price of silver up, miners lobbied the government to buy more silver with new paper money. Farmers in the South and West supported this policy because it would lead to inflation, which would make their debts cheaper to pay off.

Back East, the bankers who controlled the government's monetary policy were horrified at the thought of unlimited silver coinage. But they needed the support of the South and West to pass a new tariff bill. So the two sides agreed to a compromise.

The Sherman Silver Purchase Act committed the government to buy 4.5 million ounces of silver each month, nearly the entire output of the western mines. About the same time, the McKinley Tariff Act was passed.

THE McKINLEY TARIFF

The McKinley Tariff was the Harrison administration's payoff to big business for its support during the campaign. A highly protective measure, it raised tariff rates to forty-eight percent, their highest peacetime level ever.

But the bill, sponsored by future president William McKinley of Ohio, backfired. The point of the high tariff was to make foreign goods expensive so that Americans would be more likely to buy U.S. goods. But greedy manufacturers raised their prices to match those of the foreign goods.

Consumers were furious, and they turned their anger on the governing Republican party. A good many were voted out of office during the 1890 midterm elections, and two years later, President Harrison was tossed out, too.

THE ELECTION OF 1892 WAS A REMATCH. ALTHOUGH both candidates faced opposition within their parties, the Republicans renominated Benjamin Harrison, while the Democrats chose former president Grover Cleveland.

An early dump-Harrison movement tried to generate support for perennial candidate James G. Blaine, but

the president's backers made sure he won renomination on the first ballot. Cleveland also won nomination on the first ballot, squeaking by despite vocal opposition from New York's Tammany Hall delegation and westerners who advocated the free coinage of silver, which Cleveland opposed.

The third candidate in the race was James Weaver, the nominee of the People's party, which met in Omaha. Weaver had run for president once before in 1880 as the choice of the short-lived Greenback party.

Once again, the election turned on the tariff issue, but this time the McKinley Tariff doomed the Republicans. Cleveland called attention to its upsetting effect on consumer prices and pointed out that he had favored a low tariff for years.

When the votes were counted, Cleveland won the popular vote by almost four hundred thousand, the biggest margin since Grant won reelection in 1872. Cleveland took the electoral vote, including New York's, by an even wider margin. But Weaver did remarkably well, becoming the only third party candidate between 1860 and 1912 to win at least one state. He carried four: Colorado, Idaho, Kansas, and Nevada.

GROVER CLEVELAND

24TH PRESIDENT
★
FROM 1893 TO 1897

BORN: March 18, 1837

BIRTHPLACE: Caldwell, N.J.

DIED: June 24, 1908

PARTY: Democrat

VICE PRESIDENT: Adlai E. Stevenson

FIRST LADY: Frances Folsom

CHILDREN: Ruth, Esther, Marion, Richard, Francis

NICKNAME: Uncle Jumbo

The Baby Ruth candy bar was named after Cleveland's daughter Ruth.

"SEPARATE BUT EQUAL" DOCTRINE UPHELD

WASHINGTON, May 18, 1896—The Supreme Court ruled today in the case of *Plessy v. Ferguson*. Its decision upheld Jim Crow laws in the South that require "separate but equal" facilities for black citizens.

The *Plessy* case hinged on an 1890 Louisiana law requiring blacks and whites to travel in separate railroad cars. When Homer Plessy refused to leave a car designated for whites only, he was arrested.

Plessy's attorneys had claimed that the Louisiana law violates their client's rights, but the Court ruled that separate accommodations are not necessarily unequal.

The Court's decision aside, the intent of the Jim Crow laws has clearly been to support white supremacy in the South. These laws, first passed at the end of Reconstruction in 1877, have segregated southern schools, parks, theaters, restaurants, and even cemeteries in addition to the railroads.

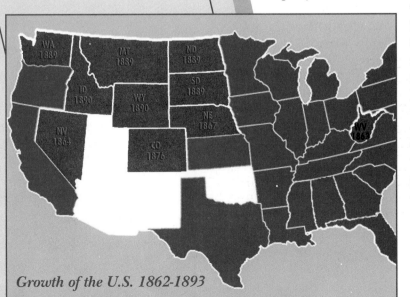

Growth of the U.S. 1862-1893

Grover Cleveland was the only president reelected after being voted out. He returned to the White House determined to lower tariff rates. But before he could do anything, the Panic of 1893 hit. The depression that followed lasted throughout Cleveland's second term.

The panic began even before Cleveland took office. In February 1893, the Philadelphia and Reading Railroad went broke, and soon others followed. By 1896, one-quarter of the nation's railroads had gone out of business.

With nearly a million workers, the railroads were the nation's biggest employers, and financing railroads was the biggest business on Wall Street. The railroad bankruptcies put hundreds of thousands of people out of work and brought Wall Street grinding to a halt.

Many of the people who lost their jobs also lost their homes and became wandering hobos. Although Cleveland genuinely wanted to help these people, his belief in a "hands-off" government prevented him from proposing any relief programs. Instead, the president focused on keeping the economy above water until the storm of depression passed.

REPEAL OF THE SILVER PURCHASE ACT The immediate crisis facing the federal government was the run on its gold reserves. Under the terms of the Sherman Silver Purchase Act, the government had to buy western silver with certificates that could be exchanged for gold. When people began using the certificates to trade their silver for gold, the government's gold supply dropped. By April 1893, the Treasury's reserves had fallen below one hundred million dollars.

Cleveland's first move was to call an emergency session of Congress to repeal the Silver Purchase Act. A terrible fight followed between conservatives, who favored the gold standard, and populists, who wanted free coinage of silver. Keeping the gold standard meant that U.S. currency would be backed by gold alone. Free coinage of silver would mean that money could be made from either silver or gold, thereby increasing the money supply.

If there were more dollars in circulation, the value of each one would go down. This prospect pleased the western and southern farmers, who didn't have much cash, but it infuriated the eastern bankers, who did.

The fight created a deep division within the Democratic party between Cleveland's "goldbugs" and the populist "silverites." The silverites were led by a dynamic young

★**SECRET SURGERY** In 1893, as Cleveland began his second term, his doctors discovered a cancerous tumor in his mouth. Believing that news of his illness might shock a nation already weakened by the Panic of 1893, Cleveland decided to have the cancer treated secretly. He quietly boarded a yacht in New York's East River, where a team of surgeons performed an hour-long operation. Working from the inside of the president's mouth so as not to leave a visible scar, they removed part of his jaw and replaced it with a rubber substitute. The operation remained a secret until one of the doctors wrote a magazine article about it in 1917.

★ **GIBSON GIRLS** Charles Dana Gibson was the highest-paid illustrator of his generation. His turn-of-the-century drawings defined the American ideal of beauty at that time. The women he drew, called Gibson girls, looked pale, dreamy, and innocent. They typically wore full, upswept hairstyles, called "pompadours," and had "hourglass" figures. Their male companions were broad-shouldered and usually clean-shaven, which started a trend. Before the appearance of the Gibson man, mustaches and beards were extremely popular.

★**BREAKFAST CEREALS** The first flaked breakfast cereal was invented by Dr. John Harvey Kellogg, the superintendent of Michigan's Battle Creek Sanitarium. The sanitarium was founded by Seventh Day Adventists, who are vegetarians. Kellogg invented cornflakes in 1895 as a healthful substitute for animal foods.

Calling his new cereal Granose, Kellogg and his brother sold ten-ounce packages for fifteen cents. About the same time, C.W. Post, a patient at the sanitarium, saw commercial possibilities in the idea of ready-to-eat breakfast cereals. In 1897, Post introduced Grape Nuts, each box of which contained his pamphlet *The Road to Wellsville*.

★**COXEY'S ARMY** In response to the depression, populist leader Jacob Coxey of Ohio proposed a half-billion-dollar public works program to help the unemployed. To rally support for this idea, he decided to lead an "army" of unemployed workers to Washington. "We will send a petition to Washington with boots on," he said.

On March 25, 1894, Coxey began the march with one hundred people. He hoped a hundred thousand more might join him, but Coxey's Army numbered just five hundred when it reached the steps of the Capitol on April 30. Police immediately arrested Coxey for trampling on the Capitol lawn, but Coxey's march heightened public awareness of the unemployment problem all over the country.

★**YELLOW JOURNALISM** In 1895, William Randolph Hearst bought the *New York Journal* and began a celebrated circulation war with Joseph Pulitzer's *New York World.* This battle over which newspaper could sell the most copies changed the newspaper business forever. Hearst and Pulitzer both tried to attract readers by playing up sensational stories, especially those relating to the rebellion in Cuba. This kind of exaggerated or unnecessarily dramatic reporting was called "yellow journalism" after a well-known comic strip, "The Yellow Kid," that was printed in the *Journal.* Hearst and Pulitzer's feverish reporting was in large part responsible for the Spanish-American War.

congressman from Nebraska named William Jennings Bryan, who held Congress spellbound with his electrifying speeches against the gold standard.

In the end, a coalition of Republicans and goldbug Democrats forced the repeal of the Silver Purchase Act. But that didn't stop the gold drain as Cleveland had expected. Now even more desperate, the president turned to Wall Street for help.

At Cleveland's request, J.P. Morgan organized a group of his fellow bankers to come to the Treasury's aid. Their loan of sixty-two million dollars in gold to the government reversed the drain and stabilized the economy. Although people's confidence in the government was restored, Morgan and his friends made a great deal of money on the loan. This led the populists to accuse Cleveland of being a puppet of Wall Street.

LABOR UNREST Meanwhile, big business used the depression as an excuse to cut workers' wages unfairly. Because the workers' quality of life was already quite low, these additional cuts merely goaded the labor movement into aggression and violence.

After the Civil War, as manufacturing industries grew larger and more powerful, companies forced workers—mostly immigrants—to accept wage cuts, longer days, and more dangerous working conditions. For most people stuck in this life of misery, unionization was the only hope.

The strikes organized by the unions usually turned violent when company bosses hired men to break up the unions by beating up the strikers. With the government, and therefore the police, on their side, the bosses usually won.

A famous example was the 1894 strike at the Pullman Palace Car

Company outside Chicago. When the Pullman Company cut wages but refused to lower rents in the company town or prices at the company store, the workers appealed for help to the American Railway Union, which Eugene V. Debs had organized only the year before.

When Pullman refused to negotiate, Debs led 120,000 workers out on strike. Although peaceful and orderly, the strike stopped nearly all the rail traffic between Chicago and the West. In fact, Debs thought he had nearly won when Cleveland's attorney general, Richard Olney, got a court injunction banning the strike. When Debs refused to obey the injunction, Olney sent in federal troops and had Debs arrested. The troops broke up the strike, and the workers were forced to return to their jobs.

Although Olney's actions temporarily ended the crisis, they also raised the level of tension between business and labor. The new labor unions, such as Samuel Gompers's American Federation of Labor, became convinced that business and government were conspiring together to enslave the working class.

THE WILSON-GORMAN TARIFF

Cleveland was so preoccupied with the economic crisis that he didn't get around to tariff reform until 1894. In that year, Representative William Wilson sponsored a bill in the House that dramatically reduced tariff rates. But the bill was reworked in the Senate by Arthur Gorman of Maryland until it barely lowered tariff rates at all. Calling the bill "party dishonor," the president refused to sign it.

Having thus failed even to reduce tariff rates, Cleveland left office as one of the most unpopular presidents of all time.

WILLIAM JENNINGS BRYAN WAS DETERMINED TO HAVE the Democratic party platform support the free coinage of silver. The platform speech he delivered to the convention, one of the most acclaimed in U.S. political history, also won him the nomination. "You shall not press down upon the brow of labor this crown of thorns; you shall not crucify mankind upon a cross of gold," Bryan said.

CAMPAIGN 1896

The Republicans nominated Governor William McKinley of Ohio on the first ballot. As a congressman, McKinley had sponsored the hated McKinley Tariff. Nevertheless, he had shown surprising strength at the 1892 Republican convention.

The campaign turned on the currency issue, which also muddied party lines. Unwilling to support either the prosilver policies of Bryan or the protective tariff advocated by McKinley, Cleveland and the goldbug Democrats backed their own candidate. Meanwhile, the Populists threw in with Bryan, who had already adopted nearly all their ideas.

The thirty-six-year-old Bryan crisscrossed the country, traveling eighteen thousand miles in three months, while McKinley stayed home and let campaign manager Mark Hanna run the election for him. Bryan had tremendous popular support in the South and West, but the Republicans controlled the East, where the money was. Raising three million dollars from leading industrialists, Hanna was able to flood the country with Republican pamphlets written in different languages so that McKinley could attract immigrant voters. By comparison, Bryan raised only five hundred thousand dollars, mostly from owners of silver mines.

Although Bryan's personal appeal was powerful, his target audience of farmers now made up less than half the population. Buoyed by the growing power of the urban manufacturing interests, McKinley won a decisive victory.

WILLIAM McKINLEY

25TH PRESIDENT
★
FROM 1897 TO 1901

BORN: January 29, 1843

BIRTHPLACE: Niles, Ohio

DIED: September 14, 1901

PARTY: Republican

VICE PRESIDENT: Garret A. Hobart, Theodore Roosevelt

FIRST LADY: Ida Saxton

CHILDREN: Katherine, Ida

NICKNAME: Wobbly Willie

Always wore a red carnation in his lapel for good luck.

REMEMBER THE MAINE!

Mysterious Explosion Sinks U.S. Ship

HAVANA, February 15, 1898—The U.S. battleship *Maine* sunk today in the harbor at Havana after an unexplained explosion punched a hole in its side. Two hundred and sixty sailors went down with the ship.

Investigators have been unable to determine the cause of the blast. The Spanish have insisted that the explosion was an accident, but unsubstantiated reports in U.S. newspapers have blamed an underwater Spanish mine.

The *Maine* had been sent to the Spanish colony of Cuba in January as a show of force to discourage the seizure of U.S. property there. The Cubans have been fighting for their independence from Spain since 1895.

Given the current war fever, the sinking of the *Maine* will almost surely lead to war with Spain.

William McKinley had a notably warm and engaging personality. It was often said of him that a person could walk into his office angry and walk out with a smile.

It helped McKinley's popularity that, like Cleveland, he was a conservative, hands-off politician. Big business was given free rein during his term, and hugely powerful trusts were allowed to develop without much restraint.

McKinley's immediate problem upon taking office was a growing budget deficit. Because the Supreme Court had recently ruled that a proposed income tax was unconstitutional, the government's revenues still came primarily from tariffs on imported goods.

Tariff rates had been the hottest issue during the last three elections. When the Democrats were in power, they lowered the rates. With Republicans such as McKinley in office, the rates went up again. The Dingley Tariff, which replaced the 1894 Wilson-Gorman Act, raised tariff rates

109

even higher than the protective McKinley Tariff had in 1890.

At first, the public protested the Dingley Tariff because it raised prices on consumer goods, especially imported ones. But the protests didn't last long as the country soon became distracted by events taking place in Cuba.

THE CUBAN REVOLT The depression caused by the Panic of 1893 hurt Cuba's huge sugar industry badly. The Wilson-Gorman Tariff, which imposed a forty percent duty on sugar, made matters even worse. By 1895, the suffering and unemployment on the island moved the desperately poor Cubans to revolt against their Spanish colonial rulers.

The Spanish responded brutally, imprisoning the Cuban rebels in concentration camps where two hundred thousand people died of disease and starvation. Whipped into a frenzy by the grisly and often exaggerated newspaper accounts of Spanish atrocities, Americans demanded that their government do something. But Grover Cleveland, who was still president, refused to interfere, and tensions continued to mount.

When McKinley became president, he tried to avoid a fight. As a veteran of the Civil War, he knew how bloody war could be. But the sinking of the *Maine* in the harbor at Havana made war inevitable.

The Spanish maintained that the explosion had been an accident, while a U.S. investigation proved inconclusive. But the popular press kept insisting that the sinking of the *Maine* had been deliberate. McKinley couldn't resist the public sentiment in favor of war. On April 11, 1898, he sent a message to Congress urging the use of military force to pacify Cuba.

The Early Years

WILLIAM McKINLEY WAS EIGHTEEN YEARS OLD when the Civil War started in April 1861. He enlisted as a private two months later and fought at **Antietam**, where he carried desperately needed rations to the front. For his bravery under fire, McKinley was promoted to second lieutenant. His new commanding officer was Colonel Rutherford B. Hayes, the future president. Of McKinley, Hayes once said, "Young as he was, we soon found that in the business of a soldier..., young McKinley showed unusual and unsurpassed capacity." McKinley's political career began when he helped Hayes win election as governor of Ohio in 1867.

★**THE FIRST LADY** McKinley met Ida Saxton in 1867 at a picnic in Canton, Ohio, where he had recently moved to set up a law practice. The future Mrs. McKinley was working as a cashier in her father's bank, an unusual job for a woman at that time. In fact, Ida McKinley was the first wife of a president to have worked in a profession other than teaching. Because the first lady suffered from a form of epilepsy that caused occasional seizures, McKinley insisted that she be seated beside him at state dinners. This broke a White House tradition of seating the first lady at the opposite end of the table from the president.

★**MOTION PICTURES** The first motion pictures were introduced by Thomas Edison in 1894. He called his viewers Kinetoscopes. People put coins into these machines and looked through peepholes to view short reels of film. The first "peep show" was *Fred Ott's Sneeze*. Fred Ott was an Edison factory worker who volunteered to sneeze for the camera.

Edison's mistake was that his Kinetoscopes played to only one viewer at a time. Two years later, the French brothers Auguste and Louis Lumière opened the world's first movie theater in Paris. Their Cinematographe was the first true movie projector. Unlike the Kinetoscope, it projected a movie onto a screen so that a large audience could view it.

★**THE KLONDIKE GOLD RUSH** Gold was first discovered along the Klondike Creek, a tributary of the Yukon River, in August 1896. But the remoteness of Canada's Yukon Territory and the onset of winter, which lasted from September until May, kept news of the Klondike strike from reaching the outside world.

The greatest gold rush in North American history began on July 16, 1897, when the news finally reached the telegraph wires. Two days later, a ship carrying two tons of Klondike gold docked in San Francisco, adding to the excitement. As the forty-niners had during the California gold rush, tens of thousands of miners hurried to northwest Canada and nearby Alaska to find their fortunes. The gold they mined expanded the money supply and helped to end the depression. It also muted populist calls for the free coinage of silver.

★**JAZZ** During the late 1890s, John Philip Sousa's military marching band played the most popular music in the country. Sousa wrote highly patriotic songs such as "The Stars and Stripes Forever." In New Orleans, however, black musicians were developing a new kind of popular music. Adding complex ragtime rhythms to the brass band melodies, they created a new style of music called jazz. Early jazz bands typically used marching band instruments such as trumpets, saxophones, trombones, and drums. Some groups also used pianos, bass fiddles, and guitars.

THE SPANISH-AMERICAN WAR Secretary of State John Hay called the Spanish-American War a "splendid little war" because it was quick and relatively painless for the United States. Only a few hundred soldiers were killed in battle, although several thousand more died from tropical diseases.

The war began in earnest on April 30, 1898, when the U.S. Pacific fleet under Commodore George Dewey sailed into Manila Bay in the Philippines. The United States had long coveted the Spanish colony, and the next day Dewey easily defeated the outdated Spanish fleet in the harbor there.

A month later, seventeen thousand soldiers left Florida for Cuba. The First Volunteer Cavalry Regiment, nicknamed the Rough Riders, was led by Theodore Roosevelt, who had just resigned as assistant secretary of the navy.

The Rough Riders were generally untrained and disorganized, but the Spanish were even more hopeless. Caught between the Rough Riders and the powerful U.S. Navy, the Spanish agreed to surrender Cuba on August 12.

In the peace talks that followed, the Cubans were granted limited independence, but the United States took possession of Puerto Rico, Guam, and the Philippines. With the annexation of Hawaii that same year, the nation was well on its way to becoming an imperial as well as a world power.

THE ANNEXATION OF HAWAII Grover Cleveland had been so outraged by U.S. complicity in the overthrow of Queen Liliuokalani that, when he regained the presidency in 1893, he immediately withdrew the Hawaiian annexation treaty submitted by Benjamin Harrison.

Cleveland tried to restore native rule to the Hawaiian islands, but the provisional government run by the white planters refused to yield its control. When McKinley replaced Cleveland as president, U.S. policy changed again, and Hawaii was annexed in July 1898.

THE OPEN DOOR POLICY One reason for U.S. interest in the Pacific was the new and potentially huge China trade. Because China was the most populous country in Asia, and also undeveloped, U.S. businesses were anxious to establish markets there.

But the Western European powers were also interested in China, as was Japan. Despite its size, China was quite weak militarily. Secretary of State John Hay worried that the Europeans and Japan would simply divide the country into "spheres of influence," leaving nothing for the United States.

To prevent this, Hay developed the Open Door policy. He sent a series of notes in September 1899 to the European powers and Japan asking them to allow equal status for all nations trading with China.

Before the Open Door policy could be adopted, however, a group of Chinese nationalists rose up in the countryside and advanced on the capital of Peking. These people were members of a secret society known as the Righteous and Harmonious Fists. Westerners called them Boxers. Their goal was to remove all foreigners from their country.

In June 1900, the Boxers rioted in Peking. The Chinese empress decided to support them. She ordered that all foreigners in China be killed. After the German minister was murdered, most of the remaining foreigners took refuge in the British embassy. The Boxer Rebellion ended when an international rescue force captured Peking on August 14.

BY 1900, THE ECONOMY HAD TURNED AROUND completely. The depression years of the early 1890s were over, in part thanks to the Klondike gold rush. The country basked in prosperity. Knowing a popular president when they saw one, the Republicans eagerly renominated McKinley for a second term.

The only suspense surrounded the choice of a new running mate to replace Vice President Garret Hobart,

who had died in office. McKinley announced that he would accept the will of the convention. Republican delegates chose Spanish-American War hero Theodore Roosevelt, then serving as governor of New York.

McKinley's opponent was once again William Jennings Bryan, the only Democratic leader with a truly national reputation. Although McKinley had beaten Bryan in 1896, the Nebraskan had kept control of his party. Winning renomination easily, he insisted that the Democrats include a free-silver plank in their

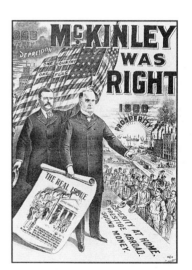

1900 party platform. His uncompromising position unnecessarily drove away gold Democrats and signaled his campaign was in trouble.

Bryan denounced McKinley for turning the United States into an imperial power by keeping the Philippine Islands after the Spanish-American War. The Republicans responded that the nation was obliged to bring "civilization" to the people who lived there.

McKinley replayed his front-porch campaign of 1896, allowing the energetic forty-one-year-old Roosevelt to campaign for him. The Republican slogan, "Four Years More of the Full Dinner Pail," emphasized the country's newfound prosperity and carried McKinley to an easy victory.

THEODORE ROOSEVELT

26TH PRESIDENT
★
FROM 1901 TO 1909

BORN: October 27, 1858

BIRTHPLACE: New York, N.Y.

DIED: January 6, 1919

PARTY: Republican

VICE PRESIDENT: Charles W. Fairbanks

FIRST LADY: Edith Kermit Carow

CHILDREN: Alice; Theodore, Jr.; Kermit; Ethel; Archibald; Quentin

NICKNAME: TR

The first president to fly in an airplane.

Although he was relatively young when he suddenly became president, Theodore Roosevelt was prepared for his new job, being both well read and well traveled. In his spare time, he read books on every conceivable subject. Sometimes he read as many as three books a night.

Yet Roosevelt was far from a shy, bookish intellectual. He loved strenuous exercise of all kinds, including horseback riding, hiking, swimming, hunting, and boxing. While he was governor of New York, he once wrestled the middleweight champion. As president, he kept in shape by boxing regularly with professional sparring partners. Every so often, he would invite political rivals to climb into the ring with him for a "friendly" round of boxing.

Roosevelt's tough image served him well as president.

ASSASSIN'S BULLET KILLS McKINLEY

Vice President Roosevelt Succeeds Him

BUFFALO, September 14, 1901—President McKinley died shortly after two o'clock this morning, eight days after he was shot by an unemployed millworker. McKinley's death surprised his doctors, who had thought the president was recovering from the bullet wound in his abdomen.

Vice President Roosevelt was sworn in today by U.S. District Court Judge John R. Hazel. At forty-two, he becomes the youngest president ever to take the oath of office. He had been vacationing at Lake Tear-of-the-Clouds in the Adirondack Mountains when a telegram reached him yesterday afternoon with news of McKinley's worsening condition.

Roosevelt traveled all night to reach a small town where he could catch a train for Buffalo. When he arrived at the station, he found another telegram waiting for him. This one told him McKinley had died during the night.

McKinley was shot on September 6 by Leon Czolgosz, who had been waiting in line to shake the president's hand. A bandage over Czolgosz's right hand concealed the revolver he used to shoot McKinley. According to Czolgosz, "I done my duty. I don't believe one man should have so much service and another man should have none."

113

One of his first policy moves was also his most controversial. Soon after he took office, Roosevelt introduced "trust-busting."

TRUST-BUSTING Trusts are companies that work together to limit competition in an industry, such as the tobacco or steel industry. The most famous trust in U.S. history was the Standard Oil trust run by John D. Rockefeller. The point of Rockefeller's trust was to fix oil prices. Rockefeller knew that if he controlled the major oil companies, he could set whatever price he wanted.

Political leaders who favored the interests of working people over those of big business were commonly called "progressives." They opposed trusts because of the unfair practices trusts used to drive small companies out of business. Progressives thought that breaking up the trusts would result in more competition and better prices for consumers.

In his first speech to Congress, Roosevelt agreed that the most ruthless trusts needed to be reformed. But there was a lot of political opposition, even within the president's own party.

THE NORTHERN SECURITIES CASE On March 10, 1902, Roosevelt brought suit under the Sherman Anti-Trust Act against a railroad trust called the Northern Securities Company. Although his action shocked Wall Street, the antitrust suit was extremely popular with the public.

It helped Roosevelt that he understood Wall Street businessmen. He was practically one of them. His father was a wealthy merchant who served on many corporate boards of directors. As a result, Roosevelt knew most of the important business leaders in the United States.

The Early Years

TEDDY ROOSEVELT WAS A SICKLY CHILD. DURING MUCH OF his boyhood, he suffered from asthma, which prevented him from attending school. He often had to sleep sitting up in a chair or his coughing would keep him awake all night.

Many years later, in 1884, after the death of his first wife, Alice Lee, Teddy moved out west to work as a rancher in the Dakota Territory. The two years Roosevelt spent in Dakota changed his life. He left a thin, spindly man but returned with his famous barrel chest and thick neck. He married his second wife, Edith Carow, shortly after his return.

Roosevelt later said that he never would have become president if it weren't for his years in the Dakota Territory. Out west, where Roosevelt's wealth and connections meant little, he mixed with cowboys, gunslingers, drunks, and gamblers.

During the Spanish-American War in 1898, Roosevelt served as commander of a volunteer cavalry unit known as the Rough Riders. On July 1, he led a charge up San Juan Hill in Cuba. Press reports made him a national hero and helped him win election as governor of New York that same year.

★**THE WRIGHT BROTHERS** Orville and Wilbur Wright operated a bicycle shop in Dayton, Ohio. They first began thinking about flying machines after reading newspaper articles about German experiments with gliders. They built their first glider in 1900.

The Wright Brothers' experiments with gliders taught them about flying machines. To build a powered airplane, the Wrights would need to develop a strong propeller and a lightweight engine, neither of which existed.

They called their first powered glider *Flyer I*. Orville made the first test flight on December 17, 1903, at Kitty Hawk, North Carolina. In the first sustained flight ever, *Flyer I* stayed aloft for twelve seconds, traveling 120 feet.

★ **HARRY HOUDINI** Harry Houdini was the most famous escape artist of all time. Beginning in the early 1900s, he made an international reputation for himself as a magician. But he was most famous for his death-defying escapes. He would often be handcuffed, bound with ropes and chains, and placed inside a locked container, such as a trunk. Sometimes the container was even submerged in water. If Houdini didn't escape quickly, he would drown.

★ **THE PANAMA CANAL** Both navigators and statesmen had long dreamed of a canal connecting the Atlantic and Pacific oceans. Without a canal, ships traveling from New York to San Francisco had to sail all the way around Cape Horn at the southern tip of South America. A canal across Central America would save seven thousand miles.

Construction of the canal began in 1904, but the work was delayed by tropical disease epidemics. A new plan by Chief Engineer John F. Stevens sped up construction. But the greatest contribution was made by Colonel William C. Gorgas, the sanitary officer. It was his work in eliminating yellow fever and malaria that made the project possible. The fifty-mile-long canal opened to shipping on August 15, 1914.

DRAWING THE LINE IN MISSISSIPPI

★ **THE TEDDY BEAR** In 1902, Roosevelt went on a bear hunt in Mississippi, but the only one he found was a small black cub caught by the hunting dogs. TR refused to shoot the cub.

After hearing the story, Clifford Berryman drew a cartoon of the incident for the *Washington Post*. Two days later, Brooklyn toy maker Morris Michtom placed a copy of that cartoon in his window next to a stuffed brown bear, which he called "Teddy's Bear." The name, which stuck, was later shortened to "teddy bear."

Although Roosevelt's approach was pioneering, it also had its moderate aspects. The president didn't want to bust all the trusts, only the worst offenders. He believed that taking no action might lead Congress to take even more radical measures later on. Roosevelt called his middle path the Square Deal.

Two years passed before the Northern Securities case reached the Supreme Court, where it would finally be decided. No one really knew how the justices would rule. In earlier cases involving the Sherman Anti-Trust Act, they had ruled in favor of big business. When the ruling in the Northern Securities case came down, however, it was five to four against the trust.

The court's decision was an important victory for Roosevelt's antitrust policy. The vote was particularly close because one of the president's own appointees to the court—Justice Oliver Wendell Holmes, Jr.—voted against him. Upon hearing the news of Holmes's dissent, Roosevelt exclaimed, "I could carve a better judge out of a banana."

THE PENNSYLVANIA COAL STRIKE The most serious domestic crisis of Roosevelt's first term came in May 1902, several months after the Justice Department first filed the Northern Securities case. At that time, coal miners in Pennsylvania went on strike for better wages and safer working conditions.

During the last quarter of the nineteenth century, U.S. presidents generally sided with business owners against striking workers. But Roosevelt was a different sort of president. He sensed that times had changed and that people thought things should be different. One of his first moves was to send in federal troops. Roosevelt said the troops were being sent to protect the mine owners' property. But the soldiers were really there to protect the striking miners as well. Business owners typically ended strikes by hiring toughs to beat up striking workers. The presence of federal troops prevented that.

Next, Roosevelt invited both sides to Washington, where he helped management and labor resolve their differences peacefully. Because the strikers won many of their demands, Roosevelt's popularity soared. With his antitrust policy and now his active intervention in the Pennsylvania coal strike, Roosevelt made it clear that his administration would protect the public interest against the greed of big business.

BIG STICK DIPLOMACY On the international stage, President Roosevelt also benefited from his tough-guy image. His motto was "Speak softly and carry a big stick." As a result, his foreign policy was called Big Stick Diplomacy. The most noteworthy example of Roosevelt's approach to foreign affairs involved the **Monroe Doctrine.**

In 1823, President James Monroe had warned European nations against further colonization of the American continents. In 1904, Roosevelt added to the Monroe Doctrine what became known as the Roosevelt Corollary. (A corollary is a statement that logically follows from a previous statement.)

At the time, the government of the Dominican Republic was deeply in debt to several European nations. France and Italy, in particular, were threatening to take over the country if the debt wasn't promptly repaid.

In a speech to Congress, Roosevelt repeated the principle of the Monroe Doctrine: The United States would not tolerate any European intervention in the Americas.

However, with the Roosevelt Corollary, he went further. The

BY 1904, WHEN THE NEXT ELECTION CAME around, Teddy Roosevelt was really enjoying himself as president. The public was fascinated by his constant activity and energy, his fun-loving family, and his boundless idealism. But Roosevelt still had to convince the Republican party that he was the man to nominate.

After all, McKinley had been the nominee in 1900, and Roosevelt had become president only as

the result of McKinley's assassination.

The older Republican leaders didn't like Teddy, whom they considered a young upstart. These men would have preferred to nominate Mark Hanna, the political boss and senator from Ohio who had helped McKinley rise to the presidency. When Hanna died in February, however, the nomination went to Roosevelt.

Traditionally, the Republicans favored big business, while the Democrats supported progressive candidates who advocated reform. Because Roosevelt was himself a progressive, the Democrats weren't sure what to do. In the end, they nominated a conservative candidate, Judge Alton Parker of New York, hoping to capture Republican votes.

The result was one of the greatest landslides in U.S. history. Roosevelt had expected to win, but not by such an overwhelming margin. "My dear," he told his second wife, Edith, "I am no longer a political accident."

president reserved for the United States the right to intervene in the affairs of any Latin American country that proved incapable of governing itself.

The Roosevelt Corollary was highly controversial. Critics argued that it would lead to U.S. imperialism of the kind that the Europeans practiced in Africa and Asia. In this way, the countries of Latin America would become colonies of the United States.

The president's supporters argued that the Roosevelt Corollary was simply common sense. The world was a dangerous place, and there was no nation better suited than the United States to police Latin America.

Whatever people thought, it was clear that Roosevelt was establishing U.S. leadership in the world as no president had before.

THE PANAMA CANAL

One of the memorable achievements of Roosevelt's first term was the Panama Canal. The president was eager to begin work on the canal before his 1904 reelection campaign. The problem was that the canal zone belonged to the nation of Colombia, which did not want to sell.

When revolution broke out in Panama in November 1903, Roosevelt supported the rebels. Once the Panamanians won their independence from Colombia, Roosevelt simply bought the canal territory from them on the same terms the Colombians had refused.

SINCLAIR'S JUNGLE EXPOSES THE MEAT INDUSTRY

Novel Leads to Passage of New Food Laws

Upton Sinclair's novel *The Jungle* was published in January 1906. In telling the story of Jurgis Rudkus, a fictional Lithuanian immigrant working in a meat packing factory, Sinclair exposed the corrupt and dangerous practices of the meat industry in the United States, and especially in Chicago.

Throughout this period, a number of crusading journalists were busy investigating corruption in U.S. industry. But it was Sinclair's novel that turned public concern into outrage. Publication of *The Jungle* led President Roosevelt to call immediately for federal regulation of food and drugs.

Two bills were quickly passed by Congress and signed by the president in June 1906. The Meat Inspection Act provided for federal inspection of meat so that consumers could be sure that the meat they bought met certain standards of freshness. Canned meats had to be accurately labeled and dated.

The second bill, the Pure Food and Drug Act, established national standards to prevent businesses from adding harmful preservatives and other hazardous ingredients to food and drugs. Never before had the federal government regulated private business so much.

A sausage factory

Roosevelt's landslide victory in the 1904 election gave him the support he needed to pursue his progressive policies. He went to work in a whirlwind of activity. A foreign crisis, however, soon captured his attention.

THE RUSSO-JAPANESE WAR

The Russo-Japanese War began on February 8, 1904, when the Japanese launched a surprise attack on the Russian troops stationed at Port Arthur in Manchuria, which had traditionally been part of China. The Russians had recently broken a promise to withdraw from Port Arthur.

For months President Roosevelt worked behind the scenes to stop the fighting. He proposed a number of cease-fire plans, but Russia and Japan could not agree on a formula for peace. Finally, on June 11, 1905, Roosevelt negotiated a breakthrough. The two warring nations announced that they would accept the U.S. president's latest plan for peace.

Formal talks began on August 9 in Portsmouth, New Hampshire. On August 29, Russian and Japanese diplomats agreed to a treaty ending the war. Roosevelt was overjoyed, having used all his skill and influence to achieve the peace.

Russia and Japan gave Roosevelt ample credit for the Treaty of Portsmouth, and Britain, France, and Germany joined in the applause for the president's accomplishment.

In 1906, Roosevelt became the first American to win a Nobel prize when he won the Nobel Peace Prize. The Nobel prizes are awarded annually in Sweden in such areas as science, medicine, and literature.

Until Roosevelt's time, it was highly unusual for a U.S. president to be so active in world affairs. During the nineteenth century, presidents tried to stay out of European and Asian disputes as much as possible.

★**THE FIRST FAMILY** Journalists who covered TR said that life in the White House often resembled a circus. The president's two youngest sons, Archie and Quentin, caused most of the uproar. One of their favorite games was sliding down the

central staircase on metal trays. Once Quentin rode his pony Algonquin upstairs into Archie's bedroom to cheer up his brother, who was sick.

TR's oldest child, his daughter Alice, was called Princess Alice by the press. Like the rest of her family, she loved to shock people. She would smoke in public, which was considered very bad manners for a woman. She also defied the standards set for women of the day by going to racetracks and betting on horses. She would even show off her pet snake on occasion. Alice was very popular, however, and her name became a favorite one for babies.

★**THE GREAT CONSERVATIONIST** Teddy Roosevelt had an especially strong love of nature. As a boy, he wanted to become a zoologist. He would later fill his Sagamore Hill home on New York's Long Island with trophies from his various hunting trips and safaris.

TR's love of nature drove him to be particularly active in the field of environmental conservation. In this work, he joined conservationists such as John Muir in California who argued that the United States must preserve its wilderness.

The country's first national park, Yellowstone in Wyoming, was established in 1872. Eighteen years later, Muir convinced the federal government to create the Yosemite and Sequoia parks in California. Roosevelt used his influence to preserve almost two hundred million acres of government land, mostly in the Northwest and Alaska.

★ *HOW THE OTHER HALF LIVES*   In the 1880s, Jacob Riis began using a camera to document the terrible living conditions of poor immigrants to this country. As a police reporter in New York City, he had plenty of opportunity to see how these people lived in urban tenement apartments. An immigrant himself, Riis crusaded for better conditions for the hundreds of thousands of people who sought a better life in the United States. In 1890, he published his photos in *How the Other Half Lives.* This book awakened public opinion and did much to fuel the progressive reforms of the Roosevelt, Taft, and Wilson administrations.

★ MUCKRAKERS   "Muckraker" was the name given to reform-minded journalists who wrote about corruption in big business. Important muckrakers included Upton Sinclair, Lincoln Steffens, and Ida Tarbell. Their articles rallied public support for progressive causes, especially government reform. Ida Tarbell's work helped bring down the Standard Oil trust.

The word "muckraker" was coined by Roosevelt, who borrowed it from *The Pilgrim's Progress* by English writer John Bunyan. Bunyan wrote about "the Man with the Muckrake. . . who could look no way but downward."

Roosevelt meant the name to be critical. He thought muckrakers focused too much on what was wrong with modern life and ignored what was good about it. The name quickly took on a positive meaning, however, because of the useful work the muckrakers were doing.

★ THE MODEL T FORD   In October 1908, Henry Ford introduced the Model T. "I will build a car for the great multitude," he said. The first Model Ts sold for $850, a fortune at the time. But Ford kept his promise. The development of assembly-line manufacturing made production more efficient, and the price of the Model T fell dramatically.

By 1927, when the car was discontinued, the price had dropped to three hundred dollars, making it widely affordable. In the meantime, Ford had sold more than fifteen million of these cars. Half the cars in the world were Model Ts.

They followed George Washington's advice to remain neutral. But as the twentieth century began, the United States was becoming a world power.

During his second term, Roosevelt became increasingly worried about the possibility of a war in Europe. Powerful European nations such as Britain and Germany were already fighting each other indirectly in colonial wars in Africa. Roosevelt feared that these conflicts might work their way back to Europe and affect the United States. For this reason, he intervened in world affairs once again.

Despite protests from Congress, Roosevelt sent U.S. representatives to a 1906 meeting held in Algeciras, Spain. The Algeciras Conference helped prevent war among Great Britain, France, and Germany over Morocco. Roosevelt's participation in the talks pointed to the end of traditional U.S. neutrality.

TAMING THE RAILROADS   Although he paid more attention to foreign policy than any president before him, Roosevelt's interest in domestic policy remained his most passionate. Roosevelt championed his progressive policies using the Square Deal slogan.

The year 1906 was particularly successful for Roosevelt. On May 18, after a long and difficult debate, the Senate passed the Hepburn Act. This law gave the president the power to regulate the prices charged by railroads on routes that passed through more than one state. It was a landmark in government efforts to control interstate business.

Progressives had long argued that the railroads, which were run by the wealthiest people in the country, charged an unfair price to move goods from one state to another. The Hepburn Act allowed Roosevelt to use the Interstate Commerce

Commission to adjust railroad shipping charges to help consumers.

AN INDUSTRIAL NATION

The United States had changed tremendously since the Civil War. Factories, not farms, now dominated the nation's economy. More and more Americans moved to the cities of the Northeast and the Great Lakes to find work in the factories there. Immigrants joined them by the millions.

Working conditions in the factories were often terrible. Adults and children worked ten- and twelve-hour days for very low wages. Meanwhile, the rich business owners got richer. There was no income tax, and other taxes were extremely low.

Dirty smoke from these factories polluted many of the cities, and overcrowding made the quality of life in them even worse. Increasingly, people thought the federal government should do something about these problems.

Theodore Roosevelt was the first national leader to adopt progressive solutions to these problems. Conservatives believed in laissez-faire economics. This French phrase refers to a hands-off approach to the economy. Progressives such as Roosevelt believed that government had the right and duty to intervene in business affairs on behalf of the public.

THE PANIC OF 1907

The Panic of 1907 began when a New York bank, the Knickerbocker Trust Company, failed in October. Knickerbocker's collapse brought down a dozen more banks and even a few railroads. Roosevelt's critics blamed his prolabor policies for cutting corporate profits. The president blamed bad business practices. A recovery began the following spring of 1908.

TEDDY ROOSEVELT MADE A BIG MISTAKE IN 1904. During that campaign, he announced that "under no circumstances" would he run for president again in 1908. This was a mistake, because now that his second term was up, he wanted to stay.

Roosevelt was only forty-nine years old. He remained full of energy and ambition. But he felt bound to keep his word. So he prepared to leave.

Roosevelt's popularity was so great that he was able to choose his successor. He picked William Howard Taft, who had served in TR's cabinet as the secretary of war.

Roosevelt's strong support ensured that Taft won the nomination of the Republican party. Meanwhile,

the Democrats chose William Jennings Bryan as their candidate. The defeat in 1904 of a conservative candidate, Judge Alton Parker, had convinced the Democratic party to return to its populist wing.

Bryan had run for the presidency twice before—in 1896 and 1900. The issues that he championed then and now—women's suffrage, prohibition of liquor, and the income tax—would eventually become law.

During the 1908 campaign, Bryan argued that Roosevelt's progressive policies should be extended further. He also promised to end government corruption and unfair business practices that existed despite Roosevelt's reforms. Bryan was a gifted public speaker, but Taft was nevertheless able to ride Roosevelt's popularity to victory.

WILLIAM HOWARD TAFT

27TH PRESIDENT
★
FROM 1909 TO 1913

BORN: September 15, 1857

BIRTHPLACE: Cincinnati, Ohio

DIED: March 8, 1930

PARTY: Republican

VICE PRESIDENT: James S. Sherman

FIRST LADY: Helen Herron

CHILDREN: Robert, Helen, Charles

NICKNAME: Big Bill

The first president to serve on the Supreme Court.

TITANIC STRIKES ICEBERG
1,513 Die as Luxury Liner Sinks

OFF NEWFOUNDLAND, April 15, 1912—The British luxury liner *Titanic* hit an iceberg shortly before midnight last night. Less than three hours later, the enormous ship sank into the icy waters of the North Atlantic. More than fifteen hundred lives were lost. The *Titanic* was on its maiden, or first, voyage from England to New York City.

Another passenger liner, the *Californian*, was less than twenty miles away from the sinking *Titanic*. But its radio operator was off duty, so no one aboard heard the *Titanic*'s calls for help. Not until ninety minutes after the *Titanic* went down did another ship, the *Carpathia*, arrive to help in the rescue.

The disaster has been particularly shocking to people because the ship's owners had bragged that the *Titanic*, the largest and most elegant ship in the world, was unsinkable.

Heroes of this ill-fated maiden voyage include Isidor and Ida Straus, who gave up their spaces on a lifeboat so that younger passengers might live.

It is certain that the sinking of the *Titanic* will lead to the passage of new safety regulations for passenger ships. The *Titanic*'s lifeboats were able to hold only 1,178 of the 2,224 people aboard.

People voted for Taft in the 1908 election because they believed he would continue the policies of Theodore Roosevelt, who had stepped aside after his first full term. Progressives expected Taft to enforce the antitrust laws and to make sure that the country's natural resources were protected from big business. They also wanted him to protect working men, women, and children in dangerous factory jobs.

Early in Taft's administration, however, progressive support for the new president began to weaken. Part of the problem was that Roosevelt was a difficult man to follow. Taft couldn't be another TR. Yet if he did something differently, he was criticized.

For instance, President Taft began his term by appointing new cabinet officers. Of course, this meant that many members of Roosevelt's cabinet were not reappointed. Newspaper editorials interpreted Taft's move as an abandonment of Roosevelt's policies. Unsympathetic headlines shouted that Taft was appointing corporate lawyers who would defend the interests of big business. Taft was by nature more conservative than Roosevelt, but the criticism was still unfair. Although not many people noticed, more of Roosevelt's programs became law during the Taft administration than during Roosevelt's.

For example, Taft's record on conservation was generally as good as Roosevelt's. In some ways, it was better. Taft was the first president to protect federal lands on which oil had been found. He also protected land that contained coal, which was even more widely used at the time than oil. Both of these decisions went against the interests of big business, which wanted to exploit these lands for their energy resources.

Taft's trust-busting record was also impressive. During the four years of Taft's presidency, there were twice as many prosecutions under the Sherman Anti-Trust Act as there had been during the seven years that Roosevelt was president.

THE STANDARD OIL CASE

The most famous antitrust case during the Taft years involved the Standard Oil Company. Roosevelt had ordered that Standard Oil be investigated for its monopoly of the oil business. But the case didn't reach the Supreme Court until Taft had become president. In May 1911, the Court found that John D. Rockefeller's Standard Oil trust violated the Sherman Anti-Trust Act. The Court ordered that the trust be broken up because it unfairly restricted the oil trade.

Also on Taft's watch, Congress passed the Sixteenth and Seventeenth

The Early Years

A S A BOY IN OHIO, TAFT LOVED TO PLAY BASEBALL. He was a good second baseman and could hit with power, but his extra weight made him a poor base runner. It helped him, however, when he would referee fights between his brothers.

After graduating from Yale University and the University of Cincinnati law school, Taft used his father's political connections to get a job as an assistant county prosecutor. He became a state judge in 1887. In 1892, he was promoted to the federal Circuit Court of Appeals.

In 1900, President McKinley appointed Taft commissioner of the Philippines, which the United States had just won from Spain in the Spanish-American War. It was Taft's job to establish a new government there.

★**THE AGE OF THE SKYSCRAPER** As the twentieth century began, so did the age of the skyscraper. The first skyscraper in the United States was the ten-story Home Insurance Company Building in Chicago, which was built in 1885.

Skyscrapers were inspiring feats of engineering, but they were also necessary. As more and more people moved to the cities, the need for space forced people to build up rather than out. There simply wasn't enough land left to build horizontally.

The new vertical architecture was made possible by two important developments. One was the introduction of safe passenger elevators. The other was the use of steel girders in construction. Because steel is both lighter and stronger than iron, it could support taller buildings. Most of the early skyscrapers were built in New York and Chicago.

★ **PRESIDENTIAL FIRSTS** During President Taft's years in office, there were an unusual number of presidential firsts. Taft bought the first cars for the White House. To house them, he had the stables converted into a garage. Taft also began the presidential tradition of throwing out the first ball on the opening day of the baseball season.

Taft was the heaviest president in U.S. history, weighing 332 pounds at his inauguration. He was so large that he once got stuck in the White House bathtub. A bathtub large enough to hold four men was installed as a replacement.

★ **MODERN DANCE** Before Isadora Duncan, classical ballet was the only dance people thought of as art. As a child, however, Isadora had refused ballet lessons. Instead, she insisted on dancing more naturally, according to her own sense of movement and rhythm.

Duncan's innovative style failed in the United States, so she moved to Europe at the age of twenty-one. Since she had very little money, she sailed to England on a cattle boat. Soon, however, she became a sensation. She scandalized Europe and filled concert halls, dancing barefoot while dressed as a woodland nymph out of Greek mythology.

★ **HULL HOUSE** Jane Addams was one of the most well-known social reformers of her time. She became famous for her work at Hull House, which she founded in Chicago in 1889. Hull House was the first settlement house in the United States. Its purpose was to help immigrants "settle" successfully.

Hull House tried to bridge the gap between the rich and the poor by establishing a day nursery, a boardinghouse for working girls, and an employment service. Classes in cooking and sewing were also offered.

Addams played an important role in the 1912 election, during which she supported Theodore Roosevelt and his Bull Moose (Progressive) party.

amendments, both of which were ratified in 1913. The Sixteenth Amendment made the income tax constitutional, and the Seventeenth Amendment provided for the direct election of senators. Previously, senators had been elected by state legislatures instead of by the people.

DOLLAR DIPLOMACY Taft's foreign policy was called Dollar Diplomacy because he used financial as well as military might to promote U.S. business interests overseas. Taft's particular focus was Latin America.

He encouraged U.S. bankers, for example, to invest in Honduras and Haiti. In 1912, he sent marines to Nicaragua to crush a rebellion there against a government friendly to U.S. business.

If Taft had so many important achievements in office, why was he so widely criticized? One problem was that President Taft always seemed to be doing the same thing—playing golf. Often, his golf partners were important business leaders.

Newspapers complained that the president shouldn't be playing a rich man's sport with people who had made unfair profits at the public's expense. Whether this was true or not didn't matter. People believed it.

But the more important reason was that Taft was always being compared to Roosevelt, whose explosive presence still captivated the nation. Taft's temperament was the opposite. His huge size and slow manner led many people to believe that he was not in charge of his own government.

ROOSEVELT IN AFRICA At the beginning of Taft's presidency, Roosevelt went on a widely publicized safari to Africa. TR said that he wanted to hunt wild game animals. But he really wanted to give Taft a chance to make his own mark on government.

Even in Africa, however, Roosevelt dominated the headlines. Stories reported that TR had been attacked by wild hippos, by a rhinoceros, and by an angry bull elephant. Each time, the articles told how the former president calmly rescued his safari group by bravely shooting the animals in question.

During his year-long trip, Roosevelt shot three hundred animals, including eighteen rhinos, eight elephants, nine lions, seven hippos, and six buffalo. Many of these animals were eventually stuffed and sent to the Smithsonian Institution.

TAFT'S PUBLIC IMAGE Taft couldn't compete. Next to fascinating stories about Teddy's exploits, newspapers wrote that Taft's favorite sport was eating. For his first Thanksgiving as president, Taft received a huge Rhode Island turkey, a fifty-pound mincemeat pie from New York, and a twenty-six-pound opossum from Georgia, said to be the largest ever shot in that state. This type of publicity didn't help matters.

In 1910, Roosevelt suggested that his support of Taft might have been a mistake. This remark unleashed a storm of newspaper stories, and it deeply hurt Taft, who had considered Roosevelt a close friend and mentor. Their friendship soon became strained. Taft later said that the loss of his friendship with Roosevelt was one of the most painful events of his presidency.

For his part, Roosevelt felt that Taft had abandoned the progressives. TR had been angry when Taft dismissed some of his cabinet officers (after privately promising to keep them), but he was even more upset when Taft chose to support conservative leaders in the Republican party.

THE 1912 ELECTION WAS A MESS. THE TROUBLE BEGAN when Theodore Roosevelt decided that choosing Taft as his successor had been a mistake. To correct this error, TR decided to run again for the White House.

President Taft, of course, had no plans to step aside, so both men went after the Republican nomination. Roosevelt was the more popular among voters, but Taft was closer to the leaders who controlled the party. As a result, Taft won the nomination.

Bitterly disappointed, Roosevelt decided to start his own party. It was formally named the Progressive party, but most people called it the Bull Moose party. This nickname came from TR's often-quoted claim that he was "strong as a bull moose."

The third man in the race was the Democratic nominee, Woodrow Wilson, who was not a particularly strong candidate. It took the Democrats forty-six ballots to nominate him. But he benefited from the fact that Roosevelt and Taft split the Republican vote.

The biggest issue of the 1912 campaign was government reform. As a result, the incumbent President Taft soon fell behind. Roosevelt became particularly radical in his calls for change. He spoke often about his Square Deal. Wilson called his program the New Freedom.

The election was close, but Wilson won because of the votes that Taft took away from Roosevelt. The big loser was President Taft, who finished a distant,

humiliating third. Wilson became only the second Democrat to be elected president since the Civil War. A decade later, President Harding appointed Taft chief justice of the Supreme Court.

WOODROW WILSON

28TH PRESIDENT
★
FROM 1913 TO 1921

BORN: December 29, 1856

BIRTHPLACE: Staunton, Va.

DIED: February 3, 1924

PARTY: Democrat

VICE PRESIDENT: Thomas R. Marshall

FIRST LADIES: Ellen Louise Axson, Edith Bolling Galt

CHILDREN: Margaret, Jessie, Eleanor

NICKNAME: Professor

The first president to hold a press conference.

Woodrow Wilson set the tone for his presidency in his first inaugural address. In that speech, Wilson outlined the issues facing the nation. He did so in terms of what was right and what was wrong. As the son of a Presbyterian minister, Wilson tended to view the job of chief executive as a moral responsibility.

Wilson began his term as president with tremendous energy, and the first two years of his administration were extremely productive. During that time, Congress passed some of the most progressive laws of the era. Wilson's first great accomplishment was the Underwood Tariff.

During the 1912 campaign, Wilson had promised to lower tariffs. With Wilson's encouragement, Congress passed the Underwood Tariff in 1913.

WORLD WAR I IN EUROPE

U.S. Stays Out of the Fighting

WHEN WORLD WAR I BROKE out in August 1914, many Americans took sides. Because of their close ties to Britain and France, most southerners and easterners supported the Allies. The children of German immigrants in the Midwest backed the Central Powers.

Despite these allegiances, almost everyone agreed that the United States should stay out of the fighting. It made little sense to become involved in a war an ocean away that seemed to mean so little to American life.

This policy of neutrality became harder to keep, however, when German submarines, called U-boats for short, began torpedoing U.S. ships bound for England.

Public opinion turned strongly against the Germans in 1915 after a U-boat sank the British liner *Lusitania.* Nearly twelve hundred passengers drowned, including 128 Americans. The Germans pointed out, however, that the *Lusitania* was carrying tons of rifle ammunition. So its voyage was not entirely innocent.

It cut the average tariff from forty-one to twenty-seven percent, the lowest rate since the Civil War.

THE FIRST INCOME TAX

To make up the shortfall in government revenue, the new tariff law established the first national income tax. The income tax had recently been made possible by the ratification of the Sixteenth Amendment, which changed the Constitution to make the income tax legal.

Despite the Sixteenth Amendment, the income tax was still a very controversial issue. Business groups fought against it, and many Americans resented paying the tax. The Underwood Tariff established a tax of one percent on all personal incomes above three thousand dollars a year. People making above twenty thousand dollars a year paid an additional amount as high as six percent.

Another of Wilson's achievements was the Federal Reserve Act, which reorganized a U.S. banking system badly in need of reform. The financial crisis known as the Panic of 1907 had caused many people to lose confidence in the country's banks.

The fight over the nation's banking system had been going on since the days of Alexander Hamilton and Thomas Jefferson, who fought over the First Bank of the United States. Forty years later, Andrew Jackson and Nicholas Biddle clashed over the Second Bank.

THE FEDERAL RESERVE ACT

Now, almost eighty years after that, the new Federal Reserve Act set up a network of twelve regional banks. Each reported to a board of governors appointed by the president. It was the job of the "Fed" to control the money supply, which is the amount of money available for

The Early Years

WOODROW WILSON'S EARLIEST MEMORY WAS AS A four-year-old boy living in Georgia. He remembered a man telling him that Lincoln had won the presidency, so there would be war between the states.

As a white child living in the South, Wilson experienced Reconstruction as a period of great injustice. Although he later pursued academic and political careers in the North, Wilson always considered himself a southerner. He believed that the South had been justified in seceding from the Union, and he also believed in the supremacy of the white race.

★THE FIRST LADIES A year and a half into his first term, Wilson's wife Ellen died. The president was so upset that he told an aide he hoped he would be assassinated. Ellen Wilson had been an active first lady, at one time lobbying Congress to pay for slum clearance in the District of Columbia.

About a year after Ellen died, the president became quietly engaged to a widow, Mrs. Edith Bolling Galt. When news of their engagement leaked three months later, people criticized Wilson for marrying so soon after the death of his first wife. Because of the bad publicity, Wilson offered to end the engagement, but Mrs. Galt said she would stand by him.

★MARGARET SANGER While working as a nurse in one of Manhattan's poor immigrant neighborhoods, Margaret Sanger saw firsthand how having too many babies kept poor families poor. The lesson was a simple one: The more children women had, the more mouths there were to feed.

Having seen the consequences for herself, Sanger devoted her life to publicizing information about birth control, even though her actions were illegal at the time. The Comstock Act of 1873 had banned pamphlets about birth control, declaring them to be obscene. But Sanger ignored this restriction because she believed strongly in the right of every woman to plan the size of her family.

★**JACK JOHNSON** Jack Johnson became the first black man to win the world heavyweight boxing championship when he knocked out Tommy Burns in Sydney, Australia, on December 26, 1908. While Johnson was champion, many white boxing fans cried out for a "great white hope" to defeat the confident, arrogant boxer. They didn't believe that a black man should be champion. Johnson further outraged white America by twice marrying white women.

In his most famous fight—on July 4, 1910— Johnson beat thirty-five-year-old Jim Jeffries, a white former champion, who had been convinced to come out of retirement to put Johnson "in his place." Johnson knocked out Jeffries in fifteen rounds.

★**THE ARMORY SHOW** Modern art developed in Europe around the turn of the century. As late as World War I, however, this new style of painting was almost unknown in the United States. Among the most influential modern artists were two Frenchmen, Paul Cézanne and Henri Matisse, and Pablo Picasso, a Spaniard living in France.

Modern art was first introduced to the United States in 1913 at an exhibition held at the Sixty-ninth Regiment Armory in New York City. The exhibition's most important works were in the modern style of cubism. Cubist painters treated people and objects as though they were geometric shapes. President Herbert Hoover's favorite cartoon of himself was one done in the cubist style.

investment. During boom times, the Fed was supposed to raise interest rates, so people wouldn't borrow and spend too much money. During recessions, the Fed would lower them, so people could get the credit they needed more easily.

Wilson's early success in convincing Congress to enact his programs proved that he was a capable administrator. Very soon, however, he would also have to prove himself as a leader during two international crises. The first involved U.S. relations with Mexico.

THE MEXICAN REVOLUTION The announcement of the Roosevelt Corollary to the Monroe Doctrine had strained relations between the United States and Latin America. Countries in Central and South America resented Roosevelt's claim that the United States could intervene in their affairs whenever the U.S. government thought Latin Americans were not governing themselves properly.

When the Mexican Revolution broke out in 1911, officials in the Taft administration became worried that the fighting might spill over into Texas and the Southwest. In 1913, Mexican general Victoriano Huerta came to power and established a dictatorship. Wilson refused to recognize Huerta's government and instead continued his policy of "watchful waiting."

Despite the public pressure for an invasion of Mexico, Wilson resisted. In an important speech in Mobile, Alabama, the president announced the Mobile Doctrine, which stated that the United States would never again acquire territory by conquest.

Six months later, in April 1914, U.S. sailors in the port of Tampico, Mexico, were arrested for no reason. Although they were quickly released,

Wilson demanded a twenty-one-gun salute to the American flag as an apology. When Huerta refused, Wilson had U.S. marines occupy the Mexican city of Veracruz. Huerta resigned in July.

The man who replaced Huerta, Venustiano Carranza, didn't fare much better. The revolutionary Pancho Villa rose up against him and took control of northern Mexico. In March 1916, the worst U.S. fears came true when Villa crossed the border and attacked Columbus, New Mexico. He set fire to the town and killed seventeen people. In response, President Wilson sent General John J. Pershing, known as Black Jack, to capture Villa and his men. Crossing the border himself, Pershing followed Villa three hundred miles into Mexico, but the wily Villa managed to escape him. The chase continued until February 1917, when Wilson ordered U.S. soldiers out of Mexico. By that time, the United States was about to enter a much greater fight, the first world war.

U.S. NEUTRALITY

Wilson had dedicated much of his first term to preventing U.S. involvement in World War I. He shared the public opinion that favored neutrality and did whatever he could to keep the country out of the war. Germany often made this difficult, however.

On February 4, 1915, the German government announced that it considered the waters around Great Britain to be a war zone. Therefore, all ships found in British waters—including neutral U.S. ships—would be subject to U-boat attack.

Wilson responded immediately to this violation of U.S. neutrality. He warned the Germans that continued attacks would force the United States to take military action. Wilson's threats helped convince Germany's

WILSON WON RENOMINATION EASILY AT THE Democratic convention in St. Louis, where the party unveiled its campaign slogan for the fall: "He kept us out of war."

The Democrats believed that World War I and American neutrality would be the biggest issues of the campaign. Their party platform, which listed the party's position on a number of issues, also supported new health and safety standards, a ban on child labor, and the right to vote for women.

The Republican nominee was Justic Charles Evans Hughes of the Supreme Court. The Republicans attacked Wilson for failing to protect American

interests abroad. They believed that the United States should take a much tougher stance with Germany and at the same time build up its military. Hughes supported a ban on child labor, benefits for workers who were disabled on the job, and women's suffrage.

As expected, the war in Europe did dominate the election. Because Theodore Roosevelt advocated U.S. entry into the war, he supported the hawkish Republicans, and other progressives followed his lead.

As the election neared, some newspapers predicted that Hughes would win. For three days after the voting, the result was in doubt. But a late vote count in California gave Wilson a narrow victory there. With that state's thirteen electoral votes, Wilson finished with 277 to Hughes's 254. Had California gone Republican, Charles Evans Hughes would have been president.

military leadership that the U-boat attacks might bring the United States into the war on the side of the Allies. The Germans suspended the U-boat attacks in the fall of 1915.

ENTRY INTO WORLD WAR I The world was a much more interconnected place in the twentieth century than it had ever been before. Even the vast Atlantic Ocean could not insulate the United States from Europe's problems. The country was slowly but surely being dragged into the war.

While Wilson's first term was marked by the enactment of his progressive domestic policies, his second term was consumed by the country's entry into World War I. One of the reasons that most presidential scholars rate Woodrow Wilson so highly is that he proved his leadership abilities both at home and abroad.

Wilson had long believed that a neutral United States could play an important role in ending the war in Europe. In a January 1917 speech before the Senate, he called on both the Allies and the Central Powers to accept "peace without victory." But Wilson's efforts at peacemaking, while respected, were generally ignored.

The United States moved closer to war when Germany announced in January 1917 that it would resume unrestricted submarine warfare in British waters. This meant that U.S. neutrality would no longer be respected at sea. On February 3, Wilson broke off diplomatic relations

WORLD WAR I ON THE HOME FRONT

Baruch, Hoover Lead Mobilization Efforts

The United States entered World War I in the late spring of 1917. But U.S. soldiers weren't ready to fight yet. The country wasn't ready, either.

To help him manage the war effort, President Wilson recruited business leaders, many of whom worked for the token salary of one dollar per year.

Wilson named Wall Street baron Bernard Baruch to head the new War Industries Board. In that position, Baruch directed U.S. heavy industry. Wilson also made mining engineer Herbert Hoover the national food administrator.

Because the war had already been going on for three years, European food supplies were running out. Hoover worked tirelessly to increase food exports to both soldiers and civilians in Europe.

But the patriotism of the war effort had its spiteful side. Propaganda against Germany led to discrimination at home against many German Americans, who were suspected of being spies and traitors.

Food *is* Ammunition— *Don't waste it.*

with Germany. The American public was outraged by submarine warfare, which it regarded as particularly devious and cruel. But the country was still not ready to enter the war.

All that changed on March 1, when the text of the Zimmermann Telegram was made public. This telegram from German foreign minister Arthur Zimmermann to his ambassador in Mexico had been intercepted by British intelligence agents, and a decoded copy was provided to Wilson.

In the telegram, Zimmermann proposed an alliance between Germany and Mexico. In the event that the United States entered the war, Germany offered to help Mexico reconquer its "lost territories" in Texas, New Mexico, and Arizona. After the text of the telegram was released, public opinion turned quickly in favor of war. On April 2, Wilson asked Congress to declare war on Germany. In his speech, he said, "The world must be made safe for democracy."

During much of 1917, Wilson attended to preparations for the war. He ordered General John J. Pershing to muster an American Expeditionary Force for overseas duty. He also looked to the future. He believed that making a lasting peace would be an even greater task than winning the war.

THE FOURTEEN POINTS

On January 8, 1918, Wilson gave a speech outlining the Fourteen Points upon which he thought peace should be based. These included free navigation of the seas, self-determination for colonies, and arms reduction. The last point of the president's plan called for the formation of an ambitious League of Nations, which could avoid catastrophic wars in the future by guaranteeing the rights and

★WHITE HOUSE SHEEP

Edith Wilson was devoted to the war effort. During her husband's second term, she permitted a flock of sheep to graze on the White House lawn. The wool from these sheep was auctioned off to raise money for the Red Cross.

Meanwhile, she spent many nights busy at her sewing machine, which she used to make surgical clothing for Red Cross doctors. She also promoted wartime rationing by observing gasless Sundays, meatless Mondays, and wheatless Tuesdays.

★PROHIBITION

During the nineteenth century, many social reformers objected to the high rate of alcohol consumption among American men. Activists sought to remove the temptation of strong drink by passing "dry" laws prohibiting its manufacture and sale.

Many business leaders favored Prohibition because they thought it would reduce absenteeism at work. Religious groups supported it because they believed drinking was sinful. Progressive groups even argued that poverty, disease, and crime were largely due to alcoholism.

The 1916 election swept a large majority of "dry" candidates into office. As a result, the Eighteenth Amendment was soon passed and ratified by the states. This amendment, combined with the Volstead Act of 1919, began the Prohibition era in America.

★THE GREAT MIGRATION

The movement of southern blacks to northern cities began around 1910. During World War I, nearly half a million blacks left the rural South for urban centers such as New York, Detroit, and Chicago. By 1940, almost two millions blacks had participated in the Great Migration, which changed the racial geography of the nation.

Southern blacks were drawn to the North because of the potential for work there during the wartime and postwar boom. Many of the jobs they found were on assembly lines that had been only recently racially segregated. The need for workers, however, outweighed employer bigotry. "Prejudice vanishes when the almighty dollar is on the wrong side of the balance sheet," one black newspaper in Chicago wrote.

★CHARLIE CHAPLIN

English-born Charlie Chaplin was one of the earliest American movie stars. He began his film career in 1913 making brief film comedies, called "shorts," for Mack Sennett's Keystone Company. Sennett was already famous for his slapstick Keystone Kops shorts.

While making his second film, *Kid Auto Races at Venice,* Chaplin developed his famous "tramp" character—or as Chaplin called him, "the little fellow." Within two years, Chaplin's derby hat, cane, baggy pants, and small mustache became internationally known trademarks.

★WOMEN'S SUFFRAGE

Women finally won the right to vote when the Nineteenth Amendment was ratified in August 1920. Until then, only women in a few western states were permitted to cast ballots. The presidential election of 1920 was the first in which every woman who was a U.S. citizen could vote.

Women first began organizing for the right to vote during the 1840s. Although the women's suffrage movement gained momentum after the Civil War, its ultimate success can be traced to three contemporary factors: the contributions of American women during World War I,

the support of President Wilson, and the confrontational tactics of Alice Paul and others. These "suffragettes" marched and picketed to demand the vote. Sometimes they were arrested and jailed.

independence of all the world's nations.

In the spring of 1918, before the bulk of the U.S. troops arrived in Europe, the Germans launched a huge, desperate offensive. The attack failed, and by September 1918, there were more than one million Americans in France and Belgium. During the night of October 3-4, the German government sent a note to Wilson asking for a truce and peace negotiations based on the Fourteen Points.

THE PARIS PEACE TALKS

Wilson's goal for years had been to promote world peace based on democratic principles. The peace talks in Paris gave him an opportunity that he couldn't pass up. Not surprisingly, but perhaps not wisely, he decided to lead the U.S. delegation to the peace talks personally.

The president was greeted enthusiastically as he toured England, France, and Italy. He was considered a hero because of his role in ending the war. In 1919, he won the Nobel Peace Prize, becoming the second U.S. president to do so. (Theodore Roosevelt had won the award in 1906 for his work in ending the Russo-Japanese War.)

Wilson stayed in Europe for more than six months while he helped negotiate the Treaty of Versailles. During his long absence, his health began to fail him. He also began to lose control of the U.S. government. When he finally returned to the United States in 1919 with his precious treaty, the Senate was far from ready to ratify it.

From Wilson's point of view, the most important section of the Treaty of Versailles was the one that established the League of Nations. But his opponents in the Senate wanted to eliminate the League of Nations from the treaty because they believed the United States should stay out of international affairs. These senators were known as "isolationists."

Republican senator Henry Cabot Lodge led a determined fight against the treaty. But Wilson was a stubborn man. Even with his health in question and his patience exhausted, he refused to compromise. He would not renegotiate the treaty.

WILSON'S STROKE Instead, in September, Wilson went on an ill-advised nationwide speaking tour to rally support. After visiting twenty-nine cities in three weeks, he broke down physically in Pueblo, Colorado. Then, after returning to Washington, he suffered a stroke. The president recovered, but never completely.

While Wilson recuperated, he continued to make the most important governmental decisions. But he trusted his second wife, Edith, to handle the lesser details of government and to decide which matters were important enough to merit his attention. She reviewed all his papers and ran the White House in the name of the president. Wilson never offered to step down temporarily, and no one confronted him.

After Wilson refused to renegotiate the Treaty of Versailles, the Senate defeated it in March 1920. Its terms still went into effect, however, because the other Allies had already agreed to them. The terrible financial burden the treaty placed on a defeated Germany would lead to the rise of Adolf Hitler only a decade later. The League of Nations was established, but without the United States, it was never effective. The world was no safer for democracy.

HAD WOODROW WILSON REMAINED HEALTHY, HE might have run for a third term. Instead, he was forced to retire. But the 1920 election still turned on Wilson and his policies.

The Democrats nominated Governor James M. Cox of Ohio, who earnestly embraced Wilson's record. Franklin Roosevelt was picked as Cox's running mate. Roosevelt was chosen partly because of his successful record as Wilson's assistant secretary of the navy and partly because Democratic party leaders thought his famous name might win some extra votes.

The deadlocked Republican convention nominated a compromise candidate, Senator Warren G. Harding

of Ohio. Harding's breakthrough came in Suite 404 of the Blackstone Hotel in Chicago, where the party bosses met secretly to work out a deal. At two o'clock in the morning, they called Harding to their "smoke-filled room" and asked him whether he had anything to hide. Harding thought for ten minutes and replied that he did not. The next day, he was nominated. Governor Calvin Coolidge of Massachusetts was chosen as his running mate.

The Republicans campaigned against Wilson's record. They claimed the president had been unprepared for the war, and they attacked his cherished League of Nations. Meanwhile, Cox urged Americans to work even harder for peace and progressive reform. He pointed to the still-unstable international situation and to the fact that one in six Americans was still illiterate. But the war-weary public was in no mood to meet his idealistic challenge. Instead, Americans embraced Harding's campaign slogan, which offered a "Return to Normalcy." The Republicans won in a landslide.

WARREN GAMALIEL HARDING

29TH PRESIDENT
★
FROM 1921 TO 1923

BORN: November 2, 1865

BIRTHPLACE: Corsica, Ohio

DIED: August 2, 1923

PARTY: Republican

VICE PRESIDENT: Calvin Coolidge

FIRST LADY: Florence Kling De Wolfe

CHILDREN: None

NICKNAME: Wobbly Warren

The first president to speak over the radio.

Warren Harding's "Return to Normalcy" campaign was a rejection of Woodrow Wilson's idealism. During the campaign, candidate Harding had avoided taking a position on the League of Nations. By being vague, he hoped both supporters and opponents of the League might vote for him. A month after taking office, however, President Harding announced to Congress that he would not support U.S. membership in that organization.

To help manage the executive branch, Harding proposed a new government office called the Bureau of the Budget. To run this office, he appointed Charles G. Dawes, an engineer and banker from Ohio. Dawes's job was to make a formal budget for government spending. Before the Bureau of the Budget was created, each department of the government handled its own budget. Now that process could be unified and streamlined.

Harding also signed into law two new tariffs. These replaced the 1913 Underwood Tariff and

TEAPOT DOME SCANDAL

Harding's Interior Secretary Caught in Corrupt Deal

Interior Secretary Albert Fall made a secret deal with the Mammoth Oil Company in 1922. Fall arranged for Mammoth to lease the government's Teapot Dome oil fields in Wyoming on terms that were very favorable to Mammoth. In exchange, Mammoth Oil president Harry Sinclair paid Fall a bribe of three hundred thousand dollars in cash and government bonds.

Some people asked questions when the lease was first signed, but the full story didn't come out until the release of a Senate report in October 1923. By that time, Harding was already dead, having passed away two months earlier.

The president may have learned enough before he died to know that his administration was about to unravel. That knowledge may have been a factor in his own collapse. There was no evidence in the Senate report, however, that Harding ever profited personally from any of these corrupt dealings.

raised tariff rates to an average of thirty-eight percent. Singled out for special protection were new industries that had grown up during World War I, especially the drug and chemical industries.

Harding found the role of president difficult. Despite years in the Senate, he was often confused by the complexities of legislation. For instance, one tax reform bill eluded him completely. "I can't make a damn thing out of this tax problem," Harding admitted. "I listen to one side and they seem right, and then— God!—I talk to the other side and they seem just as right, and here I am where I started."

IMMIGRATION Harding responded to the national concern about high levels of immigration by signing the Immigration Restriction Act of 1921. This law established the first general quotas, or limits, on immigration in the nation's history.

The wave of immigration from eastern and southern Europe that took place before World War I was the largest ever. Businessmen appreciated the cheap labor, but many feared that poor Europeans would bring with them dangerous ideas about socialism. Workers who had come over during previous waves of immigration feared the loss of their jobs. The Immigration Restriction Act limited immigration from each country to three percent of the number of people from that country already in the United States in 1910.

On the issue of civil rights, Harding was remarkably ahead of his time. In October 1921, he became the first president since the Civil War to deliver a speech in the South on behalf of equal rights for blacks.

Harding's biggest accomplishment came in foreign affairs. Because the victorious nations of World War I were

HARDING GREW UP ON A FARM IN CALEDONIA, OHIO, where his chores included milking the cows, tending to the horses, and painting the barns. In 1884, when he was not yet nineteen, Harding and two friends purchased an almost bankrupt newspaper in Marion, Ohio, for three hundred dollars. Before long, Harding became the sole owner of the *Marion Star*.

The Early Years

When Harding was twenty-five, he married Florence Kling De Wolfe, a thirty-year-old divorced woman with one son. Florence's father warned her not to marry Harding and at one point even threatened Harding's life. But the couple got married anyway.

Florence Harding became an excellent circulation manager. It was largely her work that built the newspaper into a business profitable enough to launch her husband's political career.

★**POKER** As a senator, Harding voted for Prohibition. But as president, he secretly stocked the White House with illegal bootleg liquor. He liked to have some on hand for his poker games, which often ran late into the night. Harding especially enjoyed playing poker with members of his cabinet. Among the regulars in what Harding called his "poker cabinet" were Secretary of War John Weeks, Attorney General Harry Daugherty, and Interior Secretary Albert Fall. Both Daugherty and Fall were key figures in Harding administration corruption scandals. During one unfortunate game, Harding gambled away a complete set of the White House china.

★**WOMEN'S WORK** The development of the typewriter gave women new opportunities in the workplace. For female high school graduates, secretarial work became an attractive alternative to traditional women's work such as teaching and nursing. It was also far less backbreaking than farm or factory work. Soon huge "pools" of neat young women clattered away at manual typewriters in city offices nationwide. By 1930, there were eleven million women in the work force, more than double the number in 1900.

WARREN GAMALIEL HARDING 1921-1923

★THE ROARING TWENTIES

In a peculiar way, the outrageousness of the 1920s was caused by the restrictions of Prohibition. Because most people didn't take Prohibition seriously, business at illegal speakeasies, or bars, was always good. Once people broke one law or social taboo, it became easier to break others.

The prosperity of the 1920s produced a thrilling popular culture. Fashionable young women called "flappers" discarded their puffy prewar dresses and instead wore short ones that clung tightly to their bodies. Dancing the nights away at speakeasies, the flappers scandalized older Americans with their freedom. They were the first women to smoke cigarettes in public, and their favorite dance was the wild, flailing Charleston.

★NEGRO LEAGUES

In the 1920s and 1930s, blacks were not allowed to play major league baseball. Instead, black players formed their own leagues. The most famous of these was the Negro National League, formed in 1920.

Teams in the Negro leagues were often as popular as major league clubs in the same town. In Chicago, for instance, the Chicago American Giants sometimes drew more fans than either the White Sox or the Cubs across town.

Perhaps the biggest Negro league star was the flamboyant pitcher Satchel Paige of the Kansas City Monarchs. Negro league games often had a carnival-like atmosphere. Sometimes Paige would dazzle the crowd by calling in his outfielders and pitching to a batter without them. He was sure that the opposing hitters couldn't hit his famous fastball.

already beginning to maneuver for power, Harding convened an international meeting on arms control. The Washington Conference for the Limitation of Armament was held in the nation's capital between November 1921 and February 1922.

The conference concluded when the United States, Great Britain, Japan, France, and Italy all agreed to limit the total size of their navies. Under the terms of this agreement, the United States and Britain were granted the largest navies. The size of the Japanese navy was capped at slightly more than half the size of the U.S. and British navies. The French and Italian fleets were limited to a little more than half the size of the Japanese fleet.

The conference also led to the Four Power Pact among the United States, Great Britain, Japan, and France. With this treaty, the four nations agreed to respect each other's territory in Asia. They also promised to resolve peacefully any disagreements among them.

TEAPOT DOME

Nevertheless, by early 1923, Harding's presidency was unraveling. The rumors circulating about corruption in his administration were beginning to get louder. Senator Thomas Walsh of Montana started a formal investigation into them. His committee began collecting evidence of what became known as the Teapot Dome scandal.

Harding's problem began with the people he brought with him to Washington. The only qualification most of them had was a longtime political loyalty to the president, and they were usually more interested in private gain than public service. Because Harding was rather weak-willed, he found it difficult to refuse friends who asked for jobs. Few voters doubted Harding's own integrity, but Walsh's investigation proved that many of his appointees were crooks.

PRESIDENT HARDING WAS DEEPLY TROUBLED BY the growing charges of corruption in his administration. In late June 1920, just as the Senate investigation was getting under way, Harding set out on a nationwide speaking tour that he called the Voyage of Understanding. He wanted to explain his policies and assure the American people that he was an honest man.

The trip by railroad was unwise, however, because Harding was suffering from high blood pressure and heart trouble. His tiring schedule weakened him. When he reached San Francisco at the end of July, he was exhausted and had to be carried from the train. On August 2, he died unexpectedly in his room at the Palace Hotel.

After the president's death, some people claimed that Florence Harding had poisoned her husband to spare him the indignity of impeachment. Others whispered that she poisoned him because he had been unfaithful to her. (As a senator and president, Harding had two long-term affairs and fathered a child by one of these women.) The rumors were fanned by the first lady's refusal to allow an autopsy.

Nothing was ever proven, however, and historians today believe Harding died of natural causes.

Harding Dies in Office

IN 1924, THE COUNTRY WAS PROSPEROUS AND at peace. Under normal circumstances, these two conditions would ensure the reelection of a president. But Republican party leaders were worried. They weren't sure whether voters would hold the scandals of the Harding administration against them.

Republicans were lucky that Calvin Coolidge happened to be Harding's vice president.

Coolidge's direct, upright manner enabled him to restore confidence in the government in a very short time. As a reward, he was nominated unanimously at the first national party convention broadcast on radio.

The Democratic convention, however, produced the longest deadlock in history. For more than one hundred ballots, Californian William McAdoo, the candidate of the rural South

and West, battled New York governor Al Smith, who had the backing of the eastern cities. In the end, both men withdrew, and the nomination went to compromise candidate John W. Davis on the 103rd ballot.

Davis, a West Virginia lawyer, campaigned hard. But the Republican's "Keep Cool with Coolidge" campaign proved unbeatable. The independent Republican senator Robert M. LaFollette ran a strong campaign as the Progressive party candidate, winning seventeen percent of the vote. But his strength was spread much too thin. The only state he carried was his home state of Wisconsin.

CALVIN COOLIDGE

30TH PRESIDENT

★

FROM 1923 TO 1929

BORN: July 4, 1872

BIRTHPLACE: Plymouth, Vt.

DIED: January 5, 1933

PARTY: Republican

VICE PRESIDENT: Charles G. Dawes

FIRST LADY: Grace Anna Goodhue

CHILDREN: John, Calvin

NICKNAME: Silent Cal

Had an electric horse installed in his White House bedroom.

LUCKY LINDY LANDS SAFELY IN PARIS

PARIS, May 21, 1927— Yesterday Charles Lindbergh, a twenty-five-year-old airmail pilot, took off in his monoplane from New York. Today, he landed at Le Bourget airfield outside Paris. In the intervening 33½ hours, Lindbergh became the first person to fly solo across the Atlantic Ocean.

The nonstop flight has made Lindbergh an international hero. It has also increased public acceptance of the airplane as a mode of transportation.

For his 3,600-mile journey aboard the *Spirit of St. Louis*, Lindbergh took with him a few sandwiches and a quart of water. He also brought letters of introduction.

Lindbergh grew up in Little Falls, Minnesota, and Washington, D.C., where his father was a congressman. Consumed by a passion for flying, he dropped out of college during his second year and instead enrolled in flying school. Lindbergh traveled around the country performing as a stunt pilot before becoming an airmail pilot in 1926.

Vice President Calvin Coolidge was vacationing at his father's home in Plymouth Notch, Vermont, when President Harding died in San Francisco. The Coolidges didn't have a telephone, so a messenger had to be sent by car from a nearby town. It was after midnight when Coolidge was awakened with the news that the president had died.

The shocked vice president knelt to say a prayer. Then he went downstairs to a sitting room, where he was sworn in as president shortly before 3:00 A.M. His father, a justice of the peace, administered the oath of office at this informal ceremony. Afterward, Coolidge went back upstairs and back to sleep.

The new president had a big job ahead of him. Within months, the nation would be shaken again by news of the Teapot Dome scandal.

Quickly, the phrase Teapot Dome became common shorthand for government

137

bribery and corruption. It was Coolidge's task to restore faith in the government and faith in the governing Republican party. Republican leaders were worried that the entire party would be tainted by the Harding corruption scandals.

"Silent Cal" Coolidge succeeded beyond anyone's expectations. His quiet style of governing, in contrast to the wildness of the Roaring Twenties, proved to be his greatest asset. The new president moved aggressively to root out corruption. By remaining calm, Coolidge soon convinced the public that the country's problems were over. As a result, he became a much celebrated symbol of integrity in office.

Throughout his term, people identified Calvin Coolidge with the values of old-fashioned America. The New England Puritan ethic that he lived by honored thrift, industry, dignity, morality, frugality, and faith. Coolidge's convictions stood out prominently because they contrasted so vividly with the exuberance and extravagance of the time.

THE BUSINESS OF AMERICA Coolidge believed that prosperity was closely linked to the success of the business community. "The chief business of America is business," he often said. Almost everything Coolidge did was designed to benefit business. In many ways, his conservative presidency made possible the lighthearted frolics that captured the attention of the nation.

In his 1925 inaugural address, Coolidge proposed tax cuts. He argued that reducing the tax burden on the wealthy would benefit everyone by increasing business activity. It was a very appealing policy, and it worked as long as the economy continued to grow.

The tax laws Coolidge shepherded through Congress were extremely

The Early Years

COOLIDGE SPENT HIS CHILDHOOD IN PLYMOUTH, Vermont, where his father was a shopkeeper active in local politics. It was from his father that Calvin inherited his New England thrift and restrained nature. After college, he became a lawyer.

The event that made Coolidge nationally famous occurred during his term as governor of Massachusetts. In 1919, the police force in Boston went on strike, leading to a crime wave in that city. Coolidge sent in state troops and upheld the decision to fire the strikers. When American Federation of Labor president Samuel Gompers appealed to the governor to reconsider his decision, Coolidge sent him a characteristically terse reply. The telegram was reprinted throughout the country. "There is no right to strike against the public safety by anybody, anywhere, any time," Coolidge wrote.

★**SILENT CAL** President Coolidge was widely known as a man of few words. His nickname, Silent Cal, reflected his reserved nature. But Coolidge was also quite witty.

On one occasion at the White House, a dinner guest made a bet with a friend that she could get Coolidge to say more than two words. When she told the president about her bet, Coolidge thought for a moment. "You lose," he said.

★**RADIO** Beginning in the early 1920s, radio truly changed American life. The number of stations broadcasting programs exploded from thirty in 1922 to more than five hundred in 1923. A decade later, two-thirds of homes in the United States had radios, which was twice the number of homes with telephones.

At first, Americans resisted advertising on the radio. Commercials were only one of a number of ways that stations financed programming. During the Great Depression, however, radio commercials gained acceptance and became the norm. Soap manufacturers, for example, sponsored popular daytime dramas that became known as "soap operas."

★WALT DISNEY In 1928, little-known animators Walt Disney and Ub Iwerks produced the first animated cartoon with sound. Their short film, *Steamboat Willie*, starred a new character called Mickey Mouse.

From the moment that Mickey first appeared in movie theaters, people loved him. Disney, who provided the voice for Mickey, went on to make other cartoons. Mickey's huge number of fans convinced Disney that the public liked to see animals who talked and behaved like humans. To satisfy the popular demand, Disney created Donald Duck and the dogs Pluto and Goofy.

★HARLEM RENAISSANCE After World War I, the neighborhood of Harlem in New York City became a center for the creative outpouring of many African Americans. This was the Harlem Renaissance. Older black writers, especially James Weldon Johnson, encouraged younger writers, artists, and musicians to create works of art that described the unique experience of being black in the United States. Authors such as the poet Langston Hughes and the novelist Zora Neale Hurston were the first to write with awareness and pride about the black experience.

★BABE RUTH When the Boston Red Sox sold Babe Ruth to the New York Yankees in 1920, the price of $125,000 was both unheard of and a bargain. The Roaring Twenties were a golden age for sports, and no star shone brighter than the Babe's. Ruth's popularity had such a powerful effect on ticket sales that sportswriters called the new Yankee Stadium "The House That Ruth Built."

Such astounding feats as the sixty home runs he hit during the 1927 season earned the Sultan of Swat unprecedented salaries. Before the 1930 season, he signed a contract for eighty thousand dollars a year. When asked how he felt about making more money than President Hoover, the Babe said, "I had a better year," referring to the 1929 stock market crash.

favorable to business. They lowered income taxes and eliminated a number of other taxes that had been used to raise money during World War I. To a great extent, the apparent prosperity of the Roaring Twenties was a result of Coolidge's tax policy.

At first, as Coolidge had predicted, the tax cuts encouraged rich people to invest more money in business. What the frugal president hadn't expected, however, was that many more people would begin taking risks with their money in the hope of even quicker, higher returns. Such unrestrained speculation has been widely blamed for the 1929 stock market crash.

AVIATION One of Coolidge's most successful initiatives was his promotion of commercial aviation. Ever since the sensational experiments of the Wright Brothers at the turn of the century, the aviation industry had grown by great leaps, and now passenger aircraft were becoming available.

In 1926, Congress passed the Air Commerce Act. The purpose of this bill was to place commercial aviation under government regulation so the fledgling industry could be nurtured. The bill also approved the first two commercial airline routes, one north-south and the other east-west.

FARM POLICY Coolidge was also successful in defeating bills he didn't like. Twice Congress passed the McNaury-Haugen farm bill, and twice the president vetoed it. By the terms of this bill, the government would buy surplus crops from U.S. farmers at a fixed price and then sell them abroad, often at a loss. The purpose was to protect farmers from unstable crop prices.

Coolidge attacked the bill as contrary to the free-market economy that he championed. He argued that government had no business fixing crop prices and that the farmers should make do with the laws of supply and demand. According to the president's economic philosophy, crops should cost what people were willing to pay for them. Coolidge's action may have seemed sensible at the time, but it contributed greatly to the suffering of farmers during the Great Depression.

THE KELLOGG-BRIAND PACT

In foreign affairs, Coolidge followed a policy of isolationism. One exception was the treaty negotiated by Secretary of State Frank Kellogg and the French foreign minister Aristide Briand.

The countries that signed the Kellogg-Briand Pact of 1928 agreed not to use war as a tool of national policy. It was the most ambitious peacemaking effort yet. Eventually, all but five of the world's nations signed the treaty, and it was celebrated as the beginning of a new era in international relations.

However, the Kellogg-Briand Pact didn't end war because the treaty was entirely unrealistic and impractical. There was no way to enforce it and no punishment for those who broke it. The treaty did nothing, for example, to stop the growth of Nazi Germany or any of the other factors that would lead to World War II. The pact was well intentioned, but it was a complete failure.

When Coolidge's first full term came to an end in 1928, the country was still prosperous, but the president decided not to run for reelection. In a characteristically tight-lipped announcement, Coolidge said, "I do not choose to run for president in 1928." He gave no further explanation. Instead, Coolidge retired to write his autobiography, which was naturally a very short book.

CAMPAIGN 1928

WHEN PRESIDENT COOLIDGE ANNOUNCED THAT HE would not run for reelection in 1928, Secretary of Commerce Herbert Hoover became the Republican front-runner. Hoover's support—which came primarily from women, progressives, and immigrants—was strong enough to win him the Republican nomination. In his acceptance speech, Hoover said, "We shall soon with the help of God be in sight of the day when poverty will be banished from this nation."

Hoover was quiet and shy. In contrast, the Democratic candidate, Governor Alfred E. Smith of New York, was colorful and witty. He was also the first Roman Catholic to be nominated for president by a major political party.

Smith campaigned for religious tolerance, but he was largely unsuccessful. Republicans put out pamphlets, without Hoover's knowledge, claiming that Smith would be the servant of the pope in Rome. Many Protestants in the Midwest and West believed what they read.

In the northern and eastern cities, Smith attracted huge and enthusiastic crowds, but his appeal remained regional. Hoover ran a quieter campaign, emphasizing the prosperity of the Republican Coolidge administration. In November, he carried forty of the forty-eight states.

HERBERT CLARK HOOVER

31ST PRESIDENT
★
FROM 1929 TO 1933

BORN: August 10, 1874

BIRTHPLACE: West Branch, Iowa

DIED: October 20, 1964

PARTY: Republican

VICE PRESIDENT: Charles Curtis

FIRST LADY: Lou Henry

CHILDREN: Herbert, Jr.; Allan

NICKNAME: Chief

The first president to have an asteroid named for him.

STOCK MARKET CRASHES
"Black Tuesday" Ends Boom Years

NEW YORK, October 29, 1929—Wall Street collapsed today. Prices on the New York Stock Exchange fell disastrously in very heavy trading. In just a few hours, stock in the nation's companies lost ten billion dollars in value.

Stocks that had been selling for twenty, thirty, and forty dollars a share only a few weeks ago were dumped for pennies in the desperate rush to sell. The nosedive taken by the stock market last week was nothing compared to today's disaster.

The predictions of prominent bankers that the worst was over turned out to be tragically wrong, as did President Hoover's claim that the business of the country was "on a sound and prosperous basis." Evidently, the panic had already set in.

Experts say that the leading cause of the crash was wild and unregulated stock speculation financed by borrowing. As long as prices went up, everyone made money. But when prices started to fall a week ago, brokers called in their customers' debts.

Because these investors had all their money tied up in stocks, they had to sell in order to pay the brokers. These sales drove down the market even further until a stampede developed.

At the beginning of his presidency, people thought of Hoover as a new, modern leader who could organize the government for the benefit of the people. Everyone knew of his accomplishments during World War I, when he managed the food distribution to Europe. Hoover masterfully provided more than eighteen million tons of food to starving people there. A new verb, to "hooverize," meant to conserve food for the war effort.

Hoover was also a self-made millionaire, which made him seem the right person for the times. The country was prosperous and believed that Hoover could lead it to even greater economic heights. People were not jealous of his wealth, because they knew he had been orphaned as a child and had worked hard to make his fortune. Early on, Hoover announced his hope that Americans could create a "new day" that would fulfill the country's potential, especially in the area of science.

Then came the stock market crash. Hoover responded to this crisis with energy and determination. He met with business leaders and delivered many speeches designed to restore confidence in the economy. He was quite active, in fact, more so than any president before him when faced with an economic crisis. But never before had the emergency been so great.

THE GREAT DEPRESSION The crash immediately bankrupted many high rollers who had been speculating in the stock market. But its lasting effects touched everyone. The crash led to the failure of five thousand banks, wiping out the savings accounts of nine million ordinary people. During the next three years of the Great Depression, an average of one hundred thousand jobs were lost each week.

President Hoover simply failed to understand how bad things were. In March 1930, he announced that "the evidences indicate that the worst effects of the crash upon unemployment will have passed during the next sixty days." Instead, unemployment got worse.

People who were scared of losing their jobs, or had already lost them, stopped making unnecessary purchases. As a result, businesses suffered more. Then, as demand fell, even more jobs were lost.

As people's savings ran out, they became unable to repay their debts. Many lost their homes. Farmers couldn't make a living, either, because crop prices were so low. By 1930, four million people were unemployed. By 1932, twelve million people were out of work, which meant that one in four Americans had lost his or her job.

During the worst years of the Great Depression, starving people lined up for free soup and bread in towns and cities across the nation. Resorts became ghost towns.

The Early Years

ERBERT HOOVER WAS BORN IN WEST BRANCH, Iowa, which made him the first president born west of the Mississippi River. After the death of his father when he was six, Herbert was sent to live with relatives.

For eight months, he lived with an uncle on the Osage Indian reservation in Oklahoma. There, he played with Osage children and learned how to hunt with a bow and arrow. When he was nine, his mother died and he was sent to live permanently with another uncle in Oregon.

At Stanford University, Hoover studied geology. After his graduation, he got a job as a mining engineer with a company that sent him to Australia, Burma, and China. Hoover and his wife, Lou, learned Chinese so well that they often spoke the language in the White House to protect themselves against eavesdroppers.

★**FLY FISHING** Hoover was a dedicated fly fisherman. Occasionally on weekends, he liked to forget the worries of the presidency by taking fly fishing trips. He often traveled to the Rapidan River in nearby Virginia in what is now the Shenandoah National Park.

★**AL CAPONE** For organized crime, Prohibition meant good business. Making liquor illegal didn't end the demand for it, so bootleggers prospered, especially in Chicago. The biggest of the mob bosses there was Al "Scarface" Capone.

Capone ordered a great many killings. The most famous of these was the St. Valentine's Day Massacre. On February 14, 1929, members of Capone's gang disguised themselves as policemen and raided a garage run by rival gangster Bugs Moran. Capone's men lined the Moran gang up against a wall and machine-gunned them to death. Newspapers later dramatized the event, which became a symbol of the violence that engulfed Prohibition-era Chicago.

★THE MARX BROTHERS Americans often sought emotional relief from the Great Depression in Hollywood movies. Watching a silly comedy usually helped people forget their troubles, at least for a time. The Marx Brothers kept many Americans laughing when they might otherwise have been crying.

There were originally five Marx Brothers: Groucho, Chico, Harpo, Gummo, and Zeppo. But Gummo left the act before the brothers began making movies in the late 1920s. In those movies, Groucho, Harpo, and Chico were the central characters. Their comedy was particularly popular because it poked fun at stuffy rich people from the point of view of poor, disadvantaged outsiders.

★THE DUST BOWL Depression life in Oklahoma was made much worse by a severe drought that hit the region in the early 1930s. Conditions there became so bad that sometimes huge dust storms completely blocked the sun.

Hoping for a better life in California, many "Okies" headed west to work as migrant fruit pickers. John Steinbeck's novel *The Grapes of Wrath* and the songs of Woody Guthrie describe the terrible disappointments they found in California: low wages, brutal working conditions, and little hope.

Passenger trains rolled along the tracks with empty cars because no one could afford the fare.

THE SMOOT-HAWLEY TARIFF Congress's response was the Smoot-Hawley Tariff of 1930, which raised tariff rates to record levels. Hoover knew the bill was dangerous, but he signed it anyway, thinking he had no other choice. The intention of the tariff was to increase sales of U.S. products by raising the cost of imported goods.

But the new rates quickly led to an international trade war as other nations raised their tariffs as well. This drastically reduced sales of U.S. goods overseas. Overall, the worldwide depression worsened.

By 1931, most Americans thought it was obvious that the government should provide direct aid to the people. Other nations, such as Great Britain, were already making payments to the unemployed and the elderly. But the president refused to support these programs.

Hoover wanted to help people who were suffering. But he was not willing to give up his traditional American faith in individual responsibility. Hoover thought that direct aid to people would make them dependent on the government and undermine their ability to earn a living.

HOOVERVILLES Hoover himself soon came to symbolize the hardships of the Great Depression for many people. Homeless families who lived in shacks made out of discarded lumber and cardboard called their shantytowns "Hoovervilles." The newspapers that people used to cover themselves were known as "Hoover blankets." The wild rabbits they killed for food were "Hoover hogs."

A short decade before, Hoover had been hailed as the Great Humanitarian for his efforts to feed starving Europeans. By 1932, however, his reassurances that conditions would improve were greeted with jeers. No one believed him anymore, and his campaign promises of 1928 came back to haunt him. While running for president, Hoover had said, "We shall soon with the help of God be in sight of the day when poverty will be banished from this nation." Of course, things didn't work out that way.

Throughout his term, Hoover refused to allow government aid to the unemployed and the homeless. But in 1932, he did create the Reconstruction Finance Corporation. This agency loaned two billion dollars to businesses, banks, and state governments to help them through the Great Depression. Hoover believed that the money would eventually trickle down to the people who needed it. But it was much too little and much too late.

THE BONUS MARCH In May 1932, World War I veterans organized the Bonus March on Washington, D.C. In 1924, in appreciation for their service during the war, Congress had awarded them pay bonuses in the form of insurance that could be redeemed in 1945. Because of the Great Depression, the veterans wanted Congress to move up payment of these bonuses. Many veterans argued that they might not live until 1945 unless the bonuses were paid immediately.

When Congress turned them down, some members of the Bonus Army went back home. But others remained camped near the Capitol. In July, Hoover lost his patience and ordered the U.S. Army to drive away the Bonus Army. The use of tear gas and fixed bayonets against the veterans and their families was widely criticized. Once again, Hoover seemed insensitive to the suffering caused by the depression.

THE GREAT DEPRESSION DOMINATED THE 1932 campaign. The Republicans renominated President Hoover. To have given up on him would have meant admitting that the economic crisis was the fault of his Republican administration.

The Democrats nominated Franklin Roosevelt, the innovative governor of New York. Although crippled by polio in 1921, FDR had made a dramatic comeback. After his nomination, Roosevelt flew to Chicago, where he became the first presidential candidate to deliver an acceptance speech in person. Among his most wealthy and influential supporters was Joseph P. Kennedy, whose son John would later run for president himself.

Because Roosevelt was confined to a wheelchair, most people thought he would run a quiet campaign. But FDR surprised everyone with an energetic trip around the country during which he delivered more than fifty speeches.

Roosevelt promised to get the country back on its feet with public works projects and government aid to farmers. He called his program a "new deal for the forgotten man." It was no accident that FDR's New Deal sounded a lot like Teddy Roosevelt's popular Square Deal.

President Hoover insisted that Roosevelt's policies would not work and continued to warn against government aid. But the voters didn't believe the country would pull out of the Great Depression by itself. In November, Roosevelt carried forty-two of the forty-eight states.

144

FRANKLIN DELANO ROOSEVELT

32ND PRESIDENT

★

FROM 1933 TO 1945

BORN: January 30, 1882

BIRTHPLACE: Hyde Park, N.Y.

DIED: April 12, 1945

PARTY: Democrat

VICE PRESIDENTS: John N. Garner, Henry A. Wallace, Harry S. Truman

FIRST LADY: Anna Eleanor Roosevelt

CHILDREN: Anna; James; Franklin; Elliot; Franklin Delano, Jr.; John

NICKNAME: FDR

The first president to appear on television.

Like Lincoln, Franklin Roosevelt became president during a time of grave national crisis. The Great Depression, the worst in U.S. history, had closed banks around the country and cut industrial production in half. More than thirteen million people were out of work, and one-quarter of the nation's farmers had lost their land because banks had foreclosed on their loans.

With ordinary Americans lining up at free soup kitchens to avoid starvation, Roosevelt knew something had to be done quickly. "Action and action now" was his inaugural promise. Showing that he could be composed under pressure, Roosevelt tried to reassure people. "The only thing we have to fear is fear itself," he said.

Roosevelt's cabinet appointments reflected his plan to make changes in the way government was run. He chose

OWENS FOILS HITLER

Sprinter Wins Olympic Gold

BERLIN, Germany, August 16, 1936—The Summer Olympics ended here today with the host nation, Nazi Germany, winning the most medals. But the U.S. sprinter Jesse Owens captured headlines around the world with his four gold-medal performances.

Owens won the two sprint events and the long jump. He also ran the anchor leg for the winning sprint relay team. He tied or broke Olympic records in each of these events.

German dictator Adolf Hitler had intended to use the Berlin Olympics to show the world how completely his country had recovered from World War I. He also hoped to use the games to prove his theories that the whites of Northern Europe are by nature superior to other races.

The medals that Owens, an African American, won here have proved to the world that Hitler's theories are wrong.

liberals who were not afraid to experiment with bold reforms. The president even appointed the first female cabinet officer, Secretary of Labor Frances Perkins.

THE BANKING CRISIS

The most immediate of Roosevelt's problems was the banking crisis. Because so many banks had already failed, the public was fast losing confidence in the nation's financial institutions. Worried depositors began lining up at banks to withdraw their money. These "runs" threatened the entire banking system. On the day Roosevelt took office, nearly half the states had declared bank "holidays" to keep the remaining banks in business.

Two days later, on March 6, Roosevelt called a halt to all banking operations. Three days after that, Congress, which had been called into special session, passed the Emergency Banking Act. This law endorsed the president's action and kept the banks closed until federal auditors could examine their books.

In his first "fireside chat," Roosevelt explained the government's new banking policy, which restored much of the public's faith in the system. By the end of March, more than twelve thousand banks with ninety percent of the nation's deposits were back in business. With the unsound banks closed, the runs stopped. Roosevelt's handling of the banking crisis displayed early on his determined, energetic leadership.

The president followed this up with serious bank reform. In June 1933, Congress established the Federal Deposit Insurance Corporation to guarantee individual deposits up to five thousand dollars. As intended, the new law gave the depositors confidence that even if a bank failed, they would not lose their money.

The Early Years

AS A BOY, FDR ENJOYED THE SHELTERED LIFE provided by his wealthy and well-known family. A pampered child, he wore dresses until he was five and then kilts. Not until he turned eight did Franklin wear his first pair of pants—or take his first unsupervised bath.

Following the career path of his fifth cousin Theodore Roosevelt, Franklin entered politics in 1910, winning election to the New York State Senate. Three years later, Woodrow Wilson named him assistant secretary of the navy.

In 1921, after running for vice president on the losing 1920 Democratic ticket, Roosevelt contracted polio, a disease that paralyzed his legs. He had to wear braces and use a wheelchair for the rest of his life, which made him more sensitive to the troubles of other people. After seven years of difficult physical therapy, however, he made a remarkable political comeback, winning election as governor of New York state in 1928.

★**MARION POST WOLCOTT** In 1938, Marion Post Wolcott took a job as a photographer with the New Deal's Farm Security Administration. This government agency hired a team of photographers during the late 1930s to compile a visual record of life in the United States. She and other FSA photographers, including Walker Evans and Dorothea Lange, traveled all over the country documenting the lives of everyday people. Roosevelt's Works Progress Administration was committed to employing other types of artists as well. The Federal

Writers Project put together a state-by-state series of guidebooks, while the Federal Theater Project staged free performances, including a black version of *Macbeth* that played to more than 120,000 people.

★ FIRESIDE CHATS

Early in his first term as president, FDR began a series of informal radio speeches. He called them "fireside chats." His purpose was to explain the government's New Deal policies directly to the people.

The fireside chats reassured a worried nation. Americans listening on the radio could hear the optimism and firmness in the president's mellow voice. Speaking

from the White House, Roosevelt seemed to be talking to each member of the audience personally. As a result, people came to believe that he understood their problems as no president had before.

★ HUEY LONG

One of the country's best known and most controversial politicians during the Great Depression was Huey Long, the governor of Louisiana. Long won the support of poor whites by improving rural roads and expanding government services. He paid for these programs by taxing corporations and the rich.

Nicknamed the Kingfish, Long used folksiness to hide his ruthless manner. In 1931, he resigned as governor to enter the U.S. Senate. There he developed the Share-Our-Wealth program, promising to make "every man a king." To his critics, Long was a demagogue who charmed uneducated voters with simplistic plans and impractical promises. Long planned to run for president in 1936, but in September 1935, at the height of his influence, he was assassinated in the Louisiana state capitol by the son-in-law of a politician whose career he had ruined.

★ THE *HINDENBURG*

The German airship *Hindenburg* began the first regularly scheduled transatlantic passenger service in May 1936. The 830-foot-long, hydrogen-filled zeppelin was a source of great pride for the Nazis. It carried fifty passengers in private cabins at a cruising speed of seventy-eight miles per hour.

On May 6, 1937, as the *Hindenburg* was approaching its mooring station at Lakehurst, New Jersey, the airship mysteriously burst into flames. Thirty-six people died in the explosion, which ended the brief era of lighter-than-air transport. Coincidentally, Herbert Morrison's report of the disaster was the first coast-to-coast radio broadcast.

THE HUNDRED DAYS

During his first hundred days in office, Roosevelt demonstrated a concern on behalf of the government that President Hoover had not. He created a network of agencies whose sole purpose was to offer relief to the suffering public. "Only a foolish optimist can deny the dark realities of the moment," Roosevelt said. He compared the threat of the depression to the threat posed by war and suggested that he might assume powers usually granted to a president only during wartime.

Between March and May 1933, Roosevelt sent New Deal legislation to Capitol Hill piece by piece. An obedient and heavily Democratic Congress, desperate for recovery, approved nearly all of Roosevelt's requests. Mostly spending bills were passed. The New Deal's basic assumption was that government spending could "prime the pump" of business and get the economy rolling again.

THE CIVILIAN CONSERVATION CORPS

Unlike Hoover, Roosevelt believed it was the federal government's responsibility to address the problems of the needy. The first New Deal program to help the unemployed was the Civilian Conservation Corps, which gave jobs to men between the ages of eighteen and twenty-five.

Recruited in the cities, these young men were put to work in rural camps built by the War Department (now the Department of Defense). They made thirty dollars a month planting trees, building dams, and doing other jobs that helped conserve the environment. Twenty-two dollars of their salary was sent home each month to their families. Between 1933 and 1941, nearly three million young men spent some time living and working in CCC camps.

The first comprehensive program for unemployment relief was the Federal Emergency Relief Administration, created in May 1933. Led by Roosevelt's trusted associate Harry Hopkins, FERA at first made cash payments directly to the unemployed. But Hopkins believed that providing people with jobs was a better way to go—both for the people, psychologically, and for the economy. Eventually, FERA spent about four billion dollars on direct relief as well as on jobs that were not supposed to compete with private business.

AGRICULTURAL PROGRAMS Roosevelt also had to resolve a crisis in agriculture. Farmers had been suffering for years from low crop prices, which fell even further after the 1929 stock market crash. In April 1933, the *New York World-Telegram* wrote that "actual revolution already exists in the farm belt." In Iowa, farmers violently resisted when banks called in overdue mortgages and threw families out of their homes. Riots forced the governor to declare martial law in several counties.

The Agricultural Adjustment Act of May 1933 attempted to raise prices by cutting production. It authorized the government to pay farmers for taking land out of cultivation. This seemed a cruel thing to do while millions of people were starving in the cities, but Secretary of Agriculture Henry Wallace argued that farmers simply were not able to make a living any other way. "Agriculture cannot succeed in a capitalist society as a philanthropic enterprise," he said.

One of the boldest and most original of the New Deal programs was the Tennessee Valley Authority, an independent public company that Congress created to build and run dams in seven southeastern states.

No ONE DOUBTED THAT FRANKLIN ROOSEVELT would be nominated for a second term. In his acceptance speech at the Democratic convention, the president said, "There is a mysterious cycle in human events. To some generations much is given. Of other

generations much is expected. This generation of Americans has a rendezvous with destiny."

The Democrats used the New Deal to portray themselves as the party of ordinary people. Farmers, workers, and the unemployed were firmly behind Roosevelt, as were blacks, who abandoned the party of Lincoln for the first time since the Civil War. Meanwhile, most Americans viewed Republicans as the party of wealthy conservatives.

Roosevelt's Republican opponent, Kansas governor Alfred M. Landon, campaigned against the New Deal, which he said undermined the American traditions of individualism and self-sufficiency. He accused the Roosevelt administration of massive waste and inefficiency in its relief programs. FDR ignored these attacks and reminded the voters that the Great Depression had started during a Republican administration.

While Landon wanted the federal government to stay out of business affairs, Roosevelt believed that it had a responsibility to protect workers by regulating the economy. Roosevelt's economic activism gave the Democrats a huge advantage.

A curious poll conducted by the *Literary Digest* using names taken at random from telephone books predicted that Landon would win by a landslide. The poll was inaccurate because, during the Great Depression, many Americans were too poor to have phones. Those who did were more likely to be well-to-do Republicans. Instead of winning in a landslide, Landon lost by more than ten million votes. His defeat was one of the worst ever suffered by the presidential nominee of a major party.

In addition to generating and selling electricity, the TVA managed reforestation and flood control programs. Many of the TVA's four hundred thousand customers were rural farmers who had never before had access to electric power.

THE NATIONAL RECOVERY ADMINISTRATION
The economic cornerstone of the New Deal was the National Industrial Recovery Act passed in June 1933, which established the National Recovery Administration. The NRA's aim was to encourage business groups and trade associations to compose "codes of fair competition" for their industries. It was believed that these codes would provide a practical basis for regulating the marketplace.

In exchange for agreeing to suspend the antitrust laws so that prices and production quotas could be fixed, the government won concessions for workers. Wage scales were raised, especially among the poorest-paid workers.

The 746 different NRA codes proved to be unwieldy, however. They led to the widespread opinion among conservative business leaders that the New Deal was horrendously impractical and inefficient. Industrialists also objected to Section 7(a) of the act, which guaranteed workers the right to bargain collectively. This meant that unions could negotiate a single

"WAR OF THE WORLDS" RADIO SHOW STARTS PANIC

NEW YORK, October 30, 1938—A radio program broadcast on CBS stations tonight has caused a nation-wide panic. The Mercury Theater of the Air's "War of the Worlds" radio play about a Martian invasion has caused thousands of people to flee their homes despite repeated announcements that the broadcast was only a dramatization.

The show featured simulated news reports about a Martian landing at Grover's Mill, New Jersey. On a single block in nearby Newark, more than twenty families ran out into the street with wet towels over their faces because they believed the realistic reports of a gas raid.

The mastermind of this Halloween media hoax, twenty-three-year-old Orson Welles, has become an instant national celebrity. His work demonstrates the incredible power of radio, still a relatively new medium of communication.

contract to cover all the workers in a factory. It also led to a number of union strikes against nonunion employers.

SOCIAL SECURITY One of the most lasting of Roosevelt's innovations was the Social Security Act of August 1935. This law guaranteed support payments to people who were old, unemployed, sick, or disabled.

At the same time, Congress also passed the National Labor Relations Act, known as the Wagner Act, which made it illegal for employers to interfere with union organizers, and the Wealth Tax, which raised individual income tax rates as high as seventy-five percent for people earning over five million dollars.

What little political opposition there was to the New Deal ended in 1934 when Democrats won huge victories in the midterm congressional elections, increasing their majorities to forty-four seats in the Senate and more than two hundred in the House.

SUPREME COURT OPPOSITION The only effective opposition to President Roosevelt's programs came from the Supreme Court, which struck down many of his initiatives during 1935 and 1936. The Court ruled that the NRA codes, the Agricultural Adjustment Act, and congressional acts relating to railroad retirement, the coal industry, farm mortgages, and cities that went bankrupt were all unconstitutional.

Although the specifics of the decisions varied, the justices generally believed that Roosevelt had seized powers that rightfully belonged to Congress and the states.

Although Republican attacks on the New Deal were rejected by voters during the 1934 congressional

★**THE FIRST LADY** Shy and insecure as a young woman, Eleanor Roosevelt later blossomed into the most active and admired of first ladies. She was also the first wife of a president to make public statements on current political issues.

When both of her parents died while she was still in her teens, Eleanor was sent to an exclusive girls' school in London. When she returned to New York, she did social work in the city's slums. That same year, she met Franklin Roosevelt, her fifth cousin once removed. Once their

courtship began, Eleanor helped open Franklin's eyes to the terrible conditions endured by people who lived in the poor neighborhoods where she worked. Her uncle Theodore Roosevelt gave the bride away at her 1905 wedding.

After FDR was struck down with polio in 1921 when he was thirty-nine, Eleanor encouraged him to fight the disease and return to politics. She attended political meetings for him and, as a result, became active in human rights organizations herself. In 1939, she resigned from the Daughters of the American Revolution to protest their refusal to let the black singer Marian Anderson perform in Washington's Constitution Hall. After FDR's death, President Truman made her a member of the first U.S. delegation to the United Nations.

★**ABRAHAM LINCOLN BATTALION** In 1936, a civil war began in Spain between the Nationalist rebels and the Republicans who had been elected to govern the country. Fascist Italy and Nazi Germany sent troops and tanks to support the Nationalists, while the Republicans turned to the Soviet Union for help. Although the U.S. government decided not to get involved, many Americans personally supported the Republican cause.

Soviet officials organized the International Brigades, made up of idealistic young volunteers eager to fight for democracy and freedom in Spain. One of these brigades included the Abraham Lincoln Battalion, at first made up entirely of Americans. Nearly three thousand young men, mostly students without any military training, served in the battalion. Republican sympathizer Ernest Hemingway set his popular 1940 novel *For Whom the Bell Tolls* during the Spanish Civil War, which the Nationalists won in 1939.

★**NYLON** During the 1930s, a Du Pont chemist named Wallace H. Carothers developed the first artificial fiber, later named nylon. In 1938, the first nylon toothbrushes were sold. Two years later, the first women's stockings made from this "miracle fabric" appeared in department stores across the country.

Nylon stockings quickly became the rage, helping to define a new 1940s look. The first nylons had a noticeable dark seam that ran up the underside of the leg. Like silk stockings, they were held up by garters. When the government rationed nylon during World War II—to the horror of nearly all American women—a black market quickly developed. Others simply decorated their legs with black pencil lines that looked like stocking seams.

★**AMELIA EARHART** Like Charles Lindbergh before her, Amelia Earhart performed such remarkable feats as a pilot and adventurer that she became a national hero. Earhart was the first woman to match Lindbergh's solo transatlantic flight, and she was also the first person to fly solo from Hawaii to California, an even greater distance.

During the 1930s, she used her fame to promote two cherished causes: commercial aviation and feminism. In 1937, she attempted to fly around the world with navigator Fred Noonan. Their twin-engine Lockheed Electra disappeared on July 2 during the most dangerous leg of the trip, from New Guinea to tiny Howland Island in the middle of the Pacific Ocean. Their fate remains a mystery.

campaign, Roosevelt heeded the charges that his New Deal agencies were disorganized and inefficient.

In 1935, the president proposed a reorganization of these agencies that Congress passed as the Emergency Relief Act of 1935. Most of the New Deal agencies were brought under the control of the Works Progress Administration, directed by Harry Hopkins. The WPA hired more than eight million people for public works projects before closing its doors in 1943.

PACKING THE SUPREME COURT By the time Roosevelt began his second term in 1937, government spending had brought about a limited recovery. But the president was frustrated, especially by the Supreme Court whose aging justices believed that many New Deal programs went far beyond the powers granted to the federal government by the Constitution.

To get around this roadblock, Roosevelt proposed on February 5, 1937, a plan to reorganize the Court. He wanted to appoint a new justice for every current justice over seventy years old. Because six of the justices were already past seventy, Roosevelt could appoint six more justices, bringing the total number to fifteen.

Most people agreed that something had to be done to prevent the Court from blocking reform, but Roosevelt's plan was quite controversial. The president claimed that the bill was meant to reduce each justice's workload. But it was obvious that he was trying to control the Court's decisions by creating a new majority in favor of the New Deal.

The Senate eventually rejected the plan, but in the meantime the justices got the message. While the bill was still under consideration, a previously conservative justice began voting with the Court's liberal bloc. This switch made the difference in two important 5-4 rulings supporting minimum wage laws and the Social Security Act.

AMERICA IN ISOLATION The difficulties at home made it easy for Americans to ignore events happening in the rest of the world. During the 1930s, Germany, Italy, and Japan were all turning increasingly aggressive. Germany reclaimed land it had lost during World War I, while Italy invaded Ethiopia, and Japan conquered Manchuria on the Chinese mainland. The U.S. response was generally to ignore these events. Isolationists at home believed that the Atlantic and Pacific oceans would insulate the nation from European and Asian wars.

In keeping with this isolationism, Congress enacted a series of neutrality acts beginning in August 1935 that prevented Americans from selling arms to nations at war. After World War I, many people came to believe that arms dealers were "merchants of death" who secretly conspired to start wars because wars were good business. It was thought that banning the arms trade would stop the fighting.

Unfortunately, this policy helped the aggressor nations, who had stockpiled weapons for years and were thus better prepared to fight. During the Spanish Civil War, for example, U.S. neutrality laws prevented Americans from supporting the Republican side, while the Nationalists received huge amounts of military aid from the fascist governments in Germany and Italy.

In his "quarantine" speech of October 5, 1937, Roosevelt demanded that freedom-loving nations of the world spurn aggressor nations. Ninety percent of the world's nations wanted peace, he said. The remaining ten

DURING THE SUMMER OF 1940, ROOSEVELT KEPT HIS reelection plans secret. Not even the delegates to the Democratic convention knew what he intended. When Postmaster General James Farley, a trusted political ally, asked permission to launch his own campaign, the president told him to go ahead. Farley thought Roosevelt had decided to retire, but Roosevelt was really working behind the scenes to have the convention draft him.

Never before had a president run for a third term, and Roosevelt was worried that the voters might think him arrogant. By having the convention draft him, which it did, FDR could pretend that his campaign for a third term had been forced upon him by the will of the people.

To run against Roosevelt, the Republicans nominated Indiana businessman Wendell L. Willkie, who ran a power company. Willkie had been a Democrat as late as 1932, when he contributed $150 to Roosevelt's first campaign. Willkie later became a Republican after breaking with Roosevelt over the Tennessee Valley Authority, which competed with Willkie's own company.

Unlike FDR's first two campaigns, which had been dominated by economic issues, the 1940 race focused on the war in Europe and the prospect of a third term for Roosevelt. Both candidates pledged to keep the country out of the war, but those who wanted the United States to take a strong stand against Hitler tended to favor Roosevelt.

On economic issues, Willkie basically agreed with Roosevelt's New Deal policies, so he attacked Roosevelt for breaking George Washington's tradition of stepping down after two terms. Because Willkie was generally unable to distinguish himself from Roosevelt, the country decided to stick with a proven and trusted leader. Although three-quarters of the nation's newspapers endorsed Willkie, FDR's support in the cities and among the working class carried him to victory.

President Roosevelt with Joseph Stalin (left) and Winston Churchill (right).

JAPANESE ATTACK PEARL HARBOR!

Surprise Air Raid Sinks Pacific Fleet

PEARL HARBOR, Hawaii, December 7, 1941—At five minutes before eight this morning, Japanese dive bombers and torpedo planes launched a surprise attack on the U.S. naval base at Pearl Harbor.

Eight battleships were crippled in the harbor. At the nearby army air base, half the fighter planes were destroyed while they sat on the ground. In all, more than twenty-three hundred U.S. servicemen were killed during the raid.

The Japanese can now proceed with the conquest of East Asia unhindered by the U.S. Pacific Fleet, which has been seriously damaged.

President Roosevelt is expected to ask for a declaration of war when he appears before a joint session of Congress tomorrow.

percent needed to be controlled as though they were diseases.

"We are determined to keep out of war," the president said, but the world's interdependence "makes it impossible for any nation completely to isolate itself from economic and political upheavals in the rest of the world, especially when such upheavals appear to be spreading and not declining."

Roosevelt's speech created an uproar among isolationists, who believed the president was inching closer to war. Although FDR toned down his public statements after that, he remained privately determined to resist aggression.

THE GOOD NEIGHBOR POLICY Throughout his first two terms in office, Roosevelt worked hard to improve U.S. relations with Latin America. In his first inaugural address, he said that he wanted to "dedicate this nation to the policy of the good neighbor."

For many years, the United States had been a difficult neighbor indeed. During the 1920s, Harding and Coolidge sent U.S. troops into Panama, the Dominican Republic, and Honduras. When violence followed the withdrawal of U.S. troops from Nicaragua in 1925, Coolidge sent them back to meet our "moral responsibility" there.

Roosevelt promised to put an end to that sort of interference. At the Montevideo Conference of American States in 1933, Secretary of State Cordell Hull gave his support to a declaration that "no state has the right to intervene in the internal or external affairs of another." By satisfactorily addressing this issue, the Roosevelt administration helped to ensure Latin American cooperation later in the fight against Hitler.

PREPARATIONS FOR WAR World War II began when Nazi Germany invaded Poland in September 1939 and Britain and France came to Poland's aid. Roosevelt invoked the current Neutrality Act as he was required to by law, but he made it clear whose side the United States was on. "Even a neutral cannot be asked to close his mind or his conscience," the president said.

With Great Britain threatened, Americans debated whether or not to help. Isolationists organized the America First Committee to make sure their views were heard. Prominent spokesmen such as Charles Lindbergh warned that the United States had no business intervening in European affairs. But Roosevelt quite clearly saw the threat that Hitler posed to the world. After the fall of France in June 1940, he did everything he could within the law to help the British.

On September 3, 1940, Roosevelt issued an executive order trading fifty surplus destroyers to Britain in exchange for naval bases in Newfoundland and Bermuda. The British desperately needed the destroyers to fight German submarines in the North Atlantic. Meanwhile, Congress passed the first peacetime draft in U.S. history and appropriated sixteen billion dollars for new warships and airplanes.

In a fireside chat two months after his 1940 reelection, Roosevelt declared once again his support for Britain. "All our present efforts are not enough," he said. "We must be

★FALA
One of the most famous presidential pets was FDR's dog Fala. This little black Scottie went everywhere with the president. When Roosevelt and British prime minister Winston Churchill met at sea to sign the Atlantic Charter in 1941, Fala was there at his master's feet. On a voyage to Hawaii in 1944, sailors aboard the cruiser *Baltimore* lured Fala belowdecks in order to pluck tufts of his hair for souvenirs.

★JAPANESE INTERNMENT CAMPS In the months after Pearl Harbor, many Californians focused their anger on the 127,000 Japanese Americans living in this country, mostly on the West Coast. Rumors spread quickly that Japanese Americans planned to sabotage military bases there. In February 1942, President Roosevelt ordered all Japanese Americans, whether they were citizens or not, removed from the West Coast to internment camps as far away as Arkansas. This policy was urged on him in part by farming interests who proceeded to buy up—at bargain prices—the rich land that relocated families were forced to sell. No efforts were made to curb the freedom of German or Italian Americans, however.

★THE HOME FRONT After the United States' entry into World War II, the country mobilized to fight on three fronts: in Europe, in Asia, and at home. Between 1941 and 1945, fifteen million men—and for the first time, nearly two hundred thousand women—served in the armed forces. At home, however, those men left behind important jobs on the nation's assembly lines that had to be filled. A government campaign featuring a character called Rosie the Riveter encouraged women to do their part for the war effort. Their enthusiastic response allowed factories in crucial war-related industries to keep running both day and night.

★ **THE GEODESIC DOME** R. Buckminster Fuller was a visionary architect and engineer who devoted his life to conserving the natural resources of the planet he called Spaceship Earth. During the 1940s, he developed the geodesic dome. Fuller's revolutionary geometric design was uniquely balanced so that its size was not a limiting factor. People could build geodesic domes as large as they wanted.

Fuller's domes offered many possibilities for the future. Because their strength increased with their size, geodesic domes could be built to enclose entire cities or to protect peo- ple living under- water or on other planets. One of the most famous geodesic domes would be built to house the U.S. pavilion at the 1967 world's fair, called Expo67, in Montreal.

★ **THE MANHATTAN PROJECT** In August 1939, Albert Einstein, the most famous scientist of his time, wrote a letter to President Roosevelt on behalf of colleagues who had recently fled Nazi Germany. In his letter, Einstein warned Roosevelt that the United States should begin work on an atomic bomb unless it wanted the Germans to develop one first.

At first, Roosevelt didn't take Einstein's letter very seriously, but that changed after Pearl Harbor. The presi- dent eventually devoted two billion dollars to the research. The bomb program was code-named the Manhattan Project because most of the early work took place at Columbia University in Manhattan.

On July 16, 1945, the first atomic bomb was set off near Alamogordo in the New Mexican desert. The explo- sion produced a flash that lit mountains ten miles away, vaporized the bomb tower, and turned the desert sand to glass for eight hundred yards around.

the great arsenal of democracy." One week later, the president proposed the "lend-lease" program. Lend-lease provided arms to Britain immediately but deferred payment until after the war. The program was later extended to the Soviet Union after the German invasion of that country in June 1941.

In August 1941, Roosevelt met with British prime minister Winston Churchill aboard a battleship off Newfoundland. It was the beginning of an exceptionally close relationship between the two leaders. Together they drew up the Atlantic Charter, which detailed their common war aims. These included the rights of all people to choose their own form of government and to trade freely.

"DR. WIN THE WAR" The United States finally entered the war after the Japanese attack on Pearl Harbor. Tensions between the United States and Japan had been building since the Japanese invasion of China in 1937. In 1940, Japan joined the Triple Alliance with Germany and Italy, agreeing that war against one meant war against all.

With the same energy he brought to the New Deal, Roosevelt set about retooling the country's factories for war. Diverting funds from some New Deal programs and ending others, the president began a massive defense spending program. At a press conference, Roosevelt declared that "Dr. Win the War" had replaced "Dr. New Deal."

During World War II, nearly every resource and every person in the country played some part in the war effort. The Office of Price Administration rationed many necessary commodities such as rubber, sugar, and gasoline. Roosevelt himself spent much of his time planning strategy and meeting with the Allies.

After the Allied invasion of North Africa in late 1942, Roosevelt met with Churchill at Casablanca, Morocco. The following November, the two leaders met again, this time with Soviet premier Joseph Stalin in Teheran, Iran. Together these men were known as the Big Three.

At Teheran, Roosevelt and Churchill promised Stalin that they would open a second front in Europe the following summer. Stalin eagerly awaited the Allied invasion of France because it would force the Germans to shift troops from the Russian front in the East back to the West.

D-DAY The supreme Allied commander, General Dwight D. Eisenhower, decided that the invasion of France would take place on the beaches of Normandy. The day—code-named D-Day—was June 6, 1944. The success of the D-Day invasion, the largest naval operation in history, gave the Allies a foothold in Europe, which they kept expanding until France was liberated and Germany itself threatened.

When the Big Three met for the final time in February 1945 at Yalta in the Soviet Union, the end of the war was finally in sight. By this time, Roosevelt was quite sick.

At Yalta, Stalin forced Roosevelt and Churchill to agree to allow, at least temporarily, Communist governments in Eastern Europe. Many historians have used the president's weakened condition to explain his concessions to Stalin. But others have pointed out that Roosevelt had little choice. To oppose Stalin would have required the United States to invade Eastern Europe itself.

On April 12, 1945, as the Allies converged on Berlin, Roosevelt died at his retreat in Warm Springs, Georgia. Less than a month later, on May 7, the Germans formally surrendered, ending the war in Europe.

AFTER TWELVE DIFFICULT YEARS AS PRESIDENT, Roosevelt's health was clearly failing. Although they were certain to nominate him for a fourth term, most Democrats suspected that in choosing Roosevelt's running mate, they were choosing the next president. Because of strong opposition to incumbent vice president Henry Wallace, whom some delegates considered a socialist, Roosevelt replaced him with Senator Harry Truman of Missouri.

The Republican candidate, New York governor Thomas E. Dewey, had been the front-runner for the 1940 nomination before Wendell Willkie took it away from him. This time, Dewey won on the first ballot with 1,056 of the 1,057 votes. (The remaining vote went to General Douglas MacArthur.) Dewey had first made a name for himself during the 1930s fighting organized crime as the district attorney in New York City. As governor, he had fought corruption in the state's police department and improved conditions in its mental health facilities.

With World War II still being fought, Dewey refused to criticize Roosevelt's foreign policy. However, he did make Roosevelt's health an issue, attacking "the tired old men" in Washington who had been running the country for so long. In response to Dewey's tactic, FDR's doctor announced that the president was in excellent health.

Roosevelt also campaigned in bad weather to prove that neither he nor the nation had anything to fear on that count.

Democrats claimed that Dewey, who had no foreign policy experience, was not qualified to become president during wartime. Their slogan, "Don't change horses midstream," succinctly summed up Roosevelt's appeal. In November, FDR won again, but this time by a narrower margin than in any of his three previous victories.

HARRY S. TRUMAN

33RD PRESIDENT
★
FROM 1945 TO 1953

BORN: May 8, 1884

BIRTHPLACE: Lamar, Mo.

DIED: December 26, 1972

PARTY: Democrat

VICE PRESIDENT: Alben W. Barkley

FIRST LADY: Elizabeth (Bess) Virginia Wallace

CHILDREN: Margaret

NICKNAME: Man from Independence

The first president to travel underwater in a modern submarine.

ATOMIC BOMB DROPPED ON HIROSHIMA

HIROSHIMA, Japan, August 6, 1945—The first atomic bomb ever used in warfare was dropped today on the Japanese city of Hiroshima. Of the 344,000 people living there, approximately one hundred thousand were killed instantly. Another hundred thousand died later from burns and radiation poisoning.

The ten-foot-long bomb, code-named Little Boy, was carried by the *Enola Gay*. This B-29 bomber dropped Little Boy from an altitude of thirty-two thousand feet. The bomb exploded two thousand feet above the ground, leveling more than four square miles of the city. Waves of flame engulfed the rest of Hiroshima as the river flooded, trapping wounded people too weak to move.

President Truman justified the massive civilian casualties by pointing to the hundreds of thousands of U.S. servicemen who might have died during an invasion of Japan.

On April 12, 1945, just five weeks into his vice presidency, Harry Truman was suddenly called to the White House. He met Eleanor Roosevelt in her study. The first lady put her arm around Truman's shoulder and said, "Harry, the president is dead."

Truman's first thoughts were for the president's widow. "Is there anything I can do for you?" he asked. But Mrs. Roosevelt shook her head. "Is there anything we can do for you?" she replied. "For you are the one in trouble now."

Franklin Roosevelt had been running the country for more than twelve years when he died. For Truman—or anyone else—to succeed him was a mighty task.

Roosevelt had brought the country through the Great Depression and won the war in Europe. But Japan still remained to be tamed, and communism already seemed to be threatening the stability of the postwar world.

THE POTSDAM CONFERENCE Truman began at a great disadvantage because Roosevelt had never included him in policy development meetings. Truman wasn't even briefed on the atom bomb program until after he was sworn in as president. As a result, Truman had to learn about being president in a hurry. His first important test came in July 1945 when he traveled to the Berlin suburb of Potsdam to meet Winston Churchill and Joseph Stalin.

At Potsdam, the three leaders agreed to divide postwar Germany into four zones controlled by the United States, Britain, France, and the Soviet Union. The division roughly corresponded to the troop positions at the end of the war. Although the German capital of Berlin fell entirely within the Soviet zone, it was also divided into four sectors, one for each Allied power.

THE ATOM BOMB On July 16, the day before the Potsdam conference opened, U.S. scientists conducted the first atom bomb test near Alamogordo, New Mexico. The A-bomb had been developed with the help of the British, but the Soviets knew nothing about it. After learning of the test's success, Truman decided to tell Stalin personally about the United States' new superweapon.

On July 26, the Allied leaders at Potsdam sent an ultimatum to the Japanese: "The alternative to surrender is prompt and utter destruction." But the Japanese didn't know about

HARRY TRUMAN HAD TO WEAR THICK GLASSES during his childhood in Independence, Missouri. Because the glasses were expensive, his

The Early Years

mother would not allow him to play contact sports. Other boys sometimes teased him for taking piano lessons instead. "I was kind of a sissy," Truman later said.

After serving in World War I, Truman opened a men's clothing shop in Kansas City. The business failed in 1922. But that year, with the backing of local political boss Thomas Pendergast, Truman won election to the top job in the county. In 1934, also with the help of Pendergast, he won a seat in the U.S. Senate.

Although Truman was sometimes called the "senator from Pendergast," he was known to be a capable and honest public servant. The Pendergast machine was certainly corrupt, but Truman said Pendergast never asked him to do anything dishonest because "he knew I wouldn't do it if he asked it."

★**JACKIE ROBINSON** On April 15, 1947, twenty-eight-year-old Jackie Robinson became the first black to play in a major league baseball game. Until Robinson broke the color barrier, African Americans were forced to play in separate Negro leagues.

All through his rookie year, the Brooklyn Dodgers' new second baseman was taunted by fans and players alike, who called him "nigger" and "jungle boy." But the dignified and courageous Robinson never responded. He just played as well as he could. That year, he was named the National League's Rookie of the Year. Two years later, he won the league's Most Valuable Player award.

★ **THE UNITED NATIONS** The United Nations was created at the end of World War II. Its purpose was to prevent wars, promote human rights, and aid economic development throughout the world. Delegates from fifty nations attended the conference in San Francisco at which the UN Charter was drafted and then signed in June 1945.

Twenty-five years and one world war earlier, the U.S. Senate had debated the League of Nations Covenant to the Treaty of Versailles for eight months before rejecting it. This time, the United States became the first country to join the new international organization. After just six days of debate in July, the Senate ratified the UN Charter by a vote of 89-2.

★ **THE GI BILL OF RIGHTS** The GI Bill of Rights was the name soldiers gave to the Servicemen's Readjustment Act of 1944. Congress passed this bill to provide benefits for the GIs fighting World War II. It established a system of veterans' hospitals to guarantee them medical care. It also set aside money for low-interest mortgages, small business loans, and college scholarships. The money the GI Bill provided for tuition and living expenses allowed nearly ten million veterans to attend colleges and trade schools after the war. In this way, the GI Bill played an important role in retraining soldiers for jobs in the peacetime postwar economy.

★ **THE BUCK STOPS HERE** Truman had a particularly feisty personality. "If you can't stand the heat, get out of the kitchen," he liked to say. He occasionally lost his temper in public and was known to use vulgar language at times. But Truman's scrappiness gave him the self-confidence he needed to make difficult decisions. A sign on his desk read, "The Buck Stops Here." It meant that he never "passed the buck," or made someone else take responsibility for a decision.

the A-bomb, so they didn't see any reason to surrender.

Truman was faced with one of the most demanding choices ever made by a president: whether or not to use the atomic bomb. If he did, he would be the first to use a weapon more deadly than anything ever created. If he didn't, hundreds of thousands of U.S. soldiers might die during the planned invasion of Japan. Although he feared its consequences, Truman decided to use the bomb.

When the August 6 attack on Hiroshima still failed to produce a Japanese surrender, Truman ordered a second bomb dropped on Nagasaki three days later. On August 10, the Japanese sued for peace, and World War II was over. As one war ended, however, another began.

THE COLD WAR Stalin had made it clear at Yalta that the Soviet Union would accept nothing less than secure borders. To the Soviets, this meant that Communist governments would be established and maintained in Eastern Europe. Stalin believed that the industrious Germans would recover quickly, as they had after World War I, and he wanted a buffer.

However real Stalin's concerns about Germany may have been, Truman and other western leaders remained concerned about the spread of communism.

In a speech delivered in Fulton, Missouri, in March 1946, Winston Churchill said that an "iron curtain" was descending across Europe. On one side were the democracies of the West; on the other side, the Communists.

The struggle between these competing political philosophies became known as the Cold War. Although the United States and the Soviet Union never fought each other directly, they used surrogates, notably

HARRY S. TRUMAN 1945-1953

the Koreans and the Vietnamese, to fight their battles for them.

THE TRUMAN DOCTRINE

The first important conflict of the Cold War took place in the Mediterranean, where Communist rebels threatened the governments of Greece and Turkey. Many experts pointed out that, while these governments were strongly anticommunist, they also treated their people very harshly. Truman didn't really care. He believed it was more important for the United States to check the spread of Soviet influence wherever it could.

On March 13, 1947, the president explained his policy for the "containment" of communism in a speech he delivered to Congress. In order to justify his four-hundred-million-dollar aid request for Greece and Turkey, Truman argued that the United States must guarantee help to every nation fighting the Communist menace. This policy was later called the Truman Doctrine.

THE MARSHALL PLAN

In the spirit of the Truman Doctrine, Secretary of State George Marshall tackled the problem of war-ravaged Europe. Nearly three hundred thousand Americans had been killed in action during World War II, but almost none of the fighting took place on U.S. soil. Central Europe was not as fortunate. During the six years of the war, tank battles and Allied bombing reduced to rubble most of the industrial cities in Britain, France, the Soviet Union, and Germany. Four million Germans and more than eighteen million Soviets were dead.

Three months after Truman's speech on Greece and Turkey, Marshall announced his plan to rebuild Europe. He believed the only

MOST POLITICAL PROFESSIONALS WROTE TRUMAN OFF as a caretaker president even before the campaign began. Liberals within the Democratic party, including FDR's sons, tried to convince General Dwight

Eisenhower to run, but Eisenhower declined. Things got worse for Truman at the convention, where Mayor Hubert Humphrey of Minneapolis led a successful fight for a strong civil rights plank in the party platform. Thirty-five southern delegates walked out in protest.

After the convention, conservative southern Democrats met in Birmingham to form the States' Rights, or Dixiecrat, party, nominating South Carolina governor Strom Thurmond for president. Meanwhile, the radical Roosevelt wing of the Democratic party, upset with Truman's tough stance on the Soviet Union, put up Henry Wallace, FDR's second vice president, as the candidate of the Progressive party. Wallace promoted peace with the Soviet Union and opposed the Marshall Plan as a disguised attempt by U.S. corporations to take over Europe.

Abandoned by members of his own party, Truman wasn't given much of a chance. New York governor Thomas E. Dewey, renominated by the Republicans after losing in 1944, sat back and waited for victory. But Truman fought hard. During a thirty-thousand-mile "whistle-stop" train campaign, he made three hundred speeches to six million people. His gutsy manner and blunt attacks on the "do-nothing Eightieth Congress" caught the attention of the country. "Give 'em hell, Harry," one man at a rally in Seattle yelled.

Truman's campaign kept this positive momentum going. Still, all the polls, and even the early returns, predicted his defeat. On Election Day, the early edition of the *Chicago Tribune* ran the headline "Dewey Defeats Truman." The president later posed with this headline after victories in California and Ohio clinched his election.

Harry, Bess, and Margaret Truman with friends.

COMMUNISTS INVADE SOUTH KOREA

UN Security Council Condemns North

NEW YORK, June 25, 1950—The Communist government of North Korea launched a full-scale military invasion of South Korea today as the North Korean army crossed the Thirty-eighth Parallel border in force.

In an emergency meeting called this afternoon by President Truman, the UN Security Council voted 9–0 to hold North Korea accountable for the attack. The resolution is a prelude to sending UN troops to Korea. U.S. soldiers are expected to make up more than three-quarters of the combat troops used in this UN "police action."

As a permanent member of the Security Council, the Soviet Union had the power to veto the resolution, but the Soviet leadership continues to boycott Security Council meetings. The boycott began when the other members refused to recognize the People's Republic as the rightful government of China.

way to save the exhausted nations of Western Europe from communism was to get their economies rolling again with U.S. dollars.

Marshall even offered to include the Soviets in his reconstruction program. "Our policy is directed not against any country or doctrine, but against hunger, poverty, desperation, and chaos," he said. A suspicious Stalin turned down the U.S. offer.

Between 1948 and 1952, Congress authorized twelve billion dollars for the Marshall Plan. Half of that went to Britain, France, and West Germany, which was created in 1949 when the three western zones were merged.

THE BERLIN AIRLIFT Meanwhile, the Soviet Union decided to test the West's resolve. It considered the Allied presence in Berlin an unnecessary annoyance. To encourage the British, French, and Americans to leave, the Soviets decided to blockade West Berlin beginning in April 1948.

Truman responded quickly and decisively by ordering an airlift to the besieged city. Using a constant shuttle of cargo planes, the United States and Great Britain were able to keep the West Berliners supplied with food, coal, and other necessities. The blockade ended in May 1949 and the successful airlift two months later.

The Berlin airlift made clear the need for a united front in Western Europe. The North Atlantic Treaty Organization, created by an

161

agreement signed in April 1949, provided just that. Truman's active participation in NATO finally put an end to the isolationism that had dominated U.S. foreign policy since the days of Washington.

THE FAIR DEAL Truman had a somewhat easier time with domestic issues. Of all the nations who fought in World War II, only the United States came out of the war better off economically. After years of rationing, Americans were eager to spend the money they had saved on large purchases such as cars, houses, and washing machines.

The biggest problem facing Truman was how to handle the massive demobilization of troops. At the end of the war, there were twelve million men serving in the army and navy. Within a year, nine million of them were discharged.

Truman's economic advisors worried that the discharged soldiers would have a difficult time finding new jobs now that many of their old jobs had been taken over by women and blacks. "Rosie the Riveter isn't going back to emptying slop jars," one union leader said. "Times have changed. People have become accustomed to...new ways of being treated."

The crunch was eased by two trends. Many women did indeed leave the work force to become mothers and housewives, beginning the postwar Baby Boom. Meanwhile, the country's economic boom created a great number of new jobs, particularly in home building and consumer manufacturing.

With his Fair Deal program, Truman tried to adapt Roosevelt's depression policies to postwar prosperity. Truman's top priorities were a national health care program and a civil rights bill. Both were defeated by new Republican

★**THE FIRST FAMILY** Harry Truman first met Bess Wallace in Sunday school. "I had only one sweetheart from the time I was six," Truman later said. But he and Bess didn't start dating seriously until 1913, when they were both nearly thirty. They were married in 1919.

Their daughter Margaret was an outgoing person like her mother. During her father's presidency, Margaret tried to launch a singing career. The twenty-three-year old made her debut before a national radio audience in March 1947. In 1950, the *Washington Post* music critic wrote that she "cannot sing with anything approaching professional finish." After reading the review, President Truman sent the critic an angry letter: "I have just read your lousy review.... You sound like a frustrated old man who never made a success.... I never met you, but if I do you'll need a new nose."

★**LEVITTOWN** The return of soldiers to civilian life caused a severe housing shortage after World War II. To relieve this problem, the construction firm of Levitt and Sons built a planned community on New York's Long Island that soon provided a model for suburban developers all over the country.

The secret of Levittown's success was its construction methods. Using prefabricated materials and assembly-line techniques, construction crews were able to put up as many as thirty identical houses in a single day. The homes may have lacked individuality, but they were remarkably affordable, selling for as little as seven thousand dollars each. With a GI Bill mortgage, a veteran could buy a house in Levittown for sixty-five dollars a month with no money down.

★**THE BABY BOOM** During World War II, many families put off having children. But once the war was over, there seemed little reason to wait. Between 1946 and 1960, these new parents created the Baby Boom. Because of the extraordinary size of the Baby Boom generation, its concerns and interests have always had a powerful influence on American society.

The book used to raise most of these children was *Baby and Child Care* by Dr. Benjamin Spock. This 1946 manual sold twenty-four million copies, more than any other book except the plays of Shakespeare and the Bible. It emphasized flexibility instead of the rigid schedules and discipline favored by earlier generations.

★**THE COMPUTER AGE** Besides the atom bomb, scientists made other important discoveries during World War II. At the University of Pennsylvania, J. Presper Eckert and John W. Mauchly began the computer age when they built the first all-electronic digital computer. They called their machine the Electronic Numerical Integrator and Calculator, or ENIAC for short.

The first computers, including ENIAC, used vacuum tubes to relay information. Because these tubes took up so much space, ENIAC covered fifteen hundred square feet and weighed thirty tons. The invention of the transistor in 1948 allowed scientists to replace the vacuum tubes and shrink the size of computers substantially. A transistorized version of ENIAC would have fit inside a refrigerator.

majorities in the Eightieth Congress, elected in 1946.

Much to Truman's displeasure, the Eightieth Congress did pass, over the president's veto, the Taft-Hartley Act of 1947, which rolled back many of the legal gains unions had made since the passage of the Wagner Act in 1935.

After his remarkable reelection, Truman campaigned once more for his Fair Deal programs, this time before a friendlier Democratic Congress. He got the minimum wage raised from forty to seventy-five cents an hour and won passage of the National Housing Act, which provided money for slum clearance and low-income housing. Truman had already used an executive order in July 1948 to end racial segregation in the armed forces. But the united opposition of southerners in Congress prevented him from making any further progress on the issue of civil rights.

When Truman ordered the dropping of the atom bomb in 1945, he had hoped that its use might scare other countries, especially the Soviet Union, into maintaining the peace. But the testing of a Soviet bomb in 1949 forced the president to change his thinking. Now peace depended on a stable "balance of terror" between the two superpowers.

WHO LOST CHINA? The "loss" of China that same year also hurt the Truman administration badly. The victory of Mao Zedong's Communist Red Army over the hopelessly corrupt Nationalist forces of Chiang Kai-shek had been expected by government officials. Nevertheless, it shocked ordinary citizens, who began to ask, "Who lost China?" Republicans in Congress blamed Truman's secretary of state, Dean Acheson, whom they said was "soft on communism."

THE KOREAN WAR

Communist North Korea invaded capitalist South Korea in June 1950. Given the political situation, Truman had little choice but to send troops. Although the North Koreans were able to penetrate deeply into South Korean territory, General Douglas MacArthur's brilliant landing behind enemy lines at Inchon turned the war around. By October, United Nations forces under MacArthur's command had recrossed the Thirty-eighth Parallel border into North Korea and were advancing quickly on the Yalu River, which separated North Korea from China.

As UN forces approached the Yalu, Chinese officials warned that they would not "sit back with folded hands." But MacArthur dismissed almost casually the possibility of China entering the war. With his air force controlling the sky, the general was sure that the Chinese would be slaughtered if they tried anything.

MacArthur was tragically wrong. On November 26, Chinese soldiers streamed across the border, inflicting heavy casualties and chasing U.S. and Korean troops all the way back across the Thirty-eighth Parallel. The general's command eventually regrouped, but the best he could achieve now was a stalemate.

Once the Chinese entered the war, MacArthur began asking for permission to carry the war to China. When Truman refused him, MacArthur publicly expressed his unhappiness.

As commander-in-chief of the armed forces, President Truman was not willing to tolerate any challenge to his authority. The president relieved MacArthur of his command in April 1951.

Three months later, peace talks began, but no treaty was signed with Truman in office. Despite occasional cease-fires, the fighting continued as the negotiations dragged on.

P EOPLE HAD BEEN TRYING TO CONVINCE WORLD WAR II hero Dwight D. Eisenhower to run for president ever since the German surrender. There was a problem, however: Eisenhower didn't belong to a political party. The Democrats courted him in 1948, but it turned out that Eisenhower's views were more in keeping with the Republican party.

The Republican platform called for a strong national defense and criticized the Democrats for "appeasement of communism at home and abroad." This approach played to Eisenhower's strength as a symbol of U.S. military might. "Let's face it. The only excuse for Ike's candidacy is that he's the man best qualified to deal with Stalin," one Republican strategist said. At Thomas E. Dewey's suggestion, Eisenhower picked anticommunist crusader Richard M. Nixon of California as his running mate.

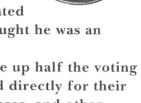

E isenhower's Democratic opponent was Governor Adlai E. Stevenson of Illinois, grandson of Grover Cleveland's vice president. Stevenson was enormously well educated and well spoken, but many voters thought he was an "egghead," or too intellectual.

Recognizing that women now made up half the voting population, the Republicans appealed directly for their votes. Stockings, nail files, makeup cases, and other women's items were printed with the slogan "I Like Ike."

For the most part, Eisenhower's campaign proceeded smoothly. The one rough spot came when *The New York Times* revealed that Nixon maintained a "slush" fund of campaign contributions, which he used to pay some of his own expenses. With Eisenhower threatening to drop him from the ticket, Nixon delivered the nationally televised "Checkers" speech on September 23. He denied using the money for personal expenses. But he did admit receiving one gift, a cocker spaniel named Checkers. "Regardless of what they say about it," Nixon declared, "we're going to keep it." Eisenhower locked up the election a few weeks later when he declared that if elected "I shall go to Korea" to get the stalled peace talks moving again.

DWIGHT DAVID EISENHOWER

34TH PRESIDENT

★

FROM 1953 TO 1961

BORN: October 14, 1890

BIRTHPLACE: Denison, Texas

DIED: March 28, 1969

PARTY: Republican

VICE PRESIDENT: Richard M. Nixon

FIRST LADY: Marie (Mamie) Geneva Doud

CHILDREN: Dwight, John

NICKNAME: Ike

Had a putting green installed on the White House lawn.

SEN. McCARTHY CHARGES COMMIES IN STATE DEPT.

WHEELING, West Virginia, February 9, 1950—Speaking before a Republican women's club, Senator Joseph McCarthy of Wisconsin shocked his audience tonight when he declared that Communists are secretly working in important positions throughout the federal government.

The senator repeatedly waved a piece of paper that he claimed was a list of 205 "card-carrying Communists" currently working in the State Department. He has not yet revealed any of the names, nor has he provided any evidence to back up his sensational charges.

McCarthy's attack comes only a month after former State Department official Alger Hiss was found guilty of lying about his Communist past. For the crime of perjury, or lying under oath, Hiss was given a ten-thousand-dollar fine and five years in jail.

Time magazine editor Whittaker Chambers, himself an admitted Soviet agent, accused Hiss of spying for the Soviet Union in testimony before the House Un-American Activities Committee. Despite his conviction, Hiss still maintains his innocence.

As the Allied commander during World War II, Dwight Eisenhower developed a reputation for smooth, effective leadership. In his two terms as president, the retired general ran the government in much the same way he ran the army. That is, he appointed staff members to create and direct national policy under his supervision.

Unlike the feisty Truman, Eisenhower always seemed to be relaxed and smiling. As a result, his years in the White House were known for peace, prosperity, and blandness. Things were not as peaceful and prosperous, however, as Eisenhower's mood made them seem.

Eisenhower believed the government should remain as

small as possible. This attitude led him to criticize the New Deal and the Fair Deal, both of which he felt neglected traditional American individualism. Above all, however, Eisenhower was a moderate who followed "that straight road down the middle" and didn't make waves.

THE KOREAN WAR ENDS

In December 1952, Eisenhower kept his campaign promise to go to Korea, where he tried to revive the stalled peace talks. The president-elect threatened to extend the war to China and even to use small-scale atomic weapons. Still, the negotiations continued for another seven months before an armistice was signed on July 27, 1953.

The supposedly limited war in Korea cost the United States fifteen billion dollars. In an attempt to avoid paying such a high price in the future, Eisenhower and Secretary of State John Foster Dulles developed the policy of "massive retaliation." In their view, the Soviet Union would not attack the United States or any of its allies as long as the leaders in the Kremlin believed that the United States would respond with nuclear devastation.

Eisenhower was particularly motivated by his desire to cut the federal budget. He assumed that nuclear weapons provided "more bang for a buck" than conventional weapons. Therefore, he ordered severe cutbacks in army ground troops and instead invested in nuclear warheads. He also spent money on the missiles and bombers needed to deliver them. But the savings turned out to be an illusion as the cost of ever more sophisticated hardware kept defense spending high.

Meanwhile, the country remained obsessed with fears of Communist

DWIGHT EISENHOWER WAS RAISED IN ABILENE, Kansas, the third of six sons born to a poor family. Other boys often teased him for wearing

The Early Years

tattered clothing and his mother's hand-me-down shoes. Young Dwight thought he would grow up to be a railroad engineer. Instead, he passed the West Point entrance exam, which earned him a free college education and a career in the army.

After graduating from the military academy, Eisenhower became a tank commander. Although he requested an overseas assignment during World War I, the army ordered him to spend the war as a training instructor. In 1932, Major Eisenhower joined the staff of Douglas MacArthur and helped the general break up the Bonus March. During

World War II, General Eisenhower led the invasions of North Africa, Sicily, and Italy before President Roosevelt named him supreme Allied commander in December 1943.

★**PRESIDENTIAL RECREATION** Golf was President Eisenhower's favorite sport, and his strong interest in the game encouraged a nationwide trend. On sunny days, the

president could often be found on the White House lawn practicing his chip shots. He usually scored in the eighties.

Eisenhower was also an accomplished cook. His best dishes were vegetable soup, charcoal-grilled steak, and cornmeal pancakes. He and his wife Mamie often hosted barbecues for their friends on the White House roof.

DWIGHT DAVID EISENHOWER 1953-1961

★ HAIL! HAIL! ROCK 'N' ROLL!

Memphis record producer Sam Phillips often boasted that, with "a white boy who could sing black," he could make a million dollars. On July 6, 1954, that boy recorded his first song for Phillips's Sun Records. Nineteen-year-old Elvis Presley sang in the rhythm-and-blues style that teenagers loved. The black musicians who had created rhythm-and-blues weren't played on many radio stations in the segregated South. But Elvis was different because his white skin made him acceptable. Many parents condemned Presley for the sexy way he shook his hips. They even tried to ban his records. But the campaigns against him and his rock 'n' roll music only made teenagers want more.

★ THE ROSENBERG CASE

In July 1950, federal agents arrested Julius and Ethel Rosenberg and charged the New York couple with transmitting top-secret information to the Soviet Union. The Rosenbergs were part of an atom-bomb spy ring involving Ethel's brother, who testified against them at their trial. The Rosenbergs claimed they were innocent, but Cold War hysteria was everywhere. Julius's active membership in the Communist party hurt their case badly. The couple was sentenced to death. Despite international protests, they were executed in June 1953. Some people believed the Rosenbergs were innocent. But even among those who thought they were guilty, many considered the death penalty to have been unjust.

★ THE MONTGOMERY BUS BOYCOTT

On December 1, 1955, in Montgomery, Alabama, a tired seamstress named Rosa Parks was told to give up her seat on a city bus to a white man. When she refused, she was arrested because in Montgomery no black person sat while a white person was standing. To protest Parks's arrest, local black ministers—led by twenty-six-year-old Martin Luther King, Jr.—organized a boycott of the bus system. For more than a year, African Americans in Montgomery used car pools, walked, and even rode horses rather than ride the segregated buses. The boycott ended when a Supreme Court decision forced the city to stop segregating black passengers in December 1956.

subversion inside the United States. President Truman had ordered a loyalty investigation of the entire government, and this bipartisan Communist witch hunt continued under Eisenhower. According to Truman's attorney general, Communists were "everywhere—in factories, offices, butcher shops, on street corners, in private business—and each carries with him the germs of death for society."

Senator Joseph McCarthy of Wisconsin quickly became famous for his crusades against the State Department, which he claimed was full of Communists. McCarthy spoke in half-truths and insinuations rather than making straightforward charges that could be proven or disproven. Often his aides would find evidence that a particular government employee had attended meetings of the Communist party during the 1930s, at a time when Communism was still considered respectable.

Although McCarthy never proved any of his outrageous charges, Eisenhower and others refrained from criticizing him. They were worried that criticizing McCarthy might make them look suspicious. People accused by Senator McCarthy, especially writers and actors, were often prevented from working because employers were also desperate not to appear disloyal. The practice of "blacklisting," or not hiring people because they were suspected of being Communists, ruined the careers of many innocent people.

THE ARMY-McCARTHY HEARINGS McCarthy's arrogance finally caught up with him in 1954. That summer, he chaired a series of nationally televised hearings about alleged Communists in the armed forces. A lawyer for the army, Joseph Welch, finally challenged the senator publicly after McCarthy tried to smear one of his young assistants. "You have done enough," Welch told McCarthy. "Have you no sense of decency, sir, at long last?"

After Welch's dignified rebuke, McCarthy's spell over Washington was broken. That December, the Senate voted to reprimand him for "conduct unbecoming a member." Since then, the term *McCarthyism* has come to mean persecution based on unproven and often unfair accusations.

FOREIGN POLICY — Eisenhower generally left the nation's foreign policy in the respected care of John Foster Dulles. The secretary of state's long experience in foreign affairs, which dated back to the Wilson administration, made it difficult for others in the White House to challenge him.

Dulles's belief, which Eisenhower accepted, was that the nations of the world were either friends of the United States or friends of the Soviet Union. No single nation, in Dulles's view, could be both.

Dulles claimed to have abandoned Truman's policy of containment so that he could press for the "liberation" of "captive nations" under Communist rule. In reality, the secretary of state did nothing of the sort. When East Germany in 1953 and Hungary in 1956 tried to free themselves from Soviet domination, the United States did nothing to prevent Soviet tanks from crushing these rebellions.

In general, U.S. foreign policy remained limited to containment. In the Southeast Asian nation of South Vietnam, for example, Dulles advised his boss to support the government there in its struggle against the Communist North.

Eisenhower was particularly concerned about what might happen if South Vietnam were to fall to the Communists. "You have a row of

THE REPUBLICANS' GREATEST CONCERN DURING 1956 was Eisenhower's health. In 1955, the president had suffered what his doctors called a "moderate" heart attack, and earlier in 1956 he had undergone serious intestinal surgery. Although the president was already back at his desk after two months of rest, some people doubted his ability to serve another four years.

On the Democratic side, Adlai Stevenson decided to try for a second nomination despite his sizable defeat four years earlier. During the primaries, Stevenson was opposed by Senator Estes Kefauver of Tennessee, nationally known for his fight against government corruption. After Stevenson was renominated on the first ballot, he surprised the convention by allowing the delegates to choose his running mate. Senator John F. Kennedy of Massachusetts made a strong pitch for the second spot on the ticket, but Kefauver beat him out.

The Democrats didn't have much to work with in terms of campaign issues. Eisenhower had ended the Korean War as promised, and he had stood up to the Soviet Union. At home, the president also had performed well. Employment was up, and people all over the country felt prosperous. The only issue the Democrats really had was Eisenhower's health. But they hesitated to bring it up for fear of offending voters.

Eisenhower and Nixon were reelected easily, winning two million more votes and two more states than they had in 1952. The president's

popularity, however, did not extend to other Republican candidates for office. Both the House of Representatives and the Senate remained Democratic. It was the first time since Zachary Taylor was elected in 1848 that a president had failed to carry at least one house of Congress for his party.

Mamie and Dwight Eisenhower in the Oval Office.

SOVIETS LAUNCH FIRST SATELLITE

BAIKONUR, Soviet Union, October 4, 1957—The Soviet Union began the space race today when it launched the first man-made object into orbit. The 184-pound satellite is called Sputnik, which means "fellow traveler" in Russian.

Sputnik is a steel sphere containing a radio transmitter and batteries to power the transmitter. Four whip aerials are attached to its outside casing.

Sputnik's orbit carries it over the Baikonur launch site every ninety minutes or so. The Soviet scientists have been able to track Sputnik's progress by moni-

toring the bleep-bleep-bleep of its radio transmitter.

The rocket that launched Sputnik into orbit was powered by the same engine that the Soviet Union uses for its new intercontinental ballistic missiles, or ICBMs.

The successful launch of Sputnik has been a blow to U.S. prestige. Many government officials also consider the Soviet lead in space to be a sign of potential U.S. military weakness.

dominoes set up," the president said, "and you knock over the first one, and what will happen to the last one is the certainty that it will go over very quickly."

In political terms, the domino theory meant that the fall of one country to communism would always lead to the fall of others. If the chain reaction wasn't stopped in time, eventually all the "dominoes" would fall, including the United States.

THE WARREN COURT At home, the Supreme Court was grabbing the headlines. When President Eisenhower appointed California governor Earl Warren to be the new chief justice in 1953, he thought that Warren would make an uncontroversial, middle-of-the-road justice. Instead, Warren led a revolution on the Court, particularly in the area of civil rights law.

Warren wrote his most important opinion for the 1954 case of *Brown v. Board of Education*. In this case, the Court unanimously reversed *Plessy v. Ferguson* (1896), which had upheld the "separate but equal" doctrine. Instead, Warren declared that segregating white and black students in public schools was unequal and therefore unconstitutional.

"To separate [black children] from others of similar age and qualifications solely on the basis of their race generates a feeling of inferiority...that may affect their hearts and minds in a way never to be undone," the chief justice wrote. "We conclude that in the field of public education the doctrine of 'separate but equal' has no place." Eisenhower later said that appointing Warren was "the biggest damn fool mistake I ever made."

THE CIVIL RIGHTS MOVEMENT In part because of the *Brown* decision, the civil rights movement gained great momentum during the Eisenhower years. Martin Luther King, Jr., became its most eloquent spokesperson. The Montgomery bus boycott that he led drew national attention to the fight for equal rights under the law.

Eisenhower personally objected to racial segregation, but he also believed that forcing integration was a political mistake. When he finally sent troops into Little Rock to force Central High School to admit black students, he did so because the governor of Arkansas had challenged federal authority, not because the president believed that integrating the school was desirable at that time.

SPUTNIK Because attention was so closely focused on Little Rock at the time, it came as a shock to most Americans when the Soviet Union announced the successful launch of Sputnik in October 1957. Sputnik was the first man-made object ever placed in orbit around the earth.

Enraged that the Soviets had jumped ahead of the United States in the space race, Congress passed the National Defense Education Act in September 1958. Its purpose was to develop scientific talent. The act provided money for new school laboratories and scholarships for college students. Before receiving the money, however, the students had to sign a loyalty oath swearing that they were not sympathetic to the Communist party. Many refused the

★**FEAR OF THE BOMB** Once the Soviets exploded an atomic bomb in 1949, the world was suddenly faced with the possibility of nuclear war. In the United States, where the Cold War was peaking, civil defense officials tried, often foolishly, to prepare people for nuclear attack.

Elementary school students were taught to "duck and cover" if they ever saw the bright flash that signaled the explosion of an atomic bomb. Meanwhile, parents invested in expensive underground bomb shelters to protect their families from the deadly radioactive fallout of an atomic explosion.

★**THE BEAT GENERATION** The Eisenhower years are best remembered for their conformity. Most people liked to do the same thing as everybody else. But other people rebelled against the safe routine of suburban life. The Beats were a group of writers, performers, and hangers-on who lived mostly in New York's Greenwich Village and San Francisco's North Beach neighborhoods. They wore black clothing (especially turtlenecks), grew beards (usually goatees), and stayed up late at night in coffeehouses listening to music (always jazz).

The most famous Beat writers were Allen Ginsberg and Jack Kerouac. Ginsberg wrote "Howl" and other works that turned poetry on its head. Kerouac wrote his novel *On the Road* during a three-week burst in 1951 on a single roll of printer's paper. The book celebrated a life of adventure unburdened by possessions or family ties.

★**THE FIRST LADY** Dwight and Mamie Eisenhower were married in 1916, when Dwight was still an army lieutenant. During their marriage, Mamie was a dutiful army wife. She adjusted quickly to life on military bases and moved twenty-eight times with her husband as he changed assignments.

As first lady during most of the 1950s, Mamie Eisenhower did what most American women did. She tried to be a good wife, mother—and in her case, grandmother. Being the wife of the president, however, required more from her than most housewives. She had to plan state dinners and supervise the White House domestic staff. She also valued her privacy and made few public appearances.

2

★**THE LITTLE ROCK NINE** After the Supreme Court's 1954 ruling in the *Brown* case, most school districts in the border states stopped operating separate schools for blacks and whites. In the Deep South, however, many schools refused to change. Little Rock, Arkansas, became the focus of southern resistance in September 1957 when Governor Orval Faubus used the National Guard to prevent nine black students from attending all-white Central High School. When a federal court ordered Faubus to admit them, the governor did. But he refused to protect the teenagers from the angry white mob outside the school. Faubus's actions forced President Eisenhower to send in federal troops. It was the first time since Reconstruction that federal troops had been used to defend the rights of blacks.

★**THE COMICS CODE** Comic books became big business during the Eisenhower years. More than a billion were sold annually. During the mid-1950s, however, parents began to complain about violence, gore, and sexuality in horror comics. To avoid legal action, comic book publishers created the Comics Code in 1954 to clean up the industry and ban the offensive stories.

   William Gaines and Harvey Kurtzman were two of the most successful creators of horror comics. To beat the new code, they began printing their comic book, *Mad*, on glossy paper. The glossy paper technically turned *Mad* into a magazine, not a comic book, so the Comics Code didn't apply. *Mad* soon became famous for making fun of everything held sacred by most Americans.

money on principle rather than sign the oath.

THE KITCHEN DEBATE In an attempt to "thaw" the Cold War, Eisenhower and Soviet premier Nikita Khrushchev agreed to a series of cultural exchanges. In July 1959, Vice President Richard Nixon visited Moscow to open a U.S. exhibition there. He met Khrushchev at the model kitchen display, where they engaged in a loud, spontaneous debate about whether communism or capitalism was the better system. The press called it the "kitchen debate."

   Two months later, Khrushchev made a goodwill tour of the United States. He was disappointed when security considerations prevented him from visiting Disneyland, but he had a useful visit with Eisenhower. The two leaders met at Camp David, the presidential retreat named after Eisenhower's grandson. Afterward, they agreed to continue working in "the spirit of Camp David" and made plans for a meeting in Paris the following May.

THE U-2 INCIDENT Less than two weeks before the Paris summit, the Soviet Union shot down a U.S. spy plane deep within Soviet airspace. At first the State Department issued vague denials, but Eisenhower later admitted that U-2 planes had been making secret high-altitude flights over Soviet territory for years.

   Although Eisenhower promised to end the flights, he refused to apologize. An angry Khrushchev canceled the Paris meeting and Eisenhower's upcoming trip to the Soviet Union.

   The early State Department denials also made Americans question their government's truthfulness. "Up until now it has been possible to say to the world that what came out of the Kremlin was deceitful and untrustworthy but that people could depend on what they were told by the government of the United States," the *Wall Street Journal* wrote. "Now the world may not be so sure that this country is any different from any other."

REVOLUTION IN CUBA In the meantime, an even more threatening situation was developing much closer to the United States. On New Year's Day 1959, the Cuban revolutionary leader Fidel Castro toppled the corrupt dictatorship of Fulgencio Batista. Although Batista had been a cruel leader, he still enjoyed a great deal of support in the United States because of his favorable treatment of U.S. business and gambling interests.

Castro at first sought friendship with the United States, but he soon seized foreign property, most of it belonging to U.S. corporations. It was the only way Castro felt he could end the colonial relationship that had bound Cuba since the Spanish-American War. When Eisenhower retaliated by halting trade with Cuba, Castro turned to the enemy of his enemy, the Soviet Union.

Before Eisenhower left office in 1961, he delivered a poignant farewell address, much as George Washington had. The first general to become president had pointed out the dangers of foreign entanglements, but Eisenhower warned Americans about a new danger at home: the dependence of U.S. industry on military spending.

The president called attention to the ties that had developed between the Pentagon and its military contractors. He called this relationship the "military-industrial complex" and warned that it was gaining too much influence. As the country became more involved in the war in Vietnam, Eisenhower's words began to sound wiser and even more prophetic.

CAMPAIGN 1960

When John F. Kennedy entered the 1960 campaign, the experts said that the young Democratic senator from Massachusetts didn't have a chance. Because Eisenhower had been a popular Republican president, most political insiders assumed that Vice President Richard Nixon would win the election easily.

Also, Democrats worried that Kennedy's Catholic religion might hurt him. Americans had never elected a Catholic president. But Kennedy's victory in the West Virginia primary proved that he could win votes in a heavily Protestant state.

Kennedy and Nixon had similar political ideas. Both believed in a military strong enough to protect the United States from Communist attack. Both also

promised to continue funding welfare programs for the poor. Throughout the summer, the race stayed close in the polls.

On September 26, Kennedy and Nixon met in the first of four debates. Although there had been presidential debates before, none had been televised nationally. Because the two candidates were so close in the polls, most people believed that the debates would decide the election.

Over one hundred million people tuned in to watch. Both men spoke well. But Nixon, who had recently been in the hospital, looked pale and uncomfortable, while Kennedy appeared tan and in charge. When Kennedy narrowly won the election six weeks later, many people thought it was due to his presidential appearance during the debates.

JOHN FITZGERALD KENNEDY

35TH PRESIDENT

★

FROM 1961 TO 1963

BORN: May 29, 1917

BIRTHPLACE: Brookline, Mass.

DIED: November 22, 1963

PARTY: Democrat

VICE PRESIDENT: Lyndon B. Johnson

FIRST LADY: Jacqueline Lee Bouvier

CHILDREN: Caroline; John, Jr.; Patrick

NICKNAME: JFK

The first Boy Scout president.

The youngest man ever elected president, John F. Kennedy is best remembered for the hope he brought to the nation. In 1961, the United States was threatened by Cold War abroad and racial injustice at home. The new president admitted these problems in his inaugural address, but he also spoke with hope to a new generation ready to solve them.

In one of the most quoted inaugural addresses ever, Kennedy set forth the goals for his program called the New Frontier. He promised to work for freedom around the world and asked people at home to give something of themselves. "Ask not what your country can do for you," he said. "Ask what you can do for your country."

MISSILES IN CUBA!

WASHINGTON, October 22, 1962—President Kennedy went on television tonight and revealed spyplane photographs of Soviet nuclear missiles currently being installed in Cuba.

After condemning the Soviet Union for lying about the missiles, the president announced a naval blockade of Cuba beginning immediately and continuing until the missiles are removed. The blockade is intended to prevent Soviet ships carrying missile parts from reaching the island.

Kennedy made it clear that the presence of nuclear missiles so close to the U.S. shore is completely unacceptable.

Before the speech, high-level sources close to the president had said that Kennedy was also considering bombing the missile bases. The president was concerned, however, that such an action would lead to a harsher Soviet military response and perhaps a nuclear war.

17 MISSILE ERECTORS

173

THE COLD WAR

Kennedy's major foreign policy concern was the Cold War with the Soviet Union. All over the world, Kennedy watched vigilantly for signs of Soviet expansionism.

When Eisenhower left office, he told Kennedy that the Central Intelligence Agency was secretly training Cuban exiles to oust Fidel Castro. Since Castro's successful 1959 revolution, Cuba had become increasingly friendly with the Soviet Union. The idea of having a Soviet ally so close to the Florida shore made most Americans, including the president, nervous. So Kennedy allowed the training to continue.

On April 17, 1961, fourteen hundred Cuban exiles landed at the Bay of Pigs. Their mission was to lead a revolt against Castro. But promised U.S. air support never arrived, and the invasion was a complete disaster. President Kennedy was forced to take the blame for a major blunder at the very beginning of his administration.

Then, in August 1961, the Soviet-backed government of East Germany built a wall dividing East Berlin from West Berlin. The United States protested, but since the wall was built entirely on the East Berlin side, it was allowed to stand.

THE CUBAN MISSILE CRISIS

Kennedy had a much more serious confrontation with the Soviet Union in October 1962 when he discovered that the Soviets were building nuclear missile bases in Cuba. The president ordered the navy to surround Cuba and dared the Soviet Union to run the blockade. Kennedy's risk paid off when Soviet premier Nikita Khrushchev agreed to remove the missiles in exchange for a U.S. promise not to invade Cuba. The Cuban Missile Crisis was the closest the world has ever come to nuclear war.

The Early Years

JOHN F. KENNEDY WAS THE SECOND OF NINE CHILDREN born into a wealthy Irish-Catholic family in Boston. His father, Joseph, was so rich that he gave each of his children one million dollars when they reached the age of twenty-one.

As a child, John (or Jack, as the family called him) was frail and sickly. He looked up to his older brother, Joe, who their father decided would one day be president. But Joe was killed during World War II.

Jack also served in the war. He was nearly killed when a Japanese destroyer rammed his gunboat, *PT-109*. But he survived the crash and won a medal for saving his crew. After the war, Jack began a career in politics, as did his brothers Bobby and Teddy.

★**THE FIRST FAMILY**   As first lady, Jacqueline Kennedy set fashion trends across the United States. Her hairdo and pillbox hats inspired thousands of

women to copy the Jackie Look. The young Kennedy children, Caroline and John, also kept the nation charmed.

John was often photographed hiding under his father's desk in the Oval Office during important meetings. His sister Caroline loved animals. One of her pets was a goodwill gift from the Soviet Union, a puppy named Pushinka, whose mother was the first dog to travel in space. Another was her horse, Macaroni.

★**SPACE RACE**   In a speech made soon after his inauguration, JFK vowed that the United States would land a man on the moon before the end of the decade. To achieve this goal, he funded a five-billion-dollar space program.

Space was yet another arena in which the United States and the Soviet Union struggled to outdo each other. At first, the Soviets held the lead. In April 1961, cosmonaut Yuri Gagarin became the first human to orbit the planet. Three weeks later, however, a Project Mercury rocket launched U.S. astronaut Alan Shepard into space.

★**CIVIL RIGHTS** During Kennedy's years in office, the civil rights movement surged ahead in its struggle for equality. In 1960, the first sit-in protested racial discrimination at a Woolworth's lunch counter. Two years later, despite a campus riot, James Meredith became the first black to enroll at the University of Mississippi.

One of the decade's most moving moments came in August 1963 when Martin Luther King, Jr., delivered his "I Have a Dream" speech in front of 250,000 people during the March on Washington.

★**POPULAR MUSIC** Life in America during the Kennedy years was sometimes silly, sometimes troubled, but most often hopeful. During the early 1960s, the songs of the Great Dance Craze replaced those sung by the leather-jacketed rebels of the Eisenhower years. Chubby Checker had Number One hits with "The Twist" and "Pony Time." In New York's Greenwich Village, however, folk singers such as Bob Dylan and Joan Baez sang political "protest songs."

★**PEACE CORPS** President Kennedy created the Peace Corps in 1961 so that Americans could help the people of developing countries directly. Doctors, teachers, scientists, and other volunteers built hospitals, started schools, and improved farming methods all over the world. Many recent college graduates were inspired to join the Peace Corps by a growing concern for the world beyond the United States.

Meanwhile, across the globe in Vietnam, the United States was becoming involved in a different type of war. Under Kennedy, the number of military advisors in that Southeast Asian country rose from a few hundred to more than ten thousand.

Historians still argue about what Kennedy would have done in Vietnam had he lived. Some claim the president was planning to pull out all the advisors. Others say he would have sent over U.S. troops just as Lyndon Johnson later did.

CIVIL RIGHTS At home, Kennedy's focus was on civil rights. Although the president supported equal rights for people of color, he also wanted to move slowly so that he wouldn't lose any of his political support. It took the work of activists such as Martin Luther King, Jr., to force Kennedy to act on his beliefs.

In May 1961, for example, thirteen Freedom Riders boarded a Greyhound bus in Washington, D.C. They were headed for the Deep South to protest segregated public transportation there. At nearly every stop, this mixed group of blacks and whites was attacked and beaten. Each time, Kennedy was pushed to protect them.

ASSASSINATION IN DALLAS Almost everyone who was alive at the time remembers what they were doing when they heard the news of Kennedy's assassination in Dallas. The event still haunts many people because it symbolizes the end of an era of hope and the beginning of a period of violence.

Kennedy once described himself as "an idealist without illusions." As president, he often showed great skill at appealing to the idealism of others, especially young people. When he was killed, much of their faith in the future was shattered.

Although Kennedy won the 1960 election by the slimmest of margins, he went on to become a very popular president. On November 22, 1963, about a thousand days into his presidency, Kennedy flew to Dallas to give a speech.

He and Jackie were greeted by huge cheering crowds all the way from the airport. As their open car entered Dealey Plaza, however, a number of shots were fired at Kennedy from the Texas School Book Depository building. Two hit the president, one in the throat and the other in the back of the head. Kennedy died at nearby Parkland Hospital half an hour later.

That afternoon, U.S. District Court Judge Sarah T. Hughes administered the oath of office to Vice President Lyndon Johnson aboard Air Force One, the president's airplane. Later, Lee Harvey Oswald was arrested and charged with Kennedy's murder.

The Kennedy Assassination

Johnson soon appointed a group of respected government officials to investigate the assassination. Led by Chief Justice Earl Warren of the Supreme Court, the Warren Commission concluded that Oswald acted alone in shooting the president.

In the years since the release of the commission's report in September 1964, many people have argued that more than one assassin was involved. The truth may never be known because two days after he was arrested, Oswald was shot in the basement of the Dallas County Jail by Jack Ruby, a nightclub owner allegedly connected to organized crime.

Had Kennedy lived, he surely would have run for reelection in 1964. With JFK gone, however, the top spot on the Democratic ticket belonged to Lyndon Johnson. At the national convention in Atlantic City, Johnson was nominated by acclamation. His slogan was "All the Way With LBJ."

CAMPAIGN 1964

To run against Johnson, the Republicans picked Barry Goldwater, an extremely conservative senator from Arizona. Goldwater's policies scared many Americans. He proposed deep cuts in social programs and a large increase in the defense budget so that he could drive the Communists out of South Vietnam. Goldwater also opposed civil rights laws and wanted to make **Social Security** voluntary, which frightened senior citizens.

Goldwater's statements about nuclear war hurt him the most. People worried that he might actually start one. Goldwater's "In Your Heart, You Know He's Right" slogan was satirized as "In Your Heart, You Know He Might." The Johnson campaign played on these fears with a powerful television commercial that implied Goldwater would use the bomb if elected.

Goldwater used the president's strong stand on civil rights to hurt him badly in the Deep South. But nearly everywhere else people voted for LBJ in overwhelming numbers, and he won a resounding victory.

LYNDON BAINES JOHNSON

36TH PRESIDENT
★
FROM 1963 TO 1969

BORN: August 27, 1908

BIRTHPLACE: Stonewall, Texas

DIED: January 22, 1973

PARTY: Democrat

VICE PRESIDENT: Hubert H. Humphrey

FIRST LADY: Claudia Alta (Lady Bird) Taylor

CHILDREN: Lynda Bird, Luci

NICKNAME: LBJ

The first president sworn in by a woman.

RIOTS RAVAGE WATTS

LOS ANGELES, August 16, 1965—The rioting in Watts, a black section of Los Angeles, finally ended today after six days of burning, looting, and death. Thirty-four people have been killed, and nearly four thousand arrested. It has taken fifteen thousand police and the National Guard to restore order.

The riots began on August 11 after a patrolman arrested a black motorist for reckless driving. When the officer drew his gun, a crowd of angry neighborhood residents attacked him.

"Martin Luther King ain't my leader," one Watts youth said as he prepared to set fire to a building. "The so-called Negro leaders have no contact with us. They don't know us; they don't know how we feel or what we want any more than you do, Mr. White Man."

The damage, covering five hundred square blocks, is estimated at upwards of forty million dollars. Two hundred businesses have been destroyed, many owned by whites. The Watts neighborhood is ninety-eight percent African American.

Growth of the U.S. 1894-1994

HI 1959

Lyndon B. Johnson had been in office only two months when he delivered his first State of the Union address. The country was still grieving deeply over the assassination of its popular young president. But John F. Kennedy's successor knew that the government had work to do.

"Unfortunately, many Americans live on the outskirts of hope, some because of their poverty and some because of their color," the new president said in his January 1964 speech. To relieve this despair, Johnson declared an unconditional "war on poverty."

As he would prove often during his presidency, Lyndon Johnson was a shrewd, down-to-earth politician who knew how to get things done. By August, with some expert arm-twisting, he had convinced Congress to approve ten antipoverty programs totaling one billion dollars. The new aid programs included a Job Corps for disadvantaged teenagers and Head Start for preschool children.

To help African Americans, Johnson pushed through the Civil Rights Act of 1964, which made it illegal for employers to discriminate on the basis of race. The new law also outlawed segregation in public places, such as hotels and restaurants, ending Jim Crow forever.

Meanwhile, the FBI continued its six-week-long search for the bodies of three civil rights workers murdered in Mississippi. Andrew Goodman, Mickey Schwerner, and James Chaney had all been taking part in the Mississippi Summer Project. The goal of the project's Freedom Summer was to organize an integrated political party to challenge the all-white state Democratic party.

After the project ended, most of the student volunteers went back to school, where many organized protests. The most compelling of these was the Free Speech Movement. This series of demonstrations at the University of California-Berkeley defended the rights of students to distribute political pamphlets on campus. But the movement also made it clear that students were not satisfied with the world as it was being run by their parents.

THE VOTING RIGHTS ACT Of all the laws passed during his administration, Lyndon Johnson was probably most proud of the Voting Rights Act of 1965. This bill outlawed literacy tests and other unfair practices that white southerners used to keep blacks from registering to vote. The Voting Rights Act made huge registration drives possible. And with more blacks registered to vote, black candidates were able to win more elections.

Prominent black mayors were elected in Cleveland, Ohio, and Gary, Indiana. And in 1966, Edward Brooke of Massachusetts became the first black senator elected since 1881.

SAM EALY JOHNSON WAS A TEXAS STATE LEGISLATOR, BUT HE was also a poor farmer. The great San Francisco earthquake of 1906 had destroyed his cotton holdings. As a result, his son Lyndon was born into hardship. When he was old enough, Lyndon worked as a shoeshine boy and trapped animals to earn extra money.

The Early Years

From an early age, Lyndon enjoyed listening to his father talk politics. Later in life he would often repeat the advice his father gave him: "If you can't come into a roomful of people and tell right away who is for you and who is against you, you have no business in politics."

For two years after college, Johnson taught public speaking, but he quit in 1931 to work for Democratic Representative Richard Kleberg of Texas. Johnson ran for the House in 1937, winning a crowded race with only twenty-seven percent of the vote. In 1948, he won a controversial Senate race by just eighty-seven votes out of nearly one million cast.

★ **BEATLEMANIA** In the months after the Kennedy assassination, grief-stricken Americans were desperate for something to lift their gloom. In February 1964, relief arrived from England. That month, the Beatles made their first U.S. appearance on the CBS Sunday night variety show hosted by Ed Sullivan. The ratings for Sullivan's show set records, and soon the Beatles had six songs in the Top Ten. Teenagers everywhere responded to the Fab Four's bouncy music, cute Liverpool accents, and mop-top hairstyles. Boys started growing their hair long, and girls rushed out to buy "mod" miniskirts popularized by British designer Mary Quant. The British Invasion that followed the Beatles included such bands as the Rolling Stones, the Animals, and the Who.

★ THE MY LAI MASSACRE

Every night, the television networks showed footage of the war in Vietnam, and every night Americans had to decide what to make of the brutality they witnessed. Even more horrible events were not televised. In March 1968, U.S. troops under Lieutenant William Calley massacred 347 unarmed civilians at the Vietnamese farming village of My Lai. The killings were kept secret for over a year. In April 1971, a military court sentenced Calley to life imprisonment, but he was freed after forty months. As his commander pointed out, singling out Calley was unfair. "Every unit of brigade size has its My Lai hidden someplace," he said. Guerrilla warfare made it difficult to recognize the enemy, and frightened soldiers often fired first and asked questions later.

★ MALCOLM X

Malcolm Little spent World War II selling drugs in Harlem and Boston. In 1946, the twenty-one-year-old hustler was arrested for burglary. In prison, he joined the Nation of Islam, a black Muslim group whose members believed that white people were devils. Malcolm changed his name to Malcolm X because "Little" was a name some white master had given his African slave ancestors.

During the early 1960s, Malcolm's fiery civil rights speeches made him famous. Unlike Martin Luther King, Jr., Malcolm preached violence as a reasonable response to violence. In 1964, however, he broke with the Nation of Islam and became a traditional Muslim, devoting himself to peace. While giving a speech in February 1965, Malcolm was shot and killed by four members of the Nation of Islam.

★ HIM AND HER

When Lyndon Johnson moved into the White House, he brought a pair of beagles with him. Their names were Him and Her. These two dogs soon became almost as popular as the president himself. In June 1964, they appeared on the cover of *Life* magazine.

The dogs were also a source of controversy. When Johnson was photographed picking them up by the ears, dog lovers around the country demanded an explanation and an apology. LBJ refused. "It's good for them," the president said.

A year later, President Johnson nominated Thurgood Marshall to the Supreme Court. In 1954, Marshall had argued the landmark *Brown* case before the Court. After his Senate confirmation, Marshall became the first black justice to sit on the Court.

THE GREAT SOCIETY

After Lyndon Johnson's landslide victory in the 1964 election, the Great Society became the theme of his domestic program. Johnson developed Medicaid and Medicare to help poor people and the elderly pay their medical bills. He also won passage of the first serious environmental and consumer laws. These bills set standards for air and water quality as well as auto safety.

Many of the Great Society initiatives were immediate successes. But there was also a problem: The Vietnam War was eating up too much government money. As the war escalated, the president urged an increasingly reluctant Congress to fund "guns and butter." Conservatives insisted that the country could not afford both.

THE TONKIN GULF RESOLUTION

In early August 1964, Johnson announced that the U.S. destroyer *Maddox* had been attacked by North Vietnamese patrol boats in international waters in the Tonkin Gulf off Vietnam. The North Vietnamese claimed that the *Maddox* had been protecting South Vietnamese raiders.

The president immediately sent Congress a resolution granting him nearly unlimited power to use U.S. military force in Vietnam. The White House staff had prepared the resolution well in advance, hoping for just such an opportunity. The Tonkin Gulf resolution passed unanimously in the House, and only two votes were cast against it in the

Senate—by Wayne Morse of Oregon and Ernest Gruening of Alaska.

In a televised speech, Johnson told the nation, "We seek no wider war." But seven months later he sent the first combat troops to Vietnam. Only thirty-five hundred Marines landed at Da Nang in March 1965, but within two years, troop levels had risen to four hundred thousand.

THE TET OFFENSIVE Johnson's military advisors promised that victory was "just around the corner." But their predictions seemed empty after January 30, 1968, when the North Vietnamese and their Viet Cong allies launched a surprise attack on major cities in the South. One Viet Cong unit even reached the grounds of the U.S. embassy in Saigon. The assault was called the Tet Offensive because it began during a cease-fire called to celebrate Tet, the Vietnamese New Year.

Although U.S. troops counterattacked successfully, the Communists had made their point. Until the Tet Offensive, it was possible for civilians to believe that the United States might actually be winning the war. After Tet, it was obvious that victory was either impossible or a very long way off. Now, many moderate Americans joined the growing antiwar movement.

In March 1968, Senator Eugene McCarthy of Minnesota, running as a peace candidate, nearly upset President Johnson in the New Hampshire Democratic primary. Johnson's slim seven-point victory forced him to rethink running for a second full term.

On March 31, the president went on national television to announce a temporary halt to the bombing of North Vietnam so that peace talks might begin. At the end of his speech, almost as an afterthought, Lyndon Johnson revealed that he would not seek another term.

PRESIDENT JOHNSON'S MARCH 31 DECISION NOT TO run again changed everything. Quickly, Vice President Hubert Humphrey declared his candidacy. Besides Senator McCarthy, Humphrey also had to battle Senator Robert F. Kennedy, the brother of the late president. Kennedy had entered the race as a peace candidate soon after McCarthy's surprising performance in New Hampshire.

Humphrey's biggest problem was Vietnam. The war was now highly unpopular, and the continued bombing of North Vietnam made it difficult for Humphrey to distance himself from Johnson, to whom he remained loyal. Meanwhile, Kennedy's campaign gained momentum. On June 5, Kennedy won the California primary, but that same night he was assassinated by a Palestinian immigrant named Sirhan Sirhan.

Kennedy's death assured Humphrey of the nomination, but it also deeply divided the party. At the Democratic convention in Chicago, thousands of antiwar activists demonstrated outside as the police beat journalists and protesters alike. An independent commission later called the chaos a "police riot."

Humphrey's Republican opponent, Richard Nixon, stood by as the Democrats self-destructed. During the campaign, the former vice president discussed issues only vaguely. Mostly he talked about law and order and his "secret plan" to end the war in Vietnam. Governor George Wallace of Alabama mounted a third-party campaign based on victory in Vietnam and an end to school busing to achieve integration.

Nixon left the Republican convention with a large lead. Humphrey made a strong comeback, especially after President Johnson ordered a bombing halt on October 31. But he couldn't close the huge gap in time. Although Nixon won the election by less than one percent of the popular vote, his electoral majority was comfortable. Even Wallace's forty-six electoral votes, all from the Deep South, weren't enough to stop Nixon.

RICHARD MILHOUS NIXON

37TH PRESIDENT

★

FROM 1969 TO 1974

BORN: January 9, 1913

BIRTHPLACE: Yorba Linda, Calif.

DIED: April 22, 1994

PARTY: Republican

VICE PRESIDENTS: Spiro T. Agnew, Gerald R. Ford

FIRST LADY: Thelma Catherine (Pat) Ryan

CHILDREN: Patricia, Julie

NICKNAME: Tricky Dick

The first president to resign his office.

During the late 1960s, demonstrations against the government increased both in size and vigor. A decade earlier, Americans had feared nuclear war with Communists halfway around the world. Now they worried about riots at home.

The assassination of Martin Luther King, Jr., in April 1968 shattered the nonviolent civil rights movement. Afterward, like Humpty Dumpty, the pieces couldn't be put back together again. Some people continued King's work, but others joined militant groups like the Black Panthers who demanded "black power." The antiwar movement also became more combative and more violent.

President Nixon ignored these protests because he believed he had the support of the "silent majority" of Americans. But no matter how hard he tried, he couldn't avoid the war in Vietnam.

ASTRONAUTS WALK ON THE MOON

SEA OF TRANQUILITY, July 21, 1969—The United States won the space race today when Apollo 11 astronaut Neil Armstrong became the first human being to walk on the moon. "That's one small step for man, one giant leap for mankind," Armstrong said as he climbed down from the lunar module *Eagle*.

Millions of people around the world watched both the moon landing last night and the moon walk early this morning on television. The landing redeemed the late president John F. Kennedy's pledge to land a man on the moon by the end of the decade.

During their single moon walk, Armstrong and fellow astronaut Edwin "Buzz" Aldrin planted a U.S. flag, set up three experiments, and collected rock samples from the lunar surface. They also spoke briefly with President Nixon.

The Apollo 11 crew of Armstrong, Aldrin, and Michael Collins is expected to bring back data of enormous scientific value. They will also be quarantined upon their return to ensure that they have brought no lunar diseases back with them.

During the 1968 campaign, he had boasted of a "secret plan" to end the war, but the peace talks that President Johnson had begun in Paris were going nowhere. The delegates couldn't even agree on what shape the conference table should be.

VIETNAMIZATION Nixon's secret plan turned out to be Vietnamization. The idea was to replace U.S. combat troops with South Vietnamese soldiers. Kennedy and Johnson had also thought it would be a good idea for the South Vietnamese to fight their own war. But both Democratic presidents had concluded that the result would be disastrous. Nixon went ahead anyway because it was the only way he could withdraw U.S. soldiers and still keep the war going.

To make up for the loss of combat troop strength, Nixon stepped up the bombing of North Vietnam. More bomb tonnage was dropped on North Vietnam than on Germany, Italy, and Japan during all of World War II. The president also ordered the secret bombing of nearby Cambodia, where the Viet Cong had supply bases.

NIXON IN CHINA As he tried to bring about "peace with honor" in Vietnam, Nixon looked forward to the greatest foreign policy coup of his career. All his life, Richard Nixon had fought Communists. His hostility toward them had been well known since his first political campaign.

That is why Nixon's August 1971 announcement that he would visit the People's Republic of China stunned the world. During that visit in February 1972, arranged by top aide Henry Kissinger, the president met with Communist leader Mao Zedong. Diplomatic relations were not yet restored, but Nixon's trip ensured that they soon would be.

RICHARD NIXON WAS BORN IN A HOUSE HIS FATHER built. Every morning before school, he helped his father truck in produce from nearby Los Angeles to sell at Nixon's Market in Whittier, California. As a student, Frank Nixon's second son was bright, serious, and quiet.

The adult Richard Nixon worked as a lawyer until 1946, when he won election to Congress. There he made a name for himself with his dogged cross-examination of alleged Soviet spy Alger Hiss. In 1950, Nixon ran for the Senate against Helen Gahagan Douglas. Referring to Douglas as the Pink Lady, Nixon distributed "pink sheets" that were supposed to show how Douglas's voting record served Communist aims. Because of this political trick, a Southern California newspaper nicknamed the new senator Tricky Dick.

★**THE ENEMIES LIST** Historians have sometimes called Nixon paranoid, meaning that he often thought people were out to get him. As proof, they point to the list of enemies Nixon ordered his staff to keep. This list included not only political opponents, but also journalists, businessmen, athletes, and movie stars. Names on the Enemies List included Bill Cosby, Jane Fonda, and quarterback Joe Namath. Nixon ordered FBI director J. Edgar Hoover to collect damaging information on some of these people using illegal wiretaps. After the Watergate hearings revealed the existence of the Enemies List, Nixon claimed that the wiretaps were justified because of "national security concerns."

★**EARTH DAY** On April 22, 1970, a number of environmental groups organized the first Earth Day. The environmental movement and its goals were still new to most people. So "teach-ins" were held on college campuses around the nation to focus public attention on such ecological issues as pollution of the air, land, and water. Since then, Earth Day activities have included beach and park cleanups as well as tree plantings.

★ THE BLACK PANTHERS

Bobby Seale and Huey P. Newton (right) founded the Black Panther Party for Self-Defense in Oakland, California, in 1966. The group's original purpose was to patrol black neighborhoods to protect residents there from police brutality. Soon the organization set up chapters in other cities, particularly Chicago, and became much more political. Chief spokesman Eldridge Cleaver encouraged blacks to buy guns because the Panthers believed that an armed showdown between blacks and whites was inevitable. Trouble between the police and the Panthers led to a number of shoot-outs. Newton, the Panthers' minister of defense, was later convicted of killing a police officer during one of these gun battles.

★ WOODSTOCK NATION

During the late 1960s, many college-age Baby Boomers developed their own distinctive styles of dress and music as well as new ways of speaking and behaving. They called their new way of living a "counterculture." Referring to themselves as "freaks" and "hippies," they gathered together at rural communes and in city neighborhoods such as San Francisco's Haight-Ashbury.

One of the most memorable countercultural events was the Woodstock Music and Art Fair held in upstate New York in August 1969. More than three hundred thousand people showed up to listen to Jimi Hendrix, the Jefferson Airplane, and many other performers. Because of the massive crowd and the lack of proper food, medical care, and sanitation, the concert site was declared a disaster area. But the show went on.

WOODSTOCK MUSIC and ART FAIR
SUNDAY
AUGUST 17, 1969
10:00 A. M.
Good For One Admission Only
$7.00
A 03400   NO REFUNDS GLOBE TICKET COMPANY

DÉTENTE In opening the door to China, long considered an enemy of the United States, Nixon played on the strained relations between the People's Republic and the Soviet Union. Although both countries were run by Communist governments, they didn't trust each other. Nixon hoped that by forging ties with China he could weaken the power and influence of the Soviet Union, which remained the United States' greatest concern.

Nixon referred to his foreign policy as "détente," which means a relaxing of strained relations or tensions. Soon after his return from China, he followed up his success there with another remarkable trip. This time, the president went to Moscow.

Nixon had been to Moscow once before, in 1959, when he and Nikita Khrushchev met in the Kitchen Debate. The highlight of this May 1972 trip was the signing of a nuclear arms control treaty. The agreement was known as the SALT treaty because it had been negotiated at the Strategic Arms Limitation Talks.

PEACE WITH HONOR Nixon's foreign policy triumphs proved that détente could work. They also did wonders for his reelection campaign. So did Henry Kissinger's announcement in October 1972, just two weeks before the election, that "peace is at hand" in Vietnam. The "breakthrough" proposal, which Kissinger and North Vietnamese negotiator Le Duc Tho had developed during secret meetings in Paris, called for an immediate cease-fire followed by a general election in the South.

After the U.S. election, however, the agreement hit a snag when each side accused the other of bargaining in bad faith. To convince the North Vietnamese to renew the talks, Nixon ordered the heaviest bombing of the war. During the "Christmas bombing" of December 1972, more than two hundred B-52 bombers flew missions around the clock over North Vietnam.

A formal peace agreement was finally signed on January 27, 1973. The South Vietnamese government retained control of Saigon, while the Viet Cong remained in place in the countryside. The United States agreed to remove all its combat troops within sixty days in return for the release of prisoners of war. Publicly Nixon claimed that he had achieved "peace with honor," but Kissinger predicted privately that South Vietnam wouldn't last eighteen months. What Kissinger didn't know was that the Nixon administration wouldn't last much longer.

THE WATERGATE BREAK-IN

On June 17, 1972, police arrested five men caught breaking into Democratic National Committee headquarters in Washington. One of the men arrested at the Watergate office building was James McCord, a former FBI agent now working for the Committee to Reelect the President. When asked about the break-in, President Nixon denied everything, insisting that no one at the White House had any knowledge of this "bizarre incident." The cover-up had begun.

At first, the scandal was limited to Nixon's reelection committee, commonly known as CREEP. But in October, Bob Woodward and Carl Bernstein began writing stories in the *Washington Post* that suggested the break-in was part of a larger Nixon campaign of "dirty tricks." Woodward and Bernstein's allegations were soon confirmed by McCord in a letter to Judge John Sirica. In his letter asking for leniency, McCord admitted that witnesses had lied. McCord later

TWO IMPORTANT CHANGES IN THE WAY DELEGATES WERE selected made the 1972 Democratic convention a world apart from the one held in 1968. First, the party's rules were changed to include more women and minority delegates. Then, in 1971, the Twenty-sixth Amendment lowered the voting age to eighteen. These changes, along with the ongoing Vietnam War, made it possible for a liberal candidate like Senator George McGovern of South Dakota to win the Democratic nomination. McGovern promised an immediate withdrawal of U.S. troops from Vietnam. He also supported legislation banning handguns. He even proposed that the government give every person in the United States one thousand dollars.

During the primaries, Alabama governor George Wallace had challenged McGovern, winning in Maryland and Michigan. These victories proved that the conservative Wallace appealed to voters outside the South. He was especially popular with blue-collar workers who felt that the Democrats had given too much power to minority groups. Wallace's campaign was cut short when a gunman shot him at a rally. He survived but was left paralyzed below the waist. Although Wallace was now out of the race, his followers seemed unlikely to support McGovern.

Richard Nixon and Spiro Agnew easily won renomination at the Republican convention. Although the Watergate burglary had already taken place, nobody paid much attention to it. What bothered voters more was the news that McGovern's running mate, Senator Thomas Eagleton of Missouri, had once undergone electric shock therapy for depression. Although McGovern at first stood by Eagleton, he later bowed to public opinion and replaced him with former Peace Corps director Sargent Shriver.

McGovern charged that the Nixon administration was the most corrupt in U.S. history, but few people believed him. Instead they listened to Henry Kissinger announce that peace was "at hand" in Vietnam. On Election Day, Nixon's margin of victory was nearly twenty million votes. McGovern lost every state but Massachusetts.

named former attorney general John Mitchell as "the overall boss."

In February 1973, the Senate established a special committee to look into "any illegal, improper, or unethical activities" that might have occurred during the 1972 campaign. During the committee's televised hearings, Senator Howard Baker of Tennessee asked nearly every witness, "What did the president know, and when did he know it?"

On July 16, presidential assistant Alexander Butterfield revealed in passing that President Nixon had been secretly recording his Oval Office conversations. The Senate committee immediately subpoenaed, or legally demanded, the tapes, as did Watergate special prosecutor Archibald Cox.

But Nixon refused to turn over the tapes. He argued that the president's executive privilege allowed him to keep his conversations private. Cox decided to fight Nixon in the federal courts.

VICE PRESIDENT FORD

One factor saving Nixon from impeachment was the reality that Vice President Spiro Agnew would succeed him. Most Democratic congressmen despised Agnew for his attacks on intellectuals as "an effete corps of impudent snobs" and reporters as "nattering nabobs of negativism." These Democrats considered the possibility of an Agnew presidency even more horrifying than the prospect of Nixon staying on.

On October 10, 1973, however, Agnew was forced to resign the vice presidency after pleading no contest to charges of

FOUR STUDENTS KILLED AT KENT STATE

KENT, Ohio, May 4, 1970— National Guardsmen fired into an antiwar demonstration at Kent State University today, killing four students. The guardsmen were using live ammunition rather than the rubber bullets typically used for crowd control.

The noon demonstration, attended by one thousand students, was held to protest the invasion of Cambodia announced last week by President Nixon. The president's action led many students to believe that he was widening the war in Vietnam instead of ending it, as he had promised.

The National Guard was called to the campus yesterday after a demonstration on May 2 turned into a riot.

That night, students burned an army-related building to the ground. This afternoon's demonstration also spun out of control when students began chanting at the armed soldiers, "Pigs off campus! We don't want your war!"

Students have held protests against the war in Vietnam since the early 1960s. But antiwar efforts have become much more vigorous since the Tet Offensive caused many Americans to reconsider whether the government has been telling the truth.

STOP THE WAR NOW

accepting bribes while governor of Maryland. Two days later, President Nixon nominated Michigan congressman Gerald Ford to be the new vice president.

Meanwhile, the tapes case, *U.S. v. Nixon*, had reached the Court of Appeals, which ordered the president to turn over the tapes.

On Saturday, October 20, Nixon tried to quash the original subpoena by ordering Attorney General Elliot Richardson to fire Cox. Richardson resigned rather than carry out Nixon's order. So did his deputy, William Ruckelshaus. Eventually Solicitor General Robert H. Bork agreed to fire Cox and terminate the office of Watergate special prosecutor.

The public response to the "Saturday night massacre" was decidedly negative. Three days later Chairman Peter Rodino announced that the House Judiciary Committee would begin impeachment hearings.

RESIGNATION Throughout the winter and spring of 1974, the subpoenas for tapes continued to be issued, and Nixon continued to avoid them. He released a few recordings and provided edited transcripts of others, but the House committee kept pressing for actual recordings of the most sensitive conversations. Finally, on July 24, 1974, the Supreme Court ruled unanimously that Nixon must turn over all the tapes. Three days later, the Judiciary Committee approved the first of three articles of impeachment against him.

On August 5, the president released transcripts of three June 23, 1972, conversations that proved he knew about and directed the cover-up. Three days later, speaking on national television, he announced his resignation. The embattled president blamed a loss of congressional support and confessed nothing.

★ **THE FIRST FAMILY**
Richard Nixon first met Pat Ryan in 1938 at auditions for a local play in Whittier. Nixon proposed that first night. "I thought he was nuts," the future Mrs. Nixon remembered. She turned him down then, but they dated for two years until she finally accepted. In the meantime, Nixon became so devoted to her that he sometimes drove her to meet other dates because she didn't have a car.

The Nixons and their daughters were an unusually close family. In 1968, Julie married David Eisenhower, grandson of the former president. Three years later, Tricia married Edward Cox in a Rose Garden ceremony. Throughout the Watergate ordeal, the president's family stood by him and reportedly urged him not to resign.

★ *ROE V. WADE* **AND ABORTION** During the late 1960s, abortion became an important political issue, especially to the women's movement. "Pro-life" advocates believed that an unborn fetus had the right to live and that it was wrong to interfere with a pregnancy. "Pro-choice" forces believed it was a woman's right to decide whether or not to have an abortion. In states with laws against abortions, many women risked their lives having them performed illegally. In 1973, however, the Supreme Court ruled in the case of *Roe v. Wade* that every woman had a legal right to end a pregnancy during the first three months. Although the women's movement praised the decision, it was widely criticized by some religious groups as immoral and by conservative scholars as bad legal reasoning by the Court.

★ **WOMEN'S LIBERATION**
The women's liberation movement drew strength from the civil rights and antiwar protests of the 1960s. While taking part in these other movements, many women discovered that men rarely treated them as equals. They were often expected to make coffee instead of speeches and policy. Soon these women banded together to demand equal treatment. Some founded organizations like the National Organization for Women to promote issues such as day care for the children of working mothers and equal pay for equal work. Men who believed that a woman's proper place was in the home were ridiculed as "male chauvinist pigs."

GERALD RUDOLPH FORD

38TH PRESIDENT
★
FROM 1974 TO 1977

BORN: July 14, 1913

BIRTHPLACE: Omaha, Neb.

PARTY: Republican

VICE PRESIDENT: Nelson A. Rockefeller

FIRST LADY: Elizabeth Anne (Betty) Bloomer Warren

CHILDREN: Michael, John, Steven, Susan

NICKNAME: Mr. Nice Guy

His daughter Susan held her senior prom in the White House.

THE WAR IS OVER
Communists Capture South Vietnam

SAIGON, Vietnam, April 30, 1975—The Vietnam War ended today when General Duong Van Minh surrendered the South Vietnamese capital of Saigon to a combined force of North Vietnamese and Viet Cong soldiers.

The cease-fire agreement of January 1973—which had guaranteed the United States, in President Nixon's words, "peace with honor"—lasted less than a year. By 1974, the war had restarted. A March 1975 strategic retreat ordered by South Vietnamese president Nguyen Van Thieu quickly turned into a rout.

Sensing on April 18 that the end of the war was near, Secretary of State Henry Kissinger ordered all U.S. citizens in South Vietnam to leave immediately.

Operation Frequent Wind, which ended today when the grounds of the U.S. embassy were captured, has been the largest helicopter evacuation in history. Nearly seven thousand people, including fourteen hundred Americans, have been airlifted to U.S. ships waiting offshore.

Gerald Ford was sworn in as president on August 9, 1974, just minutes after Richard Nixon's resignation took effect. "Our long national nightmare is over," Ford said after the ceremony.

Ford had been a football star at the University of Michigan, and as a congressman from that state, he became widely known as a fair and decent man. For twenty-five years in the House of Representatives, he spoke out for Middle American values. But despite his athletic and political accomplishments, Ford also had a reputation for being mentally slow and physically awkward. It was often said jokingly that Ford couldn't walk and chew gum at the same time.

Exactly one month after taking office, President Ford pardoned Richard Nixon for any crimes Nixon may have committed during his term in office. It was Ford's belief that the country should be spared the spectacle of a former president standing trial.

Some critics suggested that a deal had been made, while others pointed out that Nixon had been pardoned while Vietnam draft resisters had not.

Ford's pardon of Nixon contributed to the low expectations people had for him. He was the first president ever to serve who had never been elected either president or vice president. Consequently, people tended to view him more as an honest caretaker than as a leader.

THE ARAB OIL EMBARGO Although the Vietnam War was finally over, its enormous cost had a lasting effect on the national economy. Under Ford, the country suffered the worst inflation and unemployment rates since the Great Depression.

Aggravating the problem was an oil embargo, which ended the era of cheap energy in the United States. In 1973, Israel and its Arab neighbors had fought the Yom Kippur War. Afterward, the Arab oil-producing nations decided to punish the United States for helping Israel by cutting off U.S. oil imports. Within a year, gasoline prices jumped seventy percent.

Ford's most publicized solution to the country's economic woes was the Whip Inflation Now campaign. Buttons were printed up with the initials WIN, but the program went nowhere. Ford later admitted that the idea was "probably too gimmicky."

When Ford became president, he promised to "heal the nation." Betty Ford took these words seriously. As first lady, she became an outspoken advocate of women's rights, supporting both liberalized abortion laws and the Equal Rights Amendment. After she developed breast cancer, she talked about her condition so that other women could learn about the importance of early detection.

KNOWING THAT THE WATERGATE SCANDAL WOULD make it difficult for Republicans to keep the White House, more than a dozen Democrats announced they would run for president in 1976. The first was Georgia governor Jimmy Carter, who entered the race

in December 1974. At first, Carter didn't even show up on the public opinion polls. People often said, "Jimmy who?" But early primary victories in Iowa and New Hampshire made Carter the front-runner. At the Democratic convention, he had more than enough votes to win a first-ballot victory.

Carter had an informal manner and a big, toothy smile. He talked a lot about restoring people's faith in government. Being a Washington outsider helped him convince voters that his election could make a difference.

Although Gerald Ford was a sitting president, winning the 1976 Republican nomination was by no means a sure thing. Former California governor Ronald Reagan ran against him and won a number of important primaries. Ford barely held off Reagan, taking the nomination with 1,187 votes to Reagan's 1,070.

Early in the general election campaign, opinion polls showed Carter more than thirty points ahead of Ford. During the early fall, however, the president closed the gap. By the time of the debates in early October, the election seemed too close to call. Ford probably lost the race in the second debate when he mistakenly said that Poland was free of Soviet domination.

The election attracted one of the lowest turnouts of the century. Barely half the eligible voters cast ballots. Only African Americans went to the polls in large numbers, nearly all of them pulling the lever for Carter. In the end, their support made the difference in a very tight race.

JIMMY CARTER

39TH PRESIDENT
★
FROM 1977 TO 1981

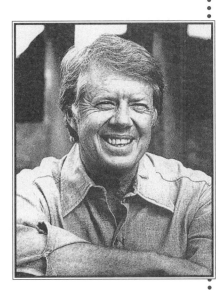

BORN: October 1, 1924

BIRTHPLACE: Plains, Ga.

PARTY: Democrat

VICE PRESIDENT: Walter F. Mondale

FIRST LADY: Eleanor Rosalynn Smith

CHILDREN: John, James Earl III, Jeffrey, Amy

NICKNAME: Hot

The first president born in a hospital.

EGYPT AND ISRAEL SIGN CAMP DAVID PEACE ACCORDS

CAMP DAVID, Maryland, September 17, 1978—President Anwar el-Sadat of Egypt and Prime Minister Menachem Begin of Israel signed two unprecedented peace documents today after thirteen days in isolation at the presidential retreat here.

One of the Camp David accords outlines a proposed peace treaty between Egypt and Israel. The other is a framework for peace in the Middle East. Begin and Sadat have both applauded President Carter for the role he has played as host and mediator.

Before this, the last major advance in the peace process came in November 1977, when President Sadat made a courageous trip to Jerusalem to address the Israeli parliament. Sadat's trip was criticized harshly by other Arab leaders who still refuse to recognize Israel's right to exist.

Carter invited Sadat and Begin to Camp David after peace talks between the two nations had broken down. Despite Sadat's visit, Israel and Egypt have been in a formal state of war since Israel was founded in 1948. The Camp David accords are expected to bring peace soon.

Jimmy Carter came to Washington determined to change the way government worked. His informal public image helped him in that task. After promising in his inaugural address to return government to the people, the president and First Lady Rosalynn Carter walked hand in hand from the Capitol to the White House rather than ride in a limousine.

Later, when he traveled, the president often carried his own luggage. And he also insisted on using the name Jimmy Carter rather than his full name, James Earl Carter, Jr.

Gerald Ford's Whip Inflation Now campaign had focused public attention on inflation, which was six percent at the time Carter took office. In other words, prices were increasing at an average rate of six percent each year. Because earnings weren't growing as fast, people were steadily losing their buying power. Under Carter, things got

Anwar El-Sadat (left) and Menachem Begin with Jimmy Carter (center)

much worse. During his years in office, inflation doubled to twelve percent.

THE ENERGY CRISIS Carter's biggest obstacle in solving the country's economic problems was the energy crisis. Throughout Carter's term, oil prices kept going up. In 1979 alone, the Organization of Petroleum Exporting Countries, known as OPEC, doubled oil prices from fourteen to more than twenty-eight dollars a barrel. This led to a shortage of affordable gasoline. When lines at the pumps reached a mile and a half long, most states introduced gasoline rationing.

The gas shortage was a disaster for U.S. automakers. With gas prices soaring, people began to buy smaller and more fuel-efficient Japanese cars rather than the "gas guzzlers" built by U.S. companies. As many as three hundred thousand autoworkers lost their jobs. Meanwhile, Congress approved more than one billion dollars in federal loan guarantees to save one carmaker, Chrysler, from bankruptcy.

To limit dependence on foreign oil, Carter proposed an energy bill with strict rules for conservation. Carter's bill also included money for the development of new energy sources. For eighteen months, the president struggled with Congress before a watered-down version of his bill was passed in November 1978.

Carter's status as a Washington outsider helped him as a candidate, but it hurt him as president. Although he enjoyed a Democratic majority in both houses, he didn't work well with Congress, and he rarely got his way.

HUMAN RIGHTS The basis of Carter's foreign policy was the issue of human rights. The president believed it was immoral for the United States to support

The Early Years

JIMMY CARTER GREW UP NEAR PLAINS, GEORGIA, WHERE his father owned a peanut warehouse. Although the Carters were better off than most families, their farmhouse had neither electricity nor running water. Jimmy's nickname as a boy was Hot, short for Hot Shot.

After Carter graduated from the naval academy in 1946, he studied nuclear physics and served aboard one of the first nuclear submarines. He planned to make a career in the navy, but when his father died in 1953, Carter moved back to Plains, where he took over the family peanut business. He soon entered local politics, helping to ease the process of desegregation after the *Brown* decision. Carter was elected to the Georgia state senate in 1962 and to the governorship in 1970.

★**THE FIRST FAMILY** Jimmy Carter projected a down-home style to show that he was a man of the people. He dressed casually, often in sweaters. He also preferred to stay in ordinary people's homes when he traveled instead of in hotels. His youngest child, Amy, was nine years old when the Carters moved into the White House. She attended public school in Washington and often brought friends home to play in her tree house on the White House grounds. Her dog was named Grits and her cat, Misty Malarky Ying Yang.

★**PROPOSITION 13** Fed up with skyrocketing property taxes, Howard Jarvis and Paul Gann began circulating a petition in California during the late 1970s to limit those taxes. Jarvis and Gann collected over a million signatures, more than twice the number they needed to put their proposal on the ballot. California's voters then approved Proposition 13 in 1978 by a two-to-one margin. California's "tax revolt" cut property taxes by nearly sixty percent. But governmental services also had to be cut, especially those to cities and schools.

★**THE ERA** Passage of the Equal Rights Amendment, known as the ERA, was one of the chief goals of the women's movement during the 1970s. The ERA stated that "Equality of rights under the law shall not be denied or abridged...on account of sex." Women's groups saw the ERA as a way to include women's rights in the Constitution. Critics claimed that women already had equal rights under the Constitution.

The ERA passed both houses of Congress and was sent to the states for ratification in 1972. By 1978, thirty-five of the necessary thirty-eight states had approved the amendment, but the number stuck there. The ERA's leading opponent, Phyllis Schlafly, claimed that the new law threatened women's traditional family role. Schlafly finally won the battle in June 1982 when the time allowed by Congress for ratification ran out.

★**NO NUKES** During the late 1970s, people began to oppose the construction of nuclear power plants. At first, the protests were small and local. In May 1977, fifteen hundred demonstrators were arrested trying to stop construction at Seabrook in New Hampshire. However, in March 1979, a nearly disastrous accident at the Three Mile Island plant near Harrisburg, Pennsylvania, awakened the public to the possible dangers of nuclear power.

In May 1979, sixty-five thousand people went to Washington to protest nuclear power. In September, more than two hundred thousand people attended a No Nukes rally and concert in New York City. These protests halted plans to build a number of new facilities and led to improved safety at the nuclear plants that continued to operate.

governments that abused their citizens—even if those governments also opposed communism. Proving that he meant what he said, the president cut off aid to brutal military dictatorships in Argentina, Ethiopia, and Uruguay.

The United States also withdrew support from longtime ally Anastasio Somoza Debayle in Nicaragua. When Somoza's tyrannical regime was overthrown in July 1979, Carter provided immediate financial support for the new Sandinista government despite its obvious Communist sympathies.

Carter's policy in Nicaragua followed an earlier success in Central America. In September 1977, the president reached agreement with Panamanian leader Omar Torrijos Herrera on the fate of the Panama Canal. The new treaty called for turning over the canal to Panama by the end of 1999.

Conservative Republicans, notably former California governor Ronald Reagan, opposed the treaty as a giveaway, but Carter lobbied heavily from the White House. After months of debate, the Senate voted to approve the treaty. The vote was 68-32, just one vote more than the two-thirds required for ratification.

SALT II With regard to the Soviet Union, Carter continued Nixon's policy of détente The Strategic Arms Limitation Talks produced another treaty, which Carter and Soviet premier Leonid Brezhnev signed in June 1979.

Before SALT II could be ratified, however—and its prospects were not good—the Soviet Union invaded Afghanistan. Waging a war that resembled the U.S. effort in Vietnam, the Red Army spent nine years fighting unsuccessfully to defend the Soviet-backed government against Islamic rebels. In response to the invasion, President Carter cut off

U.S. grain sales and led a sixty-four-nation boycott of the Moscow Olympics held during the summer of 1980.

Carter's successes in foreign affairs, however, including his triumph at Camp David, were soon overshadowed by the hostage crisis that eventually destroyed his chances for reelection.

THE HOSTAGE CRISIS

On November 4, 1979, a mob of Islamic students attacked the U.S. embassy in Iran and took the staff hostage. Earlier that year, an Islamic revolution had toppled the U.S.-supported government of Shah Mohammad Reza Pahlavi. The student radicals demanded that the shah, then undergoing cancer treatment in New York, be returned to Iran in exchange for the release of the hostages.

President Carter did not approve of the torture the shah had used to control Iran. But neither was he willing to submit to terrorism. Instead, he tried to free the hostages through diplomatic means, all of which failed.

As the months passed, public pressure on Carter continued to grow. When nothing else seemed to work, the president approved a military rescue mission in April 1980. Unfortunately, helicopter problems forced the mission to pull out, and eight servicemen were killed when one helicopter hit a transport plane. Secretary of State Cyrus Vance, who had opposed the raid, resigned in protest, and the president's public image suffered badly.

It wasn't until January 19, 1981, his last full day in office, that Carter finally negotiated the hostages' release, ending 444 days of captivity. The former president spent the first day of his retirement welcoming the hostages back at a military hospital in West Germany.

IN HIS CAMPAIGN FOR reelection, President Carter was in trouble from the very beginning. Inflation was pushing down the value of money, and soaring interest rates made borrowing expensive. Meanwhile, the Iranian hostage crisis kept dragging on. All this made Carter's term in office seem a failure. During the primary campaign, Carter was challenged by Senator Edward Kennedy of Massachusetts.

The liberal wing of the Democratic party rallied to the youngest of the Kennedy brothers, but an incident from his past doomed him. In 1969, Kennedy had driven off a bridge in Chappaquiddick, Massachusetts. A female passenger died in the accident, but Kennedy didn't report it right away. Although no criminal charges were filed, many people questioned Kennedy's conduct. Carter beat Kennedy in the primaries, but the struggle weakened him and disrupted the party.

After nearly winning the Republican nomination in 1976, Ronald Reagan took it easily this time around. His strongest challenger, George Bush, withdrew before the convention. When it came time to pick a running mate, Reagan tried to work a deal with former president Gerald Ford. Being an extreme conservative, Reagan was afraid of losing the support of moderates. But the deal fell through, and Reagan picked Bush.

Republican John Anderson of Illinois dropped out early to run a third-party campaign. He combined the conservative economic policies of Reagan with the commitment to social welfare shown by Carter.

Both he and Carter attacked Reagan for not caring about civil rights and for the frightening statements he made about getting tough with the Soviet Union.

None of these attacks stuck, however, because Reagan's staff shaped his image brilliantly. Voters watching on television saw not a dangerous warmonger but a strong leader. Reagan's vision was so attractive that he won in a landslide. The defining moment of the campaign came during the single televised debate when Reagan looked into the camera and asked, "Are you better off than you were four years ago?"

RONALD WILSON REAGAN

40TH PRESIDENT
★
FROM 1981 TO 1989

BORN: February 6, 1911

BIRTHPLACE: Tampico, Ill.

PARTY: Republican

VICE PRESIDENT: George Bush

FIRST LADY: Nancy Davis

CHILDREN: Maureen, Michael, Patricia, Ronald

NICKNAME: Dutch

The first president to have been divorced.

DRIFTER SHOOTS PRESIDENT

Reagan Survives Assassination Attempt

WASHINGTON, March 30, 1981—President Reagan was shot in the chest today outside the Washington Hilton Hotel, where he had just delivered a speech. The president was rushed to a nearby hospital, where an emergency surgical team was standing by.

"I forgot to duck," Reagan joked as the doctors prepared him for surgery to remove the bullet lodged in his left lung. Despite the seventy-year-old president's age, doctors say he appears to be making a remarkable recovery.

Also injured in the attack were a policeman, a secret-service agent, and presidential press secretary James Brady, who suffered permanent brain damage from a bullet wound to the head.

Reagan's would-be assassin is a twenty-five-year-old drifter named John W. Hinckley, Jr. The shooting appears to have no political motive. Instead, Hinckley claims that he shot the president as a love offering to actress Jodie Foster, whom he has never met.

At sixty-nine, Ronald Reagan was the oldest president ever elected, but he worked hard to remain youthful. A veteran of cowboy movies, Reagan liked to play the tough guy. His image was very important to him—and to the way he governed.

Reagan owed much of his enormous personal appeal to the way he made people feel about the country. His speeches and television appearances encouraged people to believe that the nation's social and economic problems could be solved easily and painlessly. Uncomfortable with detail, the president liked to speak in folksy generalities like "a rising tide lifts all ships." He meant that good times for some Americans would bring good times for all.

Reagan always presented himself as a man of deep conviction and principle. For example, even after he was shot, he remained firmly opposed to gun control laws. By keeping his focus on the

193

big picture, Reagan was able to avoid mistakes that many new presidents tend to make. Aware that presidents with too many proposals often get nothing done, Reagan concentrated on just a few ideas. Because he had won in a landslide, Congress passed his bills without a fight.

In Reagan's view, all government spending (with the possible exception of the defense budget) was wasteful. "Government is not the solution to our problems," he said in his inaugural address, "government is the problem." Uniting Republicans and conservative Democrats into a working coalition, he lowered taxes, raised defense spending, and cut deeply into such social programs as food stamps and unemployment benefits. Reagan argued that social spending could be handled much better by the individual states.

President Reagan immediately set about reversing the liberal policies of previous administrations. Environmentalists were outraged when the Environmental Protection Agency cut the endangered species list in half and the Interior Department moved to open federal lands to private developers.

REAGANOMICS When Reagan took office, the inflation rate was over thirteen percent, and economic growth was slow. But the new president had a radical plan for fixing things. The plan was based on supply-side economics. According to this theory, increasing the amount of money in people's pockets will increase both investment and consumer spending. These, in turn, will make the economy stronger and more productive.

To begin this beneficial chain of events, Reagan proposed a major tax cut for the rich, because they were the people most likely to invest. Reagan assured the public that

The Early Years

As the son of a shoe salesman in Dixon, Illinois, Ronald Reagan grew up collecting butterflies and bird eggs and watching cowboy movies at the local movie theater. In high school, he was elected president of the student body and acted in school plays. At Eureka College, his grades were more often Cs than As. After college, he looked for work as a radio announcer.

Reagan moved to Hollywood in 1937 after signing an acting contract with the Warner Brothers studio. A year later, he met actress Jane Wyman during the filming of *Brother Rat*. They were married in 1940 but divorced eight years later while Reagan was president of the Screen Actors Guild. In 1952, Reagan married another actress, Nancy Davis.

Reagan began his political career as a **New Deal Democrat**, but his views gradually changed. He joined Democrats-for-Eisenhower in 1952 and the Republican party ten years later. In 1966, he won the governor's race in California by nearly twenty percentage points. Reagan soon gained national attention for reforming California's welfare system, balancing its budget, and ordering gas attacks on antiwar demonstrators.

★**THE GREAT COMMUNICATOR** Ronald Reagan was the first professional movie actor to become president. In *Knute Rockne—All American* (1940), he popularized the phrase "win one for the Gipper," and in *Bedtime for Bonzo* (1951), he played a college professor trying to raise a chimpanzee as a child.

Early in his career, Reagan had worked as a radio sportscaster. In those days, the briefest descriptions of out-of-town baseball games were telegraphed to radio stations, where the announcers had to make up the details. Later Reagan was a spokesperson for General Electric. Because of his ability and experience in front of a microphone, White House reporters called Reagan the Great Communicator. More so than any other president, Reagan used carefully planned television appearances to promote his policies.

★**MICHAEL JACKSON** *People* magazine once called Michael Jackson the most famous man in the world. His 1983 album *Thriller* set new sales records, moving more than forty million copies and winning an unprecedented eight Grammy awards. His dancing also captivated the public. In his "moonwalk" routine, Jackson appeared to be walking forward as he actually moved backward. The single, sequined glove that he wore on his right hand started a fashion trend all over the world.

★**SANDRA DAY O'CONNOR**
During his presidential campaigns, Ronald Reagan promised to reverse the direction of the Supreme Court by appointing conservatives to replace liberal justices as they retired. The decision he most wanted the Court to reverse was *Roe v. Wade* (1973), which had legalized abortion. In 1981, Reagan made his first appointment to the Court. He picked Arizona judge Sandra Day O'Connor. She became the first woman ever to serve on the Supreme Court. Although O'Connor generally sided with the new conservative majority, she refused to support a complete reversal of *Roe v. Wade*.

★**PERSONAL COMPUTERS** Early computers were huge, expensive, and complicated to use. Only large businesses could afford them. Around 1980, however, companies such as IBM and Apple developed personal computers, or PCs, that ordinary people could use and afford. Apple was founded in a California garage in 1976 by two college dropouts in their twenties. Their Apple II computer, introduced in 1977, used a regular television set for a monitor and stored data on audiocassettes, but it also sold for just $1,298. IBM introduced its first PC in 1981.

economic prosperity would "trickle down" to everyone else. During the campaign, Vice President George Bush had called this plan "voodoo economics," but now he supported the president loyally.

As enacted by Congress, the Reagan tax cut added up to a twenty-five percent reduction in individual tax rates over three years. People were left with more money, but most didn't invest it. Rather, they spent it on things like videocassette recorders and aerobics classes.

Very little money trickled down to the middle class and even less to the poor. Meanwhile, the country moved deeper into the worst recession since World War II.

During the recession, high interest rates and a drop in world oil prices combined to reduce inflation to two percent. But unemployment soared from seven to nearly eleven percent in November 1982. Record numbers of people went bankrupt and lost their family farms.

BUDGET DEFICITS As many Democratic economists had predicted, the national debt ballooned. The billions saved by cutting social programs were erased by even larger increases in the defense budget. The economy didn't grow very quickly, but the budget deficit did.

President Reagan often called for a constitutional amendment to require a balanced budget. But he never submitted one himself. During his eight years in office, the national debt more than doubled. Interest payments of more than $150 billion on that debt became the third-largest item in the budget. Before Reagan, the government had never run a budget deficit higher than one hundred billion dollars. Now deficits of two hundred billion dollars and more became commonplace.

THE EVIL EMPIRE

During his first term, Reagan's foreign policy focused on the Soviet Union. His attitude toward the Soviets was remarkably similar to the Cold War mentality of the 1950s. He believed that the United States, which stood for democracy and freedom, was engaged in a mortal battle against the Soviet Union, which he called "the focus of evil in the modern world."

In March 1983, the president proposed in a nationally televised speech that the United States build a space-age missile defense system that would use satellites to shoot down incoming nuclear warheads. Because Reagan's Strategic Defense Initiative would cost trillions of dollars, it became immediately controversial on Capitol Hill.

The program was dubbed Star Wars because it reminded people of special effects they had seen in science-fiction films. After the president's speech, many reputable scientists declared that the missile shield, as Reagan had described it, could not work. But the president insisted on going ahead with the project. He believed that the surest and safest way to beat the Soviets in the arms race was to outspend them.

NICARAGUA

In Central America, Reagan fought another type of Cold War. During his first term, he sent large amounts of economic and military aid to the anticommunist government in El Salvador despite evidence that official "death squads" were murdering that government's political enemies.

During his second term, Reagan focused his attention on Nicaragua. After the 1979 revolution there, the remnants of the Somoza dictatorship took the name *Contras,* which means "against" in Spanish.

PRESIDENT REAGAN WAS PRACTICALLY ASSURED OF winning reelection in 1984. The recession had bottomed out, and a sustained boom had cut unemployment in half. Also, the country was at peace.

The early Democratic front-runner was former vice president Walter Mondale. His most significant challengers were Senator Gary Hart of Colorado and the Reverend Jesse Jackson of Chicago. Hart stressed "new ideas" and attacked Mondale for his close ties to Democratic special interest groups. Jackson was the first African American to run a national primary campaign. He built a "rainbow coalition" to speak for poor and minority voters.

Mondale proved to be unstoppable, however. At the convention, he surprised most people by declaring that he would raise taxes to control the budget deficits. "Mr. Reagan will raise taxes, and so will I," Mondale said. "He won't tell you. I just did." Then came an even bigger surprise. For his running mate, Mondale chose Representative Geraldine Ferraro of New York, the first woman ever to run on a major-party ticket.

Reagan hit Mondale hard on taxes, promising to raise them only as a last resort. He also pointed out that most Americans were indeed better off than they had been four years before. Reagan's friendliness and good humor had wide appeal, as did his vision of national progress and strength. "It's morning in America," his television commercials began.

Mondale criticized Reagan's economic policies, which benefited the rich at the expense of the poor and middle class. But he stopped short of condemning Reagan directly, because he worried that voters might object to personal attacks against the popular president. On Election Day, Reagan won an even more impressive victory than in 1980, taking the electoral vote 525-13.

From bases in neighboring Honduras, they fought a guerrilla war against the new Sandinista government in Nicaragua.

In 1981, the Reagan administration cut off aid to the Sandinistas and instead began supporting the Contras, whom Reagan called "freedom fighters." By 1983, the Contras had grown into a trained army of seventy-five hundred soldiers.

After learning that the CIA had been secretly mining Nicaraguan harbors and giving lessons in political assassination, Congress passed the Boland Amendment, which prohibited further military aid to the Contras. To get around this law, administration officials assigned Lieutenant Colonel Oliver North of the National Security Council to help the Contras quietly raise money from private sources.

TERRORISM During the 1980 campaign, Reagan had repeatedly attacked Jimmy Carter for his handling of the Iranian hostage crisis. Reagan promised that he would never negotiate with terrorists. But he found that promise difficult to keep once more hostages were taken. This time, the

SPACE SHUTTLE EXPLODES
Seven Aboard Challenger Die in Crash

KENNEDY SPACE CENTER, Florida, January 28, 1986—The space shuttle *Challenger* exploded seventy-three seconds after liftoff this morning, killing all seven members of its crew.

Low temperatures preceding the launch have been blamed for the disaster. Last night was unusually cold, and this morning there were icicles on the launch tower.

It is believed that the cold caused a seal in the shuttle's booster rockets to fail. Once the seal failed, the shuttle was immediately engulfed in a fireball.

The *Challenger* crew included Christa McAuliffe, chosen from among eleven thousand applicants to become the first teacher in space. McAuliffe had prepared several lessons on space science that she planned to broadcast directly from the orbiting shuttle to U.S. classrooms.

Because of McAuliffe's participation in the mission, millions of schoolchildren were watching the launch of the *Challenger* on television when it exploded.

kidnappers were Lebanese Muslims with ties to Iran.

Lebanon was then in the middle of a civil war between Muslims and Christians, which the United States had been trying to settle. Marines had already been brought ashore into Beirut, the Lebanese capital, for peacekeeping duty. In October 1983, a van filled with explosives rammed into their barracks. The blast it created collapsed the building. Hundreds of soldiers were buried in the rubble, and 241 were killed.

Terrorist attacks weren't limited to Lebanon. In October 1985, Palestinian terrorists hijacked the Italian cruise ship *Achille Lauro*. They killed an American in a wheelchair, throwing his body overboard. Elsewhere, an April 1986 explosion at a West Berlin discotheque killed one U.S. serviceman and injured sixty others.

Charging that Libya was responsible for the discotheque bombing, Reagan ordered a raid on that country in retaliation. A squadron of F-111 bombers attacked on April 15, striking military targets as well as the living quarters of Libyan leader Muammar Qaddafi and his family.

THE GORBACHEV ERA Meanwhile, in March 1985, an extraordinary new leader named Mikhail Gorbachev came to power in the Soviet Union. The fifty-three-year-old Gorbachev was open-minded enough to realize that his country could no longer afford to compete with the massive U.S. arms buildup. Gorbachev knew that the Soviet economy would continue to suffer unless Soviet society was itself reformed.

The two basic principles of Gorbachev's new program were *glasnost,* or openness, and *perestroika,* or restructuring. Under *glasnost,*

★**LIVE AID** In 1984, Bob Geldof produced a record featuring fellow British rock stars singing "Do They Know It's Christmas?" Proceeds from this song were donated to famine relief efforts in Ethiopia. A similar project, "We Are the World," raised money in the United States. During the summer of 1985, Geldof organized a benefit concert that would take place simultaneously in London and Philadelphia. The July 13 event, called Live Aid, was broadcast via satellite to 152 countries around the world. Performers included U2, Sting, Paul McCartney, and Madonna. The seventeen-hour show raised more than seventy million dollars for famine relief.

★**THE FIRST LADY** Nancy Reagan was one of the most controversial first ladies ever. Because she had helped her husband build his political career, many people questioned how much she still influenced him. The president obviously adored her, and White House staffers feared displeasing her.

Mrs. Reagan was criticized early in her husband's first term when she spent nearly a million dollars redecorating the White House. Later she was attacked for accepting free gowns from famous designers. Her expensive tastes in furniture and clothing seemed out of place at a time when social programs to aid the poor were being cut. During President Reagan's second term, the first lady improved her image by devoting her energies to the "Just Say No" campaign against drug use.

★**C. EVERETT KOOP** One of the most controversial figures of the Reagan administration was C. Everett Koop. The president picked Koop for the post of surgeon general because he thought the pediatrician shared his conservative values. Pro-choice groups opposed Dr. Koop's nomination for the same reason. They felt that Koop would let his personal feelings against abortion influence his judgment. But Koop's critics greatly underestimated his devotion to public service. Often during his eight years in office, the surgeon general enraged conservatives by choosing public health over politics. Koop's most controversial moment came in October 1986 when his report on the **AIDS** epidemic recommended that AIDS education begin in elementary schools as early as the third grade.

★**THE MORAL MAJORITY** President Reagan wanted to outlaw abortion and bring prayer back into the public schools. Although he made little progress on these issues, he spoke about them often. His greatest ally in this war of words was the Moral Majority, an ultraconservative religious group founded by Baptist minister Jerry Falwell in 1979. Falwell himself was one of a number of television evangelists who had far-reaching influence during the 1980s. Televangelism raised hundreds of millions of dollars, but it came crashing down in 1987 when television minister Jim Bakker was exposed for cheating his followers out of $150 million.

★**WALL STREET GREED** The deal-making on Wall Street was remarkably fast-paced during the Reagan years. The highest of the high-flyers was Michael Milken, who invented the "junk" bond. Milken's junk bonds used very high interest rates to lure insurance companies and banks into investing with him. The money the bondholders put up was used to buy companies. These companies were usually worth much more than the amount put up in cash, so the deals were called leveraged buy-outs, or LBOs. In 1987, Milken made an estimated $550 million. Three years later, he pleaded guilty to insider trading and went to prison.

censorship was eased so that people could express their ideas more freely. Meanwhile, *perestroika* attempted to revitalize the Communist system with a bit of capitalist private enterprise.

Although U.S.-Soviet relations were tense during Reagan's first term, Gorbachev's willingness to make peace helped wind down the Cold War. In December 1987, he and Reagan signed the Intermediate-Range Nuclear Forces agreement. For the first time, both sides actually agreed to reduce the number of nuclear warheads in their arsenals by destroying an entire class of missiles.

THE IRANIAN ARMS SALE Beginning in 1980, the Persian Gulf countries of Iran and Iraq fought an eight-year border war. The Iranians desperately needed arms because President Reagan had repeatedly asked U.S. allies not to sell them any. At the same time, however, members of Reagan's staff were secretly negotiating to sell arms to Iran. In exchange, so-called "moderates" in Iran agreed to help win the release of Americans held hostage in Lebanon.

Using a group of private dealers as middlemen, Reagan's National Security Council staff sold the arms to Iran at hugely inflated prices. In return, three hostages were released. But three more were soon taken. All the time, the arms sale was kept hidden from Congress and the public.

For a long time, the Reagan administration had been frustrated by Congress. The Boland Amendment was particularly irritating because the Contras were important to the president. To get around this law, White House officials decided to use some of the lavish profits from the Iranian arms sale to buy more weapons for the Contras.

The arms sale and the diversion of money to the Contras took place amid great secrecy. Later, the president claimed that even he didn't know what was going on. When his own staff members were asked direct questions during congressional hearings, they either gave misleading answers or lied. News of the arms sale was finally published in a small Beirut magazine in November 1986.

THE IRAN-CONTRA SCANDAL The first investigation of the scandal was conducted by Attorney General Edwin Meese. Meese's confirmation hearings had taken more than a year because Senate investigators had to look into a number of serious charges against him. A special prosecutor later concluded that Meese had probably broken the law a number of times, but that there was not enough evidence to prosecute him successfully.

Meese's early investigation of the Iran-Contra affair was badly bungled. While his aides conducted interviews in one room, Oliver North and his boss, National Security Advisor John Poindexter, shredded important documents in another. Poindexter later admitted that he had destroyed Reagan's signed authorization for the Iranian arms sale in order to save the president embarrassment. Other officials tried to protect the president by lying under oath about the order in which events took place.

During the congressional investigations and criminal trials that followed, administration officials portrayed President Reagan as a passive man, detached from details and overly willing to delegate authority to his aides. Because people knew the president liked to leave work early in the day and often got confused when he had to talk about the specifics of his policies, they tended to believe that he hadn't known what the National Security Council staff was doing.

WITH PRESIDENT REAGAN RETIRING, PRIMARY RACES in both parties were wide open. Vice President George Bush was embarrassed when he finished third among Republicans in Iowa. But he came back quickly to win New Hampshire and never looked back.

The Democratic campaign began wildly. After Colorado senator Gary Hart was forced out by a sex scandal, Governor Michael Dukakis of Massachusetts became the front-runner. With each primary, Dukakis added to his lead as his rivals dropped out one by one—except for Jesse Jackson. The Rainbow Coalition leader stayed in all the way to the convention. Jackson wanted the vice-presidential nomination, but Dukakis disagreed with some of Jackson's ultraliberal policies. Instead he picked conservative senator Lloyd Bentsen of Texas.

Bush's acceptance speech at the Republican convention called for an end to the greed of the 1980s. He said he wanted to lead a "kinder and gentler nation." However, when public opinion polls showed he was twenty points down, Bush ignored his own words and went on the offensive. His campaign was one of the most negative in history.

Avoiding serious but complicated issues, Bush attacked Dukakis for vetoing a bill that would have required schoolchildren to recite the Pledge of Allegiance. While Dukakis explained his new health insurance plan, Bush visited a flag factory. About the only thing Bush said regarding his own policies was, "Read my lips: No new taxes!" The election became a battle of media consultants, and the Democrats were unable to respond quickly or well to the attacks.

As Bush turned the word *liberal* into an insult, Dukakis's lead in the polls disappeared. The vice president's promise to carry on the Reagan Revolution carried him to victory. Bush became the first sitting vice president to be elected president since Martin Van Buren succeeded Andrew Jackson in 1836.

GEORGE HERBERT WALKER BUSH

41ST PRESIDENT
★
FROM 1989 TO 1993

BORN: June 12, 1924

BIRTHPLACE: Milton, Mass.

PARTY: Republican

VICE PRESIDENT: J. Danforth Quayle

FIRST LADY: Barbara Pierce

CHILDREN: George, Robin, John, Neil, Marvin, Dorothy

NICKNAME: Poppy

The first president to refuse publicly to eat broccoli.

UNITED NATIONS HOLDS EARTH SUMMIT

RIO DE JANEIRO, Brazil, June 14, 1992—The United Nations Earth Summit ended today as representatives of 153 nations signed treaties designed to reverse disturbing trends in the environment.

These agreements concern such issues as global warming and biodiversity. Global warming involves the greenhouse effect, which is the increase in worldwide temperature caused by man-made chemicals trapped in the atmosphere.

Biodiversity refers to the incredible variety of plant and animal species on the planet. Environmental scientists have warned that the continuing destruction of South American rain forests threatens many species that live there.

Environmental protection has become a particularly prominent issue in U.S. politics since March 24, 1989, when the oil tanker *Exxon Valdez* struck a reef off the Alaskan coast. The accident spilled ten million barrels of oil into Prince William Sound. The oil spill, the worst in the nation's history, killed thousands of birds, otters, fish, seals, and other animals.

Ronald Reagan may have fought the deciding battle, but the Cold War ended during George Bush's presidency. In a December 1988 speech to the United Nations, Soviet leader Mikhail Gorbachev declared that the Cold War was over. Then he followed up his words with some remarkable action.

Besides undertaking reform in his own country, Gorbachev reduced and then removed the Soviet troops from Eastern Europe. For the first time since World War II, East Germans, Czechs, Hungarians, and others were permitted to run their own governments. The world was no longer dominated by two superpowers challenging each other with nuclear weapons. Instead, in Bush's words, there was a "new world order."

While President Bush monitored the situation in the Soviet Union, he became more actively involved in Panama.

This strategically located Central American country was controlled in 1989 by dictator Manuel Noriega. Under the Reagan administration, the CIA had allowed Noriega to smuggle drugs because he gave them important intelligence information. As Noriega's drug trafficking and anti-American speeches became more frequent, President Bush found it difficult to ignore Noriega's illegal activities.

At first, Bush imposed economic sanctions, or penalties, and urged Noriega's rivals to stage a coup, or government takeover. When neither of these tactics worked, Bush ordered military action. Twelve thousand U.S. troops invaded Panama in December 1989. Noriega was captured and flown to Florida to stand trial on drug charges. Most Latin American countries publicly condemned the raid, but privately they expressed satisfaction with the result.

THE PERSIAN GULF WAR A year later, Bush again considered military action. On August 2, 1990, Iraqi troops invaded the Persian Gulf nation of Kuwait. Although only a tiny country, Kuwait held about ten percent of the world's oil reserves. If Iraqi president Saddam Hussein were someday to conquer neighboring Saudi Arabia, he would control nearly half the world's oil.

President Bush immediately called the invasion "naked aggression." The United Nations Security Council imposed economic sanctions and soon gave member nations permission to enforce the sanctions using military means. Even the Soviet Union, Hussein's biggest arms supplier, stopped selling weapons to Iraq.

Six days after the invasion, President Bush began sending troops to help the Saudis defend themselves. Eventually, more than half a million

G EORGE BUSH'S FATHER WAS A WALL STREET BANKER AND later a U.S. senator from Connecticut. Prescott Bush taught his children that people of wealth and

The Early Years

privilege should give something back to their country. On his eighteenth birthday in June 1942, George put off attending Yale University and enlisted in the navy. A year later, he earned his wings as the youngest navy pilot. During World War II, Bush flew fifty-eight combat missions against the Japanese and won the Distinguished Flying Cross.

After college, Bush turned down a job with his father's Wall Street firm. Instead, he went to Texas to learn the oil business, which eventually made him a millionaire. Running as a moderate Republican, Bush

won election to the House of Representatives from Houston in 1966. Four years later, at the request of President Nixon, he ran for the Senate from Texas. When Bush lost that race, Nixon named him ambassador to the United Nations. Bush later served President Ford as the official U.S. representative to China and as director of the CIA.

★**THE FIRST LADY** Seventeen-year-old Barbara Pierce met her future husband at a Christmas dance in 1942. He was the first boy she ever kissed. George Bush later named his bomber plane *Barbara* after her. As first lady, Mrs. Bush immediately distanced herself from Nancy Reagan by getting involved in charitable causes. She founded an organization to help illiterate adults learn how to read, and she also spoke out for the homeless. It was often said that Barbara Bush was more popular than the president. One reason might be the bestselling *Millie's Book* she wrote from the point of view of the Bush family dog.

★**NELSON MANDELA** African National Congress leader Nelson Mandela was sent to prison in 1964 for planning to sabotage the white South African government. Mandela wanted to overthrow the South African system of apartheid. In South Africa, blacks could not vote, and whites got special treatment in every situation. During the 1980s, the United States and other nations used economic sanctions,

such as halting trade, to push the white minority government into sharing power with the black majority. Although Nelson Mandela served many years at hard labor, his spirit remained unbroken. He was finally freed in February 1990 by President F.W. de Klerk, who wanted Mandela to help him negotiate a peaceful end to apartheid.

★**HIP HOP** Like most trends in popular music, including rock 'n' roll, hip hop originated in the black community. Its popularity spread quickly after MTV, the cable music television network, began airing "Yo! MTV Raps" in 1989. That show brought hip hop music, fashion, and dance styles into the mainstream. Soon baggy pants, baseball caps, gold jewelry, and hooded sweatshirts were being worn all over the country by young people who wanted to look cool. Although a handful of white performers, including Vanilla Ice, hopped onto the hip hop bandwagon, the music never lost its black urban roots.

★**MAGIC JOHNSON AND AIDS**
On November 7, 1991, basketball star Earvin "Magic" Johnson told a packed news conference that he was retiring from the Los Angeles Lakers because he had become infected with the virus that causes AIDS. Magic's announcement

stunned the world. Many people had refused to believe that such a skilled and popular athlete could get AIDS. For that reason, Johnson said he planned to devote the rest of his life to educating teenagers about how people become infected with AIDS. George Bush quickly appointed Johnson to the presidential AIDS commission, but he resigned in September 1992 after criticizing Bush for the president's lack of support.

U.S. soldiers took part in Operation Desert Shield. Meanwhile, the president and Secretary of State James Baker worked tirelessly to convince other nations to join a great coalition against Iraq. Great Britain, France, Egypt, and Syria all provided troops, while other nations sent planes and ships.

OPERATION DESERT STORM In November, the Security Council set a deadline of January 15, 1991, for the complete withdrawal of Iraqi troops from Kuwait. If the Iraqis did not obey, member nations could then force an Iraqi pullout. On January 12, after a lengthy debate, Congress voted to give President Bush the authority to wage war against Iraq. Seven hours after the deadline passed, Bush began Operation Desert Storm.

For nearly six weeks, coalition bombers devastated the Iraqi military. More than a hundred thousand combat missions were flown. On February 23, the ground assault began. Within one hundred hours, troops under General Norman Schwarzkopf had overwhelmed the Iraqi army, the fourth largest in the world. In the meantime, Kuwait was liberated.

After the war, Bush enjoyed enormous popularity. Not only had the United States won a convincing military victory, but it had been done as part of a worldwide coalition effort. This was the new world order that Bush had been talking about. Furthermore, the president had proven conclusively that he could handle himself well during an international crisis. But a crisis at home—that was another matter.

Throughout the Bush presidency, critics complained that the president had no goals for the country. During the 1988 campaign, Bush had vaguely promised to be the Education

GEORGE HERBERT WALKER BUSH 1989-1993

President and the Environmental President. Congress waited for proposals addressing these issues, but little came from the White House. What happened instead was a banking scandal followed by a deep recession.

THE SAVINGS AND LOAN SCANDAL

During the 1980s, financial speculation grew as the Reagan administration relaxed federal regulation of the savings and loan industry. Many savings and loan owners used this new freedom to make risky loans. Others simply cheated their depositors. One of the worst owners, Charles Keating, made sizable campaign contributions to five senators in exchange for their help in warding off the few federal bank examiners still on the government payroll.

By the time the roof fell in on the savings and loan industry in 1989, hundreds of billions of dollars in government-insured deposits had disappeared. The taxpayers ended up footing the bill, and only a very few people went to jail. The Keating Five may have been the worst offenders, but most congressmen had accepted contributions from the savings and loan industry. These campaign contributions made legislators reluctant to control the problem before it got out of hand.

In late November 1990, the economic news got even worse. After four months of declining economic indicators, Federal Reserve Chairman Alan Greenspan announced that the economy was having a "meaningful downturn." A month later, unemployment reached a three-year high. At first, the president and his advisors blamed the recession on the rise in oil prices during the Persian Gulf War. They predicted growth would begin again soon, but it didn't come soon enough for Bush.

I N EARLY 1991, AFTER THE END OF THE PERSIAN GULF War, George Bush was hugely popular. His eighty-nine percent public approval rating seemed to guarantee him election to a second term. But the recession soon weakened people's confidence in his leadership.

Although there were some dramatic ups and downs during the primary season, the Democrats nominated Bill Clinton on the first ballot. The forty-six-year-old

Arkansas governor claimed that he was a "new kind of Democrat," liberal on social issues and conservative on economic ones. His theme was "change." But his campaign had been dogged for months by two controversial accusations. One was that, while married, he had carried on a twelve-year affair with another woman. The other was that he had misled his draft board to avoid fighting in the Vietnam War. Although Clinton denied these charges, it sometimes seemed as though they might sink him.

M eanwhile, people turned away from Bush because he had abandoned his "Read my lips: No new taxes!" pledge. When self-made billionaire Ross Perot entered the race as an independent candidate, he focused people's attention on the budget deficit. Lecturing the public with charts and graphs, Perot said he would run the government the way he ran his own successful business. Whether voters thought he was eccentric or capable, Perot made the deficit the most important issue of the election.

Perot took nineteen percent of the popular vote, Bush thirty-eight percent, and Clinton forty-three percent. With Perot's votes, Bush would have won in a landslide. Instead, Clinton won the election with a majority in the electoral college. Less than half the voters cast ballots for Clinton, but sixty-two percent voted for change.

WILLIAM JEFFERSON CLINTON

42ND PRESIDENT
★
1993-2001

BORN: August 19, 1946

BIRTHPLACE: Hope, Ark.

PARTY: Democrat

VICE PRESIDENT: Albert Gore, Jr.

FIRST LADY: Hillary Rodham

CHILDREN: Chelsea

NICKNAME: Bubba

The first president to have been a Rhodes scholar.

ARREST MADE IN WORLD TRADE CENTER BOMBING

NEW YORK, March 4, 1993—The FBI made the first arrest today in the World Trade Center bombing case. Agents captured Mohammed Salameh in Jersey City, New Jersey, when he attempted to collect his rental deposit on the van used in the bombing.

Salameh had told the van rental company that the van had been stolen. The FBI found Salameh by tracing the vehicle using an identification number found on a piece of twisted metal at the bomb site. Salameh is a member of a Jersey City mosque attended by radical Islamic fundamentalists.

Just last week, lower Manhattan was thrown into turmoil when a huge explosion rocked the twin towers of the World Trade Center. The February 26 blast, the worst terrorist attack ever on U.S. soil, was caused by a van loaded with explosives. The van had been parked in a public garage beneath the 110-story buildings.

Five people were killed by the explosion and at least one thousand injured. The bomb left a crater in the garage seven stories deep.

As the first Baby Boomer president, Bill Clinton was often influenced by values he adopted during the 1960s. For example, he picked his vice president, Albert Gore, in part because of Gore's concern for the environment. Yet Clinton proved in his inaugural address that he understood traditional values as well. "It is time to break the bad habit of expecting something for nothing," he said. In other words, change would require sacrifice.

Many Americans, even those who voted against him, hoped that Clinton's election would end governmental "gridlock" between the president and Congress. For the first time in twelve years, both branches of government would be controlled by the same party. Change didn't come easily, however, and early stumbles by the Clinton team didn't help.

Clinton's first nominee for attorney general, Zoe Baird, was forced to withdraw her name after admitting that she and her husband had failed to pay social security tax for their two household employees. Still, Clinton remained committed to naming a female attorney general, and his second nominee, Florida prosecutor Janet Reno, won Senate confirmation easily. Several months later, he appointed another woman, federal judge Ruth Bader Ginsburg, to the Supreme Court.

TRADE AGREEMENTS Although he often fought with Congress during his first two years in office, Clinton did win two big victories on trade issues. In November 1993, the House passed the North American Free Trade Agreement by thirty-four votes. NAFTA created a free-trade zone linking the United States, Mexico, and Canada. A year later, Congress approved the General Agreement on Tariffs and Trade, an international treaty that took seven years to negotiate.

Another major presidential effort won passage of a thirty-billion-dollar anti-crime bill in August 1994. With health care, however, the president was less successful. A commission chaired by First Lady Hillary Rodham Clinton proposed covering all Americans and guaranteeing them a minimum package of benefits. But doctors, hospitals, and insurance companies fought these reforms, and congressmen criticized them for being too expensive. Some moderate senators offered compromises, but these were also rejected, and the gridlock on heath care continued.

THE 1994 ELECTIONS The president's party often loses seats in congressional midterm elections. But the 1994 election was unusually disastrous for the Democrats. Republicans won control of both the House and the Senate for the first time since 1955. A Republican even beat Thomas Foley, who became the first sitting speaker of the House to lose his seat in an election since 1862.

BILL CLINTON'S FATHER DIED IN A CAR accident before he was born. When he was seven, his mother, Virginia, remarried. Her new husband, Roger Clinton, was a car dealer and an alcoholic who sometimes beat his wife. At fourteen, Bill confronted him. "Daddy, if you're not able to stand up, I'll help you," he said, "but you must stand up to hear what I have to say. Don't ever, ever, lay your hand on my mother again."

The Early Years

In 1963, Bill took an American Legion trip from Arkansas to Washington, where he met President Kennedy. From that moment on, he knew he wanted a career in politics. Fifteen years later, he was elected governor of Arkansas. At thirty-two, he was the youngest governor in the country. After his first two-year term, Clinton was voted out of office for raising the state gasoline tax to pay for highway improvements. He accepted the defeat as a lesson in humility and regained the governorship in 1982.

★**THE FIRST FAMILY** Hillary Rodham introduced herself to Bill Clinton in law school after she noticed Clinton staring at her. In 1974, she gave up her own chance for a political career and moved to Arkansas to marry him. In Little Rock, Mrs. Clinton worked full-time as a lawyer and became active in children's issues. "If you elect Bill, you get me," she often said during the 1992 campaign. Soon after taking office, President Clinton appointed her to head his task force on health care.

Although both Clintons have supported public education, they sent their daughter Chelsea to a private school. Once when Chelsea needed permission to take some medicine, she told school officials to call her father, the president. Her mother, she said, was too busy.

★**VIRTUAL REALITY** Imagine being inside a video game in a world controlled by a computer. If you walk forward, the image that you see moves forward, too. If you look down, you see a graphic image of your feet. This effect is called virtual reality. During the early 1990s, great advances were made in virtual reality technology. Engineers at one space research center constructed a three-dimensional computer model of Mars, which they "explored" using head-mounted displays and data gloves to control the computer program. Meanwhile, the Pentagon developed a training center for tank commanders using virtual reality to simulate the tank battles of the Persian Gulf War.

★ THE INTERNET

During the mid-1990s, the number of people "surfing the Net" grew rapidly. The Internet is the "information super-highway" along which digital information

travels. To take advantage of increased Internet traffic, many organizations began setting up "home pages" for people to visit electronically using their personal computers. For instance, the White House created a home page at http://eng.hss.cmu.edu/govt/whitehouse.html.

★ SPACE

Although hard times followed the *Challenger* disaster, the U.S. space program rebounded strongly in 1996. First, the National Aeronautics and Space Administration (NASA) announced in August that it had possibly found evidence that life once existed on Mars. The evidence was a potato-sized meteorite found near the South Pole in 1986. Using a powerful microscope, NASA scientists had discovered on the meteorite tiny features that looked like fossilized bacteria. A month later, the space shuttle *Atlantis* brought

biologist Shannon Lucid back to earth after six months in space. Her 188-day mission aboard the Russian space station Mir broke the endurance records for an American astronaut and for a woman.

★ OKLAHOMA CITY BOMBING

Just after 9:00 A.M. on April 19, 1995, a bomb hidden in a rental van exploded outside the Murrah Federal Building in Oklahoma City, Oklahoma. The force of the blast collapsed most of the building, killing 168 people. The Oklahoma City bombing was the worst terrorist attack ever committed on U.S. soil.

At first, because of parallels between the Oklahoma City and World Trade Center bombings, many people assumed that the terrorists were foreigners, perhaps Islamic fundamentalists. Instead, FBI agents traced the bomb to two Americans, Timothy McVeigh and Terry Nichols. Both men were members of the militia movement. Leaders of this extremist movement encouraged their followers to stockpile guns because they believed the government was plotting to take away their rights.

"Republicans did a good job of defining us [the Democrats] as the party of government," President Clinton said after the election, "and that [was] not a good place to be."

When it came time to govern, however, the new Republican majority in the 104th Congress ran into some unexpected problems. House speaker Newt Gingrich, in particular, learned that running the government was much more difficult than attacking it.

CONTRACT WITH AMERICA
Most new Republican congressmen had backed Gingrich's Contract with America. Among the campaign promises this document had spelled out were the application of federal laws to members of Congress, the line-item veto, and an end to unfunded mandates (federal laws that require states to pay for specific federal programs). The Contract also promised swift passage of a balanced-budget amendment and legal reform.

The first three of these measures passed the House and Senate during the first hundred days of the new Congress. But the last two, like many other parts of the Contract, stalled in the Senate, where the Republicans were much less radical than those in the House.

The battle between the White House and the Congress over the budget continued for the better part of a year, reaching its climax during the fall of 1995. In late October, the House and Senate passed a bill that would have cut taxes *and* balanced the budget by 2002. It also would have cut deeply into health, education, and environmental spending.

Citing his objections to these cuts, President Clinton vetoed the bill and offered a compromise. But the Republicans turned him down. And with no budget law in place, the government began to run out of money.

GOVERNMENT SHUTDOWNS

In mid-November, the budget impasse forced a partial shutdown of the federal government. Offices were closed, and eight hundred thousand workers were sent home. The shutdown lasted six days. Finally, when President Clinton accepted the Republican goal of balancing the budget within seven years, the House and Senate approved stopgap spending bills.

Yet the president and Congress continued to disagree over how to balance the budget. So, in mid-December, Congress forced another government shutdown. This one lasted three weeks.

But this time, the Republicans miscalculated. By early January 1996, a frustrated public had turned against them. Voters who had once encouraged the Republicans to dismantle the federal government now applauded President Clinton for defending programs like Medicare from a reckless Congress.

THE WAR IN BOSNIA

President Clinton also encountered some difficult and risky situations in the arena of foreign policy. In the former Yugoslavia, for example, Serbs, Croats, and Muslims were fighting the bloodiest war in Europe since World War II. The Serbs wanted to carve out of the state of Bosnia an ethnically pure Serbian homeland. During four years of fighting, 250,000 people had died.

In November 1995, while the budget crisis swirled around him, President Clinton brought the warring factions together at an air force base in Dayton, Ohio. After three weeks of tense and bitter negotiations, the three parties finally agreed on a peace plan.

In his riskiest foreign policy move yet, President Clinton agreed to send

ALTHOUGH PRESIDENT Clinton's popularity fell off during his first two years in office, it rose again in the aftermath of the government shutdowns. Polls confirmed that the same voters who threw out the Democrats in 1994 didn't like the way the Republicans were acting, either.

To take advantage of the Republicans' confrontational policies, President Clinton moved noticeably to the political center. In August 1996, he staged a string of White House bill signings that emphasized his moderate policies. The bills he signed included ones that raised the minimum wage, expanded access to health insurance, and overhauled the welfare system. The president signed the welfare bill despite strong opposition from liberals within his administration who believed that removing the social safety net was unfair to poor people.

Running against Clinton was Republican nominee Bob Dole of Kansas. Before resigning in mid-June to devote himself to campaigning, Dole had been the Senate majority leader. In his acceptance speech at the Republican convention in San Diego, the seventy-three-year-old Dole talked about building a "bridge to the past," to the years immediately after World War II, when Americans felt confident and prosperous. Seizing on Dole's imagery, Clinton spoke in his own convention acceptance speech about building a bridge to the future.

In the end, as is usually the case, the election turned on how voters felt about the economy. Several character issues dogged Clinton, especially his role in an Arkansas land deal known as Whitewater. But the generally good economic news buoyed him and carried him to a decisive victory.

President Clinton delivers a radio address.

IMPEACHMENT TRIAL ENDS IN ACQUITTAL

WASHINGTON, February 12, 1999— The second presidential impeachment trial in U.S. history ended today when the Senate voted to acquit Bill Clinton on the two articles of impeachment voted by the House.

In fact, from the outset of the impeachment trial, there had been little doubt that the president would be found not guilty. Because conviction required a two-thirds majority, the thirteen Republican "managers" appointed by the House to argue the case had to

hold all fifty-five Republican Senate votes and still persuade twelve of the forty-five Democratic senators to vote against a Democratic president.

On the first article of impeachment, relating to grand jury perjury, the vote was 55-45 in favor of acquittal, with ten Republicans voting for the president. The vote on the second article, relating to obstruction of justice, was 50-50, falling seventeen votes shy of the necessary two thirds.

twenty thousand U.S. troops to Bosnia to help guarantee the peace. These soldiers policed Bosnia as part of a ninety-thousand-strong United Nations Implementation Force, known as IFOR. The Dayton peace plan, which preserved the unity of Bosnia, called for limited disarmament to be followed by free elections. These elections were held peacefully in September 1996.

However, Serbian president Slobodan Milosevic continued to act aggressively elsewhere in the Balkans. Frustrated in Bosnia, he turned his attention to Kosovo, a province of southern Serbia where nine out of ten residents were ethnic Albanians. (That is, the families of these people came from, or traced their roots to, neighboring Albania.) In late 1997, systematic political and economic discrimination escalated into violence as Christian Serb security forces began "cleansing" Kosovo of its many Muslim Albanian citizens.

THE BOMBING OF KOSOVO The Serbian violence was so extreme and brutal that in October 1998, NATO issued an ultimatum to Milosevic, threatening air strikes unless Serbia immediately removed its rampaging security forces from Kosovo. Milosevic responded by recalling just enough Serbian troops to postpone the bombing. Meanwhile, negotiations between Serbia and NATO continued for several more months until another ultimatum was issued.

This time, neither side backed down, and in March 1999, NATO began an eleven-week aerial offensive, the first NATO military operation ever mounted against a sovereign country.

209

As is nearly always the case, the decision to use military force posed risks for President Clinton both at home and abroad. He knew, for example, that the American public's reluctant support for an air war would vanish entirely if it eventually became necessary to use ground troops in Kosovo (because ground wars produce much higher casualties for all concerned). Also, by personally identifying himself with the task of freeing Kosovo, he risked a massive loss of public support for his presidency should the NATO military effort fail.

RELATIONS WITH RUSSIA Furthermore, Clinton had to concern himself with the Russian reponse. The Russians, who had long been allies of the Serbs, strongly opposed what they considered bullying tactics on the part of NATO. At the time, Russia was itself experiencing a difficult transition from Communism to multiparty democracy, and its military forces were in decline. But the possibility remained that Russia might intercede on Serbia's behalf, if only to boost its sinking national morale and divert attention from the country's frustrating economic problems.

Since the end of the Cold War, the United States had done its best to promote political and free-market reforms within the former Soviet Union. This policy had included substantial economic aid as well as Clinton's personal support for Boris Yeltsin during the strongly contested 1996 Russian presidential campaign.

Helped by the president's close personal relationship with Yeltsin, the Clinton administration was able to per- suade the Russians to pressure Milosevic into conceding. On June 9, the fighting ended when a battered Serbia agreed to withdraw its troops from Kosovo while a United Nations force entered the province to govern in its place. Milosevic still clung to power, but his engineering of massive fraud during the September 2000 elections led to a civil revolt that chased him from office two weeks later.

★THE TOBACCO SETTLEMENT During the late 1990s, a number of states filed suit against cigarette makers to recover money they had spent under Medicaid treating smoking-related illnesses. These suits were helped by emerging evidence that seemed to support allegations that cigarette companies had deceived the public about the health risks of smoking, In November 1998, the nation's four largest tobacco companies agreed to the largest U.S. civil settlement ever, a $206 billion agreement that called for a twenty-five-year payout beginning in 2000, restrictions on cigarette advertising, and an industry-funded campaign to reduce teen smoking. Although it was originally contemplated that the money would be spent largely on public health programs, state governments have reportedly used these funds to pay for everything from education and tax cuts to new roads and prisons. Meanwhile, the Centers for Disease Control reported in late 1999 that cigarette smoking remained the leading preventable cause of death in the United States.

★THE HUMAN GENOME PROJECT At a White House ceremony on June 26, 2000, the leaders of two massive research efforts, the public U.S. Human Genome Project and the private Celera Genomics, announced that they had created a "working draft" of the genetic sequences that make up human DNA. (DNA determines, among other things, how people look and how they respond to infection.) This "road map" is expected to revolutionize the practice of medicine by allowing scientists to create new diagnostic tests as well as new treatments for a variety of illnesses. However, the availability of this information also raises important ethical, legal, and social issues. For example, if privacy is not protected, employers or insurance companies could use genetic information to discriminate against people who may be genetically predisposed to an illness.

★COLUMBINE During the 1990s, rising levels of school violence became one of the most important local issues in the United States. In fact, the school year 1999–2000 was the first in seven without a fatal mass shooting in a U.S. public school. The worst of these was the massacre that took place at Columbine High School in Littleton, Colorado, on April 20, 1999. That day, two students armed with semiautomatic rifles and explosives killed twelve students and a teacher before killing themselves.

★FRANKENFOOD As the skills of genetic engineers improved during the 1990s, many began working to create new foodstuffs that might ease malnutrition around the world. One such example was a rice modified genetically to contain beta-carotene, a source of vitamin A. However, despite its potential benefits to poor people whose diets depended on rice, opponents argued that there were too many risks and that combining genes from different species was itself too dangerous. For this reason, genetically modified foods were often called *Frankenfood,* after the fictional monster engineered by Dr. Frankenstein. At the same time, similar concerns about the food supply produced a boom in organic farming. Organic farmers (such as the one shown here) avoid chemical fertilizers and pesticides. Instead, they use traditional techniques such as composting and crop rotation to renew their soil and combat destructive insects in their fields.

★Y2K Until the late 1990s, computer memory was in short supply. So computer programmers used a shortcut when writing programs that contained dates. Instead of using all four digits of a year, such as "1993," they used just the last two digits, or "93." As the year 2000 approached, however, programmers realized that such programs would no longer work, because computers would think that "00" meant "1900" rather than "2000." During the years leading up to 2000, both the government and the private sector spent billions of dollars in efforts to avoid a Y2K, or Year 2000, crisis. A few people moved to the country because they feared that widespread computer shutdowns would lead to riots in the cities; however, almost everyone made sure that they had fresh batteries in their flashlights in case problems with electric company computers caused the power to go out. In the end, the transition went remarkably smoothly.

CLINTON'S PERSONAL DIPLOMACY Clinton's fondness for personal diplomacy also helped him make significant headway in two of the world's perennial trouble spots: Northern Ireland and the Middle East. He helped forge the April 1998 peace accord, negotiated by former senator George Mitchell, that created a new bipartisan form of government in Northern Ireland, and he also involved himself deeply in the ongoing discussions between Israel and the Palestinians regarding the 1993 Oslo peace accord, which granted Palestinians self-rule in the Gaza Strip and West Bank.

At Maryland's Wye Conference Center in October 1998 and at Camp David in July 2000, President Clinton spent days at a time with the Israeli prime minister (first Benjamin Netanyahu, later Ehud Barak) and Palestinian leader Yasir Arafat, trying to work out the stubborn details of this "land for peace" deal. On both occasions progress was made, yet many issues, such as the future of Jerusalem and the fate of Jewish settlements on the West Bank, still separated the parties.

BUDGET SURPLUS Clinton was able to commit a great deal of time and energy to making peace around the world because the domestic economy was booming. An important indication of the good times was the persistent rise of stock prices. In March 1999, for example, the Dow Jones Industrials Average topped ten thousand points—a level with a great deal of psychological, if not economic, significance. Meanwhile, low inflation, low unemployment, and high productivity—along with earlier government belt tightening—eliminated the troublesome budget deficits.

In February 1998, the president was able to propose the first balanced budget since 1969, and a year later the government was running a surplus. That is, its income from taxes and fees exceeded the amount it spent on programs and interest payments on the national debt.

In fact, the only problem that Bill Clinton seemed to have was the Whitewater investigation, which began soon after his inauguration and continued until nearly the end of his second term. Many of Clinton's political allies criticized Independent Counsel Kenneth Starr for needlessly prolonging the inquiry, and the first lady insisted on national television that her husband was the victim of "a vast right-wing conspiracy." But Starr's probe of the Arkansas land deal did result in jail terms for James and Susan McDougal, partners of the Clintons in Whitewater.

IMPEACHMENT As Starr's investigation of the president and first lady dragged on, other allegations emerged. The most explosive was that the president had lied under oath to conceal an earlier intimate relationship with a young White House staff member.

For months after this story broke in January 1998, the president continued to deny the affair. By August 17, however, the accumulating evidence forced him to admit that he had indeed been misleading his family, his staff, and the public.

Few Americans were satisfied with the apology. Many more believed it to be insincere and politically motivated (to break the gathering momentum for impeachment). Much of the problem had to do with Clinton's continuing insistence that his testimony, though misleading, had been "legally correct."

After the November 1998 elections, Starr presented his evidence to the Republican-controlled House, which on December 19 passed by narrow margins two of four articles of impeachment. Both related specifically to Clinton's attempt to conceal his extramarital affair.

Meanwhile, despite the widespread belief that the president had lied, voters, mindful of the national prosperity, continued to give him high approval ratings. But there was one thing that Clinton had lost: He no longer commanded the moral authority he once did.

WITH BILL CLINTON RETIRING AFTER TWO TERMS, Vice President Al Gore began the 2000 presidential campaign as the most likely candidate to succeed him. The reason was that, with prosperity at home and peace abroad, voters usually stay with the incumbent party.

On the Republican side, the party faithful rallied around Texas governor George W. Bush, son of the former president, who raised nearly forty million dollars before the primary season even began. Although this early money made him seem invincible, he had to withstand a tough challenge from Arizona senator John McCain, a longtime advocate of campaign finance reform.

McCain actually beat Bush in the first Republican primary, held in New Hampshire, but Bush was able to derail McCain's candidacy with a strong showing in the March cluster of primaries known as Super Tuesday.

During the general election campaign, both candidates followed President Clinton's 1996 tactic of hugging the political center. This caused some progressive Democrats to break away in support of Green party nominee Ralph Nader. However, opinion polls showed that most voters were looking for steadiness rather than big, bold ideas.

Gore's public stiffness helped the amiable Bush take an early lead. But the momentum shifted when the vice president unexpectedly chose Connecticut senator Joseph Lieberman as his running mate. Lieberman thus became the first Jewish nominee on a major party's presidential ticket. More important, Lieberman's advocacy of religion undercut faith-based Republican attacks against Gore.

The campaign seesawed back and forth until Election Day—and then, amazingly, it continued, with the balloting

in several states simply too close for a winner to be declared. Allegations of fraud and incompetence followed, adding to the confusion. But one thing is known for certain: Had Gore received the bulk of the Democratic votes cast for Nader, the result of the election would not have been in doubt.

George Walker Bush

43RD PRESIDENT
★
FROM 2001

BORN: July 6, 1946

BIRTHPLACE: New Haven, Conn.

PARTY: Republican

VICE PRESIDENT: Richard B. Cheney

FIRST LADY: Laura Welch

CHILDREN: Barbara, Jenna

NICKNAME: Dubya

The first president to have fathered twins.

George W. Bush became president in January 2001 of a deeply divided and discouraged America. His own election had been the closest in history, and even after the Supreme Court's December 12 ruling gave him the presidency, many Americans continued to believe that he had really lost to Al Gore. The Congress with which he had to work was also split along party lines. The Republican edge in the House had slipped to just nine votes, and the Senate was dead even at fifty votes apiece. President Bush's prospects for redeeming his campaign pledges, especially his proposed $1.3 trillion tax cut, seemed dim at the outset.

However, as governor of Texas, Bush had championed a bipartisan approach to government. As president-elect, he tried to build on Al Gore's gracious concession speech, reaching out to embittered Democrats and asking for their support. He also made an effort to be inclusive in his appointments, selecting for his cabinet people from different minority groups and even considering a few Democrats.

RULING IN BUSH V. GORE

Court Decides Election

WASHINGTON, December 12, 2000—In a ruling issued at 10:00 P.M. this evening, the Supreme Court effectively gave the 2000 presidential election to Republican candidate George W. Bush. Its controversial decision came just two hours before the deadline for state certification of presidential electors.

The justices, by a vote of 5-4, overturned the recent Florida Supreme Court decision permitting the recounting by hand of ballots in several disputed Florida counties.

With its decision in *Bush v. Gore*, the Court stopped this recounting and gave the state to Bush, who was leading at the time by 537 votes out of nearly six million cast. Whichever candidate had won Florida's electoral votes would have become the next president.

Instead of taking the White House, Democrat Al Gore became the fourth candidate in history to win the popular vote but not the presidency—joining Andrew Jackson (1824), Samuel J. Tilden (1876), and Grover Cleveland (1888). Vice President Gore is expected to deliver a televised concession speech tomorrow night.

President Vice President	Term	Candidates	Popular Vote	Elect. Vote
George Washington John Adams	1789–1797 1789–1797	George Washington John Adams Others		69 34 35
Election of 1789				
		George Washington (Federalist) John Adams (Federalist) George Clinton (Dem.-Rep.) Others		132 77 50 5
Election of 1792				
John Adams Thomas Jefferson	1797–1801 1797–1801	John Adams (Federalist) Thomas Jefferson (Dem.-Rep.) Thomas Pinckney (Federalist) Aaron Burr (Dem.-Rep.) Others		71 68 59 30 48
Election of 1796				
Thomas Jefferson Aaron Burr	1801–1809 1801–1805	Thomas Jefferson (Dem.-Rep.) Aaron Burr (Dem.-Rep.) John Adams (Federalist) Charles C. Pinckney (Federalist) John Jay (Federalist)		73 73 65 64 1
Election of 1800				
George Clinton	1805–1809	Thomas Jefferson (Dem.-Rep.) Charles C. Pinckney (Federalist)		162 14
Election of 1804				
James Madison George Clinton	1809–1817 1809–1812	James Madison (Dem.-Rep.) Charles C. Pinckney (Federalist) George Clinton		122 47 6
Election of 1808				
Elbridge Gerry	1813–1814	James Madison (Dem.-Rep.) DeWitt Clinton (Fusion)		128 89
Election of 1812				
James Monroe Daniel D. Tompkins	1817–1825 1817–1825	James Monroe (Dem.-Rep.) Rufus King (Federalist)		183 34
Election of 1816				
		James Monroe (Dem.-Rep.) John Quincy Adams		231 1
Election of 1820				
John Quincy Adams John C. Calhoun	1825–1829 1825–1829	Andrew Jackson John Quincy Adams William H. Crawford Henry Clay	151,271 113,122 40,856 47,531	99 84 41 37
Election of 1824				
Andrew Jackson John C. Calhoun	1829–1837 1829–1832	Andrew Jackson (Democrat) John Quincy Adams (Nat. Rep.)	642,553 500,897	178 83
Election of 1828				
Martin Van Buren	1833–1837	Andrew Jackson (Democrat) Henry Clay (Nat. Rep.) John Floyd William Wirt (Anti-Mason)	701,780 484,205 100,715	219 49 11 7
Election of 1832				
Martin Van Buren Richard M. Johnson	1837–1841 1837–1841	Martin Van Buren (Democrat) William Henry Harrison (Whig) Hugh L. White (Whig) Daniel Webster (Whig) Willie P. Mangum	764,176 550,816 146,107 41,201	170 73 26 14 11
Election of 1836				
Wm. Henry Harrison John Tyler	1841 1841	William Henry Harrison (Whig) Martin Van Buren (Democrat)	1,275,390 1,128.854	234 60
Election of 1840				
John Tyler	1841–1845	Succeeded to the presidency on the death of William Henry Harrison.		
James K. Polk George M. Dallas	1845–1849 1845–1849	James Knox Polk (Democrat) Henry Clay (Whig) James G. Birney (Liberty)	1,339,494 1,300,004 62,103	170 105
Election of 1844				
Zachary Taylor Millard Fillmore	1849–1850 1849–1850	Zachary Taylor (Whig) Lewis Cass (Democrat) Martin Van Buren (Free Soil)	1,361,393 1,223,460 291,501	163 127
Election of 1848				
Millard Fillmore	1850–1853	Succeeded to the presidency on the death of Zachary Taylor.		
Franklin Pierce William R. King	1853–1857 1853	Franklin Pierce (Democrat) Winfield Scott (Whig) John P. Hale (Free Soil)	1,607,510 1,386,942 155,210	254 42
Election of 1852				
James Buchanan John C. Breckinridge	1857–1861 1857–1861	James Buchanan (Democrat) John C. Frémont (Republican) Millard Fillmore (American)	1,836,072 1,342,345 873,053	174 114 8
Election of 1856				

President Vice President	Term	Candidates	Popular Vote	Elect. Vote
Abraham Lincoln Hannibal Hamlin	1861–1865 1861–1865	Abraham Lincoln (Republican) John C. Breckinridge (Democrat) John Bell (Constitutional Union) Stephen A. Douglas (Democrat)	1,865,908 848,019 590,901 1,380,202	180 72 39 12
Election of 1860				
Andrew Johnson	1865	Abraham Lincoln (Rep.-Union) George B. McClellan (Democrat)	2,218,388 1,812,807	212 21
Election of 1864				
Andrew Johnson	1865–1869	Succeeded to the presidency on the assassination of Abraham Lincoln.		
Ulysses S. Grant Schuyler Colfax	1869–1877 1869–1873	Ulysses S. Grant (Republican) Horatio Seymour (Democrat)	3,013,650 2,708,744	214 80
Election of 1868				
Henry Wilson	1873–1875	Ulysses S. Grant (Republican) Horace Greeley (Democrat)	3,598,235 2,834,761	286 66
Election of 1872				
Rutherford B. Hayes William A. Wheeler	1877–1881 1877–1881	Rutherford B. Hayes (Republican) Samuel J. Tilden (Democrat)	4,034,311 4,288,546	185 184
Election of 1876				
James A. Garfield Chester A. Arthur	1881 1881	James Garfield (Republican) Winfield S. Hancock (Democrat) James B. Weaver (Greenback)	4,446,158 4,444,260 305,997	214 155
Election of 1880				
Chester A. Arthur	1881–1885	Succeeded to the presidency on the assassination of James Garfield.		
Grover Cleveland Thomas A. Hendricks	1885–1889 1885	Grover Cleveland (Democrat) James G. Blaine (Republican)	4,874,621 4,848,936	219 182
Election of 1884				
Benjamin Harrison Levi P. Morton	1889–1893 1889–1893	Benjamin Harrison (Republican) Grover Cleveland (Democrat) Clinton B. Fisk (Prohibition)	5,443,892 5,534,488 249,819	233 168
Election of 1888				
Grover Cleveland Adlai E. Stevenson	1893–1897 1893–1897	Grover Cleveland (Democrat) Benjamin Harrison (Republican) James B. Weaver (People's) John Bidwell (Prohibition)	5,551,883 5,179,244 1,024,280 270,770	277 145 22
Election of 1892				

President Vice President	Term	Candidates	Popular Vote	Elect. Vote
William McKinley Garret A. Hobart	1897–1901 1897–1899	William McKinley (Republican) William J. Bryan (Democrat)	7,108,480 6,511,495	271 176
Election of 1896				
Theodore Roosevelt	1901	William McKinley (Republican) William J. Bryan (Democrat)	7,218,039 6,358,345	292 155
Election of 1900				
Theodore Roosevelt	1901–1909	Succeeded to the presidency on the assassination of William McKinley.		
Charles W. Fairbanks	1905–1909	Theodore Roosevelt (Republican) Alton B. Parker (Democrat) Eugene V. Debs (Socialist)	7,626,593 5,082,898 402,489	336 140
Election of 1904				
William H. Taft James S. Sherman	1909–1913 1909–1912	William H. Taft (Republican) William J. Bryan (Democrat) Eugene V. Debs (Socialist)	7,676,258 6,406,801 420,380	321 162
Election of 1908				
Woodrow Wilson Thomas R. Marshall	1913–1921 1913–1921	Woodrow Wilson (Democrat) Theodore Roosevelt (Progressive) William H. Taft (Republican) Eugene V. Debs (Socialist)	6,293,152 4,119,207 3,486,333 900,369	435 88 8
Election of 1912				
		Woodrow Wilson (Democrat) Charles E. Hughes (Republican) Allan L. Benson (Socialist)	9,126,300 8,546,789 589,924	277 254
Election of 1916				
Warren G. Harding Calvin Coolidge	1921–1923 1921–1923	Warren G. Harding (Republican) James M. Cox (Democrat) Eugene V. Debs (Socialist)	16,153,115 9,133,092 915,490	404 127
Election of 1920				
Calvin Coolidge	1923–1929	Succeeded to the presidency on the death of Warren Harding.		
Charles G. Dawes	1925–1929	Calvin Coolidge (Republican) John W. Davis (Democrat) Robert M. La Follette (Progressive)	15,719,921 8,386,704 4,832,532	382 136 13
Election of 1924				
Herbert C. Hoover Charles Curtis	1929–1933 1929–1933	Herbert C. Hoover (Republican) Alfred E. Smith (Democrat)	21,437,277 15,007,698	444 87
Election of 1928				

PRESIDENTIAL ELECTION RESULTS

President Vice President	Term	Candidates	Popular Vote	Elect. Vote
Franklin D. Roosevelt John N. Garner	1933–1945 1933–1941	Franklin D. Roosevelt (Democrat) Herbert C. Hoover (Republican) Norman M. Thomas (Socialist)	22,829,501 15,760,684 884,649	472 59

Election of 1932

		Franklin D. Roosevelt (Democrat) Alfred M. Landon (Republican) William Lemke (Union)	27,757,333 16,684,231 892,267	523 8

Election of 1936

Henry A. Wallace	1941–1945	Franklin D. Roosevelt (Democrat) Wendell L. Willkie (Republican)	27,313,041 22,348,480	449 82

Election of 1940

Harry S. Truman	1945	Franklin D. Roosevelt (Democrat) Thomas E. Dewey (Republican)	25,612,610 22,017,617	432 99

Election of 1944

Harry S. Truman	1945–1953	Succeeded to the presidency on the death of Franklin D. Roosevelt.		
Alben W. Barkley	1949–1953	Harry S. Truman (Democrat) Thomas E. Dewey (Republican) J. Strom Thurmond (States' Rights) Henry A. Wallace (Progressive)	24,179,345 21,991,291 1,176,125 1,157,326	303 189 39

Election of 1948

Dwight D. Eisenhower Richard M. Nixon	1953–1961 1953–1961	Dwight D. Eisenhower (Republican) Adlai E. Stevenson (Democrat)	33,936,234 27,314,992	442 89

Election of 1952

		Dwight D. Eisenhower (Republican) Adlai E. Stevenson (Democrat) Walter B. Jones	35,590,472 26,022,752	457 73 1

Election of 1956

John F. Kennedy Lyndon B. Johnson	1961–1963 1961–1963	John F. Kennedy (Democrat) Richard M. Nixon (Republican) Harry F. Byrd	34,226,731 34,108,157	303 219 15

Election of 1960

Lyndon B. Johnson	1963–1969	Succeeded to the presidency on the assassination of John F. Kennedy.		
Hubert H. Humphrey	1965–1969	Lyndon B. Johnson (Democrat) Barry M. Goldwater (Republican)	43,129,566 27,178,188	486 52

Election of 1964

President Vice President	Term	Candidates	Popular Vote	Elect. Vote
Richard M. Nixon Spiro T. Agnew	1969–1974 1969–1973	Richard M. Nixon (Republican) Hubert H. Humphrey (Democrat) George C. Wallace (Amer. Ind.)	31,785,480 31,275,166 9,906,473	301 191 46

Election of 1968

Gerald R. Ford	1973–1974	Richard M. Nixon (Republican) George S. McGovern (Democrat) John Hospers (Libertarian)	47,169,911 29,170,383 3,673	520 17 1

Election of 1972

Gerald R. Ford Nelson A. Rockefeller	1974–1977 1974–1977	Succeeded to the presidency on the resignation of Richard M. Nixon.		

Jimmy Carter Walter F. Mondale	1977–1981 1977–1981	Jimmy Carter (Democrat) Gerald R. Ford (Republican) Ronald W. Reagan	40,830,763 39,147,793	297 240 1

Election of 1976

Ronald W. Reagan George H. W. Bush	1981–1989 1981–1989	Ronald W. Reagan (Republican) Jimmy Carter (Democrat) John B. Anderson	43,904,153 35,483,883 5,720,060	489 49

Election of 1980

		Ronald W. Reagan (Republican) Walter F. Mondale (Democrat)	54,455,075 37,577,185	525 13

Election of 1984

George H. W. Bush J. Danforth Quayle	1989–1993 1989–1993	George H. W. Bush (Republican) Michael S. Dukakis (Democrat) Lloyd M. Bentsen, Jr.	48,886,097 41,809,074	426 111 1

Election of 1988

William J. Clinton Albert A. Gore, Jr.	1993–2001 1993–2001	William J. Clinton (Democrat) George H. W. Bush (Republican) H. Ross Perot	44,909,326 39,103,882 19,741,657	370 168

Election of 1992

		William J. Clinton (Democrat) Robert J. Dole (Republican) H. Ross Perot (Reform)	47,402,357 39,198,755 8,085,402	379 159

Election of 1996

		George W. Bush (Republican) Albert A. Gore, Jr. (Democrat) Ralph Nader (Green)	49,820,518 50,158,094 2,703,722	271 267

Election of 2000

A HISTORY OF THE WHITE HOUSE

★ This is the oldest known photograph of the White House. It was taken by John Plumbe, Jr., sometime around 1846.

IN MARCH 1791, PRESIDENT GEORGE Washington personally selected some land on the Potomac River between Virginia and Maryland for the site of the nation's new capital. A year later, as plans for the District of Columbia took shape, Washington announced a national competition to design a new house for the president there. In Washington's opinion, the president's house would be one of the most important buildings constructed in the District of Columbia before the government moved there in 1800.

Washington organized this contest at the suggestion of Secretary of State Thomas Jefferson, who was himself an accomplished amateur architect. In fact, Jefferson submitted one of his own designs anonymously, but his was not chosen. Instead, the Board of Federal Commissioners selected the work of Irish immigrant James Hoban. Hoban's winning design resembled that of an English country house. (The other entries were mostly enlarged courthouses or awkward mansions.)

President Washington's personal interest in the planning of the new house was so great that after the announcement of Hoban's victory on July 17, 1792, Washington began meeting with him regularly. Although Hoban

★ This design for the president's house was submitted anonymously by Thomas Jefferson.

JUNE 1800

President John Adams visits Washington, D.C., to inspect the public buildings under construction there. He complains that the work will not be finished before the government's arrival on November 1.

★ **Hoban's original plans called for a mansion four times as large as the one that was built. Even so, the new house, which measured 168 feet east to west and 85 feet north to south, was larger than any house built in the United States until the 1870s.**

and Washington continued revising their plans until late 1793, work moved ahead quickly. The sandstone for the walls came on ships up the Potomac River from the Aquia Creek quarry, which also supplied stone for the U.S. Capitol. Work on the president's house was carried on each year from mid-April until mid-October, when temperatures became too cold for the mortar (used between the stones) to set properly.

Ironically, its greatest patron, George Washington, was the only president never to live in the president's house. When Washington left office in 1797, the building was still just a stone shell. A year later, the exterior walls got their first coat of whitewash. The recipe for this famous paint included salt, ground rice, glue, and lime. Almost immediately, people began calling the building the "white house." That nickname first appeared in print in a November 1810 issue of the *Baltimore Whig*. It was not until 1901, however, that President Theodore Roosevelt officially changed the name of the building from the Executive Mansion to the White House.

After touring the partially completed president's house, Adams ordered the nude figures carved into the mantelpieces removed and replaced with carvings of fruit and flowers. He also asked for a bell system that he could use to summon servants. This way, he wouldn't need a servant in every room, as was then the custom in large houses.

In November, as he had suspected, the president arrived to find his new house still under construction. It smelled of plaster (mixed with horse and hog hair) and wallpaper paste (made from white flour and beer). Its floors were raw, unfinished mahogany, and the grand staircase on the north front of the house had not yet been built. Instead, wooden planks were used to span the gap from the doorway to the crude gravel road that led up to the house.

★ **Until the laundry yard was completed, Abigail Adams had her servants hang the first family's laundry in the unfinished East Room.**

★ **After the War of 1812, President James Madison ordered that the public buildings in Washington, including the White House, be rebuilt exactly as they had been before the British burned them.**

AUGUST 24
1814

After learning of the U.S. defeat at the battle of Bladensburg, First Lady Dolley Madison flees the White House around 3:30 P.M. with the Declaration of Independence, the national seal, and her pet parrot. Invading British troops reach Washington, D.C., about 7:30 P.M.

After burning the Capitol, Rear Admiral George Cockburn and Major General Robert Ross entered the president's house. They found the dining room table set (the Madisons had been expecting forty people for dinner) and the food already prepared in the kitchen. In Madison's dressing room on the second floor, the battle-stained British officers paused long enough to wash and change into some of Madison's clean underwear. Orders were then given to burn the house.

MARCH-MAY
1833

Running water is installed in the White House.

When the White House was first built, it did not have running water. Instead, water needed for the kitchen and the bathrooms was carried into the house by servants, who fetched it in buckets from two wells. These wells were located in the breezeways between the house and each of its wings. James Hoban first proposed the idea of piping running water into the White House in 1816. But Hoban's idea was rejected for being too sophisticated. In 1831, the Committee on Public Buildings finally purchased a nearby spring that could be used as a source for running water, but two more years passed before work on the project was actually begun.

The system, as designed by engineer Robert Leckie, was a deceptively simple one. Water from the spring ran downhill through iron pipes into a sand-lined fountain outside the White House. The motion of this fountain kept the water from stagnating. From the fountain, more iron pipes carried the water into the house. All that was needed to power the system was an attendant, who used a hand pump to create the necessary water pressure in the pipes.

Although many hotels and some fancy American homes already had running water, President Andrew Jackson, like most of his countrymen, was not overly impressed by the new arrangement. People during the 1830s still considered running water more of a luxury than a necessity. In fact, Leckie's system was added to the White House more for reasons of fire safety than for personal convenience.

★ Although several luxuries, including running water, were added to the White House during his administration, President Andrew Jackson worked hard to maintain his image as a man of the people. As part of his Washington's Birthday celebration in 1837, Jackson invited the public to the White House to consume a huge fourteen-hundred-pound cheese that had been given to him as a gift two years earlier. In less than two hours, the cheese was gone, but the White House smelled of it for several years afterward.

1840 *President Martin Van Buren orders construction of a centralized hot-air heating system. This system replaces the many wood- and coal-burning fireplaces that have been used to heat the house.*

Unlike Andrew Jackson, President Van Buren made no secret of his appreciation for the comforts of city life. His wealthy friends in New York City, for example, all had central heating in their homes. Thoughts of their good fortune made life in the drafty, chilly White House nearly unbearable for Van Buren.

To bring the White House up to date, Van Buren had workers install a large coal furnace in the basement. This new furnace was tied into a network of plaster-lined ducts that ran upstairs through the floor and walls. The hot air produced by the furnace warmed all the state rooms on the first floor. Unfortunately, it didn't reach the second-floor family rooms, which were still heated by fireplaces.

The White House heating system was operated by a fireman, whose job it was to feed coal into the furnace. During the winter, he was on duty twenty-four hours a day, but he got the summers off. A decade later, in 1853, during the administration of Franklin Pierce, Joseph Nason of Walworth & Nason, Boston, was hired to convert Van Buren's hot-air system into a more efficient hot-water system.

1848 *Gaslight reaches the White House during the Polk administration.*

In 1847, Congress hired the Baltimore Gas Company to build a gas plant on the Capitol grounds so that the Capitol could be lit by gaslight. Gaslight was cheaper than candles and oil lamps—and also safer, because gas lamps did not tip over and start fires. The Capitol plan was soon expanded to include the White House. Coal gas from the Capitol plant was piped to the White House along Pennsylvania Avenue, feeding streetlights along the way.

Before gaslight, the White House was lit mostly by oil lamps that burned foul-smelling lard (made from animal and vegetable fat). Candles were so expensive that they were used only on important occasions.

Most of the formal rooms in the White House had chandeliers that could be lowered on pulleys when servants needed to light or change the candles in them. In 1848, pipes and burners were attached to these chandeliers, converting them to gaslight. However, because she preferred candlelight, First Lady Sarah Polk refused to let workmen convert the chandelier in the Blue Room. At first people made fun of her for being old-fashioned, but all the teasing stopped on the night of the first gaslit state reception. No one had thought to warn the Capitol gas plant to stay open late. So when the plant shut down as usual around nine o'clock, all the lights in the White House went out—except the chandelier in the Blue Room, beneath which Mrs. Polk stood in her usual spot, bathed in candlelight.

★ In late August, when Garfield seemed to be getting better, his doctors decided to let him leave Washington for the cool ocean breezes at Elberon, New Jersey. His cot was carried out of the White House on September 6 and placed on a wagon for the trip to the railroad station.

MAY 10 1879

The National Telephone Company installs the first telephone in the White House on a trial basis. It is mounted on a wall in the telegraph room.

One problem that President Rutherford Hayes had with his new telephone was that there was almost no one to call. Because telephones were so new in 1879, very few people had them. For example, Treasury Secretary John Sherman was the only cabinet member with telephone service.

Nine months later, another invention arrived at the White House: It was the typewriter. This machine, unlike the telephone, did have an immediate impact on the way the president's staff did its work. In fact, it soon revolutionized the way the White House took care of its business on a day-to-day basis. Before Hayes's purchase of the Fairbanks & Company Improved Number Two Typewriter, his clerks, who specialized in fancy penmanship, had to write out each piece of White House correspondence by hand. Using this new machine, however, they could type out letters quickly and get a lot more done.

★ After President Garfield's death from blood poisoning on September 19, the White House was draped in black.

JULY 1881

During an emergency, the White House gets the first primitive air conditioning.

After the shooting of President James Garfield on July 2, 1881, the White House was deluged with gifts from well-wishers—everything from flowers and cards to food and clothing. Garfield's doctors, however, were particularly interested in two machines being offered by inventors. These devices were intended to help cool the wounded president, who was suffering in Washington's humid summer heat.

Both used ice to cool air, which was then piped into the president's sickroom. The problem with one machine was that the cool air moved too slowly through its pipes. The other used an innovative electric blower to move the air quickly, but the icy draft it produced made the sickroom too damp.

On the night of Friday, July 9, army doctor J. J. Woodward called Professor Simon Newcomb to the White House. Woodward wanted Newcomb, a scientist who worked for the navy, to analyze the two machines and come up with a solution to the dampness problem. Newcomb quickly developed a third, much larger machine that used several tons of ice but kept the dampness to a minimum. Working around the clock over the weekend, Newcomb built this new air conditioner with the help of R. S. Jennings, inventor of the electric-blower

★ Tiffany's work, completed for the most part by October 1882, included a dramatic stained-glass screen that was not finished until early 1883. This screen separated the White House foyer from the hall that led to the state parlors and dining room.

machine, and John Wesley Powell, then director of the U.S. Geological Survey. On Monday morning, Newcomb turned on the system, and it worked.

SEPTEMBER 1881

President Chester Arthur begins the most extensive work on the White House since it was rebuilt after the 1814 fire.

President Arthur, a New Yorker with elegant tastes, considered the White House worse than shabby and below the standards of even a third-rate Manhattan hotel. During a tour of the White House a few weeks after Garfield's death, he announced, "I will not live in a house like this." He insisted that the public rooms be completely redecorated before he moved in.

From late October 1881 until early December, Arthur personally supervised this redecoration. He inspected the work nightly and regularly made changes and additions. Then, shortly after moving into the White House on December 7, he let it be known that he considered the extensive work, which cost thirty thousand dollars, only temporary.

In early 1882, Arthur asked Congress for enough money to demolish and rebuild the White House, but preservationists blocked this plan. Instead, Arthur settled for another eighty thousand dollars' worth of renovation.

To perform this work, Arthur hired the most fashionable designer in New York, Louis Comfort Tiffany, son of the famous jeweler. During the early summer of 1882, Arthur

moved out of the White House so that Tiffany's men could work freely. Castoff furnishings, which included Andrew Jackson's desk and James Polk's dining room chairs, were carted off in twenty-four wagonloads and sold at auction. By the time Tiffany finished his work, the White House was indeed the showplace that Arthur had wanted. "History remembers only a few things about [Chester Arthur]," wrote White House historian William Seale, but "one is that he had taste."

1891

Workmen cut into the White House walls to wire the building for electricity.

In January 1891, Senator Leland Stanford of California introduced a bill that called for a major reconstruction and expansion of the White House. The plans for this work had been personally developed by First Lady Caroline Harrison. For many years, presidents and their wives had complained about the lack of space in the White House, which had not increased in size since the time of Jefferson.

Mrs. Harrison's bold plan was turned down in March. But a few months later, she bounced back and took charge of an extensive redecoration of the White House made possible by the installation of electricity there.

As a first step, workmen scraped and washed away almost all the finish that had been applied by Tiffany at President Arthur's direction. They scrubbed the walls and ceilings until the original white plaster showed. Then electricians from the Edison General Company of New York made gouges into the walls deep enough to hold the new wiring. After the wires were installed, the walls were replastered and the redecorating began.

Normally, the new electrical wires would have been pushed through the existing gas pipes, but President Harrison did not have much faith in the new technology. He wanted the gas lights kept as a backup system in case the electricity failed. In fact, throughout their stay in the White House, the Harrisons refused to operate any of the electrical switches for fear of being shocked. Instead, servants turned the lights on and off for them.

★ **Mrs. Harrison's 1891 plan called for new east and west wings to be joined to the White House by semicircular colonnades. These wings were never built.**

APRIL 15
1902

First Lady Edith Roosevelt asks New York architect Charles F. McKim to provide some quick and easy solutions to the problem of overcrowding in the White House. McKim tells Mrs. Roosevelt that a complete renovation will be necessary to keep the president living there.

Like many New Yorkers, the Roosevelts considered Washington a second-rate city. Once it became obvious that the White House needed repair, they called in McKim, a founding partner of McKim, Mead & White, one of New York's leading architectural firms. In hiring McKim, Roosevelt bypassed the Army Corps of Engineers, which normally had control over any construction at the White House.

The most pressing problem was space. The state dining room didn't seat enough people, and eight rooms upstairs were simply not enough for the Roosevelts and their large family. On June 28, Congress appropriated $475,445 for the project, which the president declared must be finished by December 1.

One of McKim's most important changes was to move the offices of the president's staff out of the White House and into another building on the grounds, known then as the Temporary Executive Offices. Removing these offices from the second floor nearly doubled the amount of living space there. In general, McKim's mission was to preserve the historic White House while making it workable for a modern president.

MAY
1909

Needing even more office space, President William Howard Taft approves plans for an addition to the Executive Office Building. These plans include the first Oval Office.

When Charles McKim built the Temporary Executive Offices on the west side of the White House in 1902, he expected the building to be just that—temporary. However, with President Roosevelt's ever-increasing need for space, the building stayed. In fact, by the time of Taft's inauguration in 1909, Congress had appropriated forty thousand more dollars to enlarge the building. McKim had moved only staff offices out of the White House, but now the president's office would be moved to the new building as well.

Taft, who had a strong personal interest in architecture, decided not to build a second floor and instead chose to extend the building southward. According to plans drawn up by Nathan C. Wyeth, the president's new office would be oval in shape, like the Blue Room in the White House. Taft first occupied the new Oval Office in October 1909.

★ **This photograph shows the first Oval Office under construction in 1909. The Executive Office Building in which the president works is today known as the West Wing.**

1913

With the help of landscape architect George Burnap, First Lady Ellen Wilson designs a rose garden for the area between the White House and the West Wing.

Even in Princeton, New Jersey, a town famous for its beautiful gardens, Ellen Wilson's plantings stood out. When Mrs. Wilson moved into the White House in 1913, she surveyed the southwest garden from her dressing room window. Edith Roosevelt had planted a colonial garden, full of old-fashioned multicolored flowers. But that sort of garden didn't appeal to Mrs. Wilson, whose taste was more formal. "Come and look, children," she said, pointing out the window. "It will be our rose garden."

they opened up the chimney in the diplomatic reception room so that FDR would no longer have to hold his fireside chats in front of a fake fireplace.

★ **This photo shows the White House on the night of December 7, 1941, after the Japanese attack on Pearl Harbor. On December 14, several government departments presented President Roosevelt with a report on how to protect the White House from enemy bombing. The suggestions rejected by Roosevelt included camouflaging the White House, painting its windows black, and setting up machine guns on the roof. However, FDR did agree to build a bomb shelter under the new East Wing.**

MARCH 14 1933

The New York Daily News *announces a campaign to raise money for a swimming pool in the White House. The pool will be built for President Franklin Roosevelt, whose paralysis (caused by polio) is sometimes eased by exercise in a pool. Most of the donors are schoolchildren, who pool their pennies to make twenty-five- and fifty-cent contributions.*

The White House pool, built indoors in the arcade between the main house and the West Wing, was designed by Lorenzo S. Winslow. Roosevelt liked Winslow's work so much that the president later made him the official White House architect. Because FDR loved building and remodeling, he and Winslow worked together on many more projects during the next twelve years, including a new East Wing built in 1942. Roosevelt and Winslow also took on numerous small projects. For example,

★ **Although President Richard Nixon was no fan of the media, during the early 1970s he ordered FDR's pool filled in so that the space could be used for a new press room.**

MAY 10 1948

Congress approves fifty thousand dollars for a structural survey of the White House, where many walls have large cracks. Just how badly the house has deteriorated becomes obvious a few months later when the leg of a piano falls through the floor in Margaret Truman's sitting room.

The moment he learned of the accident involving his daughter's piano was probably the time when President Harry Truman decided to rebuild the White House. Not surprisingly, the structural survey found that much of the building's framework was unsound. The repeated drilling into Hoban's beams for gas pipes, plumbing, and electrical wires had cut some of them completely in half.

The gutting of the White House began on December 7, 1949. Truman's plan was to raze everything but the stone walls and rebuild the interior from the ground up. As a result, all that remains today of the original White House are the same stone walls that survived the 1814 fire. The Trumans did not move back into the rebuilt White House until March 27, 1952.

Nearly half a century later, the White House remains the house that Truman rebuilt. Nine more families have lived there since the Trumans left in 1953, but none has made significant alterations.

The only noteworthy change has been the historical redecoration work begun by Mamie Eisenhower during the late 1950s and greatly expanded by Jacqueline Kennedy in 1961. These first ladies championed the idea of decorating the White House with antiques from various periods in the history of the building. On the night of February 14, 1962, Mrs. Kennedy led forty-seven million viewers on a televised tour of the White House, pointing out many of the newly acquired furnishings. It is generally agreed that her antiques program restored to the White House the sense of history that had been lost following the Truman-era reconstruction.

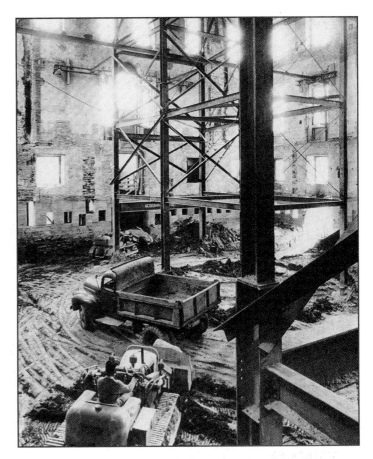

★ Perhaps because he felt guilty about demolishing the inside of the White House, Truman refused to let construction crews touch the exterior stone walls. As a result, the crews had to take apart a bulldozer, piece by piece, pass it through an opening in one wall, and then reassemble it before they could dig the new basement.

But the White House will surely not remain the way it is today. It will change again and adapt as new circumstances and tastes demand. Just as Teddy Roosevelt's desire for a larger staff forced construction of the West Wing nearly a century ago, some new presidential necessity in the future will undoubtedly force more changes. One thing will remain constant, however, and that is the White House's role as a stable, enduring symbol of the presidency.

★ The White House today.

Index

Index